Derek.

Happy 5[

Hope you enjoy reading it.

Paul

LOTUS AND CATERHAM SEVEN
Racers for the Road

Other Titles in the Crowood AutoClassics Series

LOTUS AND CATERHAM SEVEN
RACERS FOR THE ROAD

John Tipler

First published in 1995 by
The Crowood Press Ltd
Ramsbury, Marlborough
Wiltshire SN8 2HR

This impression 1997

British Library Cataloguing in Publication Data
A catalogue record for this book is available from the
British Library.

ISBN 1 85223 858 5

Typeset by Phoenix Typesetting, Ilkley, West Yorkshire
Printed and bound in Great Britain by The Bath Press

Contents

Acknowledgements

In particular I want to thank Graham Nearn, founder and managing director of Caterham Cars, without whom much of the Seven's history would be lost, and I am grateful for his historical focus, guidance and comments, and also for allowing Simon Clay and me to photograph the offices and factory, and for the opportunity of observing all aspects of the Super Seven's manufacture.

Also thanks to everyone at the Caterham Factory, particularly Paul Kite for showing me round, and Jez Coates for the lowdown on the new 21. Thanks, too, to Simon Nearn for acting as host and guide; Jan Russell and Andy Noble for liaison; Eddy Marriott and his staff at Oxted Trimming; Tony Whiting at the TSK paint shop; Bill Player at Dartford Composites; John Brigden of Brigden Coulter, Caterham's PR company.

Several of the older generation of Lotus personnel very kindly provided valuable information: many thanks indeed to Peter Brand, still at Lotus after all these years, Don Gadd of Arch Motors, and Brian Luff, both former key Lotus design personnel, and Mike Kelf who painted them; also to former Lotus sales managers Robin Read and his successor Graham Arnold for historical perspective.

Many thanks to Bob and Bruce Robinson and everyone at Arch Motors, who provided open house and all the information on chassis manufacture.

Contributions of help and information came from Patrick Peel of Lotus Cars, Clive Roberts, and John Rees, who supplied details and pictures of the Lotus Seven Club Challenge. Vauxhall HPC racer Graham Morris also supplied some excellent action shots. Others I spoke to include Russell Morgan, Pippa Newland and Magnus Laird. Geoff Rumble and Rob Cox-Allison of Black Brick fame, Iain Robertson at *Autocar*, Manning Buckle of Classic Team Lotus, Max Hora at the *Prisoner* Shop, Portmeirion, and Darren Green, KAR120C *aficionado*. Salisbury-based specialists Guy Munday and Vincent Haydon generously gave me much background information on the marque, the club, and the opportunity of driving an HPC car.

All the photographs at the Caterham factory, Oxted Trimming and Arch Motors were taken by Simon Clay of the National Motor Museum, Beaulieu; he also provided some excellent archive pictures and studio shots, for which thanks again.

My good friend and erstwhile *Carweek* colleague Andy Robinson provided Caterham photographs, and most generously lent me his camera equipment. This enabled me to get some of my own pictures for a change – at Dartford Composites and of the K-series Caterham, and especially the Series 4 and Silver Jubilee car belonging to Jeremy Bagnall-Oakley, who very kindly wheeled his cars out for a session. I am also grateful to Sarah Fowle for HPC-Vauxhall photography at Salisbury, including the hood erection and 'climbing in' sequence. My mother and daughter, Margaret and Zoë Tipler, for photographic contributions from Moreton-in-Marsh and North Weald.

Thanks also to Richard Spelberg of the Lotus Seven Club Deutschland, who went to a lot of trouble to provide some extremely fine archive material. John Watson, Lotus Seven Club archivist, and Graham Capel, historian of the Historic Lotus Register provided shelter from the storm at Silverstone. Belinda McDougall, co-ordinator of the Caterham Challenge race series furnished track passes for numerous Caterham Challenge events. Steve Davidson, *Low Flying* advertisement manager and Norfolk regional club co-ordinator, for pictures and endless chats on Caterhams. Derek Moore of the Classic Carriage Company for much useful background information. Peter Cooper, John Payne and Mick Lincoln at Redline Components for insights into the 'old days' at Caterham; Stuart Wylie of Woodcote Sports Cars; and last, but not least, James and Ruth Whiting for engine data and for lending their photo album.

I am delighted to have the Foreword to this book written by Gerard 'Jabby' Crombac, doyen of Grand Prix journalists and the author of the official Colin Chapman biography: *The Man and His Cars*. A great friend of Chapman, he was around at the birth of the Seven. As mentioned in the text, Jabby was greatly influential in promoting the Seven in France in the early 1960s, and is the proud owner of a Series 3 today.

Foreword

BY GERARD 'JABBY' CROMBAC

The Seven is one of the most important cars in automobile history. Yes, I know, this statement may seem a little pretentious. How can one place the Seven on such a pedestal, alongside cars like the Rolls-Royce Silver Ghost or the VW Beetle? Well, let me state my case before you make your own judgement.

The Seven is really the offshoot of the MkVI, whose prototype dates back to 1952. It is still in construction today, more than forty years later, because even if it is built and sold as a Caterham Seven it is a legitimate offspring, Graham Nearn having duly bought the rights to it from Colin Chapman. Only the Beetle has had a longer production run and the duration of a production run must surely be related to its success.

There are thousands of cars for which one would give one's right arm and all enthusiasts have in mind the ideal content of their garage. Obviously according to one's taste and one's age, they are not the same cars ... But above this are the cult cars, the cars which have marked their epoch, the ones which, when you mention them, people immediately associate with their image, even if it is not the type of car they are longing for at the moment. They are usually not the most expensive ones, they are the ones which millions dreamt of when they were in short pants, or the ones that introduced them to motoring; they are the cars which have changed the world's outlook towards automobiles. The earliest to spring to my mind is the Rolls-Royce Silver Ghost. It certainly wasn't more expensive than its rivals, but it boasted such high standards of performance and reliability at a reasonable price, that it laid the foundation for the cliché 'The best car in the world'. Certainly the Austin Seven was and still is considered to be a cult car: it was the first one to provide freedom of travel for many households. In France, the deux chevaux Citroën Cloverleaf fulfilled this role although it had perhaps too much of the image of a lady's first car. I suppose the famous *'Traction Avant'* of the same make, with its tremendously modern look, is more deserving of this accolade. After the war, the Americans fell for the Beetle, but we must not overlook either the MG TC or the Jaguar XKs. Surely they are the most important things to have crossed the Atlantic since tea . . . What the Seven brought to motoring is the look and the feel of a racing car at an affordable price.

And now for the punch line: the Seven is the car which has been more copied than any other in the history of the automobile. Doesn't this mean something? Of course, there are reasons for this recognized fact, which keeps Graham Nearn's solicitors busy: the Seven, as designed by Colin Chapman, was simply a triumph of functionality. Nothing is lacking to give it looks, performance, road-holding, but nothing is overdone. It's like furniture from the Bauhaus school: if one wants to create something similar, it ends up identical.

What is the attraction of the Seven? Basically, as I said above, it is a car which allows one to enjoy the feel of a racing car at a much reduced price. What is it like to drive a Seven? The sub-title of this book – Racers for the Road – is the answer! The Seven is enjoying even more success now than ever before; this is for two reasons: the first is that the progression of buying power in developed countries has made the three-car family much more frequent, and, yes, I must concede that even if many people do it (and I have done it myself), the daily use of a Seven throughout the winter is a bit of a chore. But the other reason is speed: now that increased traffic has limited the speed on most roads in most countries, there is no doubt that the best way to enjoy the thrill of tremendous speed without endangering your driving licence is to sit in a Seven – they are so close to the road that your impression of speed is nearly doubled! I know for a fact that some potential buyers of glorious supercars have settled for a Seven – it cost ten times less but brings them nearly the same pleasure.

I hope I have succeeded in convincing you if you weren't yet a devotee of the Seven, but I am sure John Tipler's book will ultimately achieve this. I was delighted when Clive Chapman suggested I should write this foreword for John, because, as you will certainly have gathered by now, I am a totally dedicated fan of this car. I bought Colin Chapman's own MkVI (1611H) at the end of its successful 1953 season and have since bought a Series 3 Seven with a cross-flow engine, mildly tweaked, which is still in my garage, separated from my living room by just a glass partition. I hope you will fall for the Seven like I did and I wish you wonderful motoring experiences with it!

Introduction

I am not prone to mystical experiences, but my first trip in a Seven certainly came close; in fact it was enough to convince me that I was about to meet my Maker. I had not been in anything quite like it at that point; it was the early 1970s and my friend Andy Weall had a Series 2 Lotus Seven powered by the 1,500cc Cortina engine. It was devastating enough in a straight line, but around the lanes of rural Essex it was truly hair-raising. This was more to do with our proximity to *terra firma* and the speed the Seven could be taken around corners than the ultimate velocity potential. I recently went to a Seven Club sprint with Weall, and the memory of this formative experience resurfaced. His recollection was chiefly of bruised hips and knees, gained from driving the car as it was intended to be driven. Anyway, we lived to tell the tale, and I was sufficiently impressed to avoid going anywhere near a Seven again for some years. Instead I went for an Elan S4SE, and I base my continued survival on its lack of reliability and consequent surrender of ownership. This is not to denigrate Lotuses. It is simply that they demand and respond to enthusiastic and committed driving – not to mention a sympathetic bank manager – and when exploring the limits, you tend to discover the underside of hedges and hay stacks.

There are two categories of sports car: there are the models produced by the major manufacturers, vehicles like the MGB and TR4, or the MX5 and MR2 today. Then there are the small-volume specialists like Lotus, Caterham, TVR and Morgan, producing no-compromise, competition-derived sports machines which can be driven straight on the race track; this used to mean they needed

From the outset, the Seven was set to thrill countless sporting motorists, as demonstrated by this tyre-smoking Series 1 at Silverstone's Woodcote bend in June 1961. The broadsiding Seven's headlights have been rotated for better aerodynamics.

regular cosseting, and if you like playing around and tinkering, it still does.

My next encounter with Sevens was right at the end of their run as a Lotus-built car, at the official switch from Lotus to Caterham Cars at a north London hostelry called Pub Lotus, a venue decked out with Lotus icons and memorabilia. Colin Chapman handed over 'the keys' to Graham Nearn in a brief but nonetheless symbolic ceremony, which included a buffet lunch for journalists and hangers-on such as myself. I was working for an agency run by erstwhile Clubmans racers Noel Stanbury and Barry Foley, doing promotional work for John Player Team Lotus, as it was known then. And as JPS press officer, along with Mike Doodson, my brief was to preach the Player's message where and whenever possible; the voice of the anti-smoking lobby had yet to be heard. We were fortunate enough to have a black and gold Elan Plus 2 as our office hack, so although Sevens were around, they did not figure as everyday transport. However, there were other highlights. In order to get advance publicity for the Player's-sponsored British Grand Prix, we used to invite the British motoring press along to Brands Hatch or Silverstone, sit them alongside Ronnie Peterson, Emerson Fittipaldi or Jacky Ickx in a Lotus road car – an Elan, Europa, Seven Series 4 as it was by then, or even the odd Granada – and they would be scared witless for a few laps, then released to stagger off weak-kneed to the bar; they would subsequently endorse the race in breathless prose. Afterwards, the hangers-on could take their turn as passengers to the stars, and I can only confirm the belief that these drivers were superhuman. Their car control was of such uncanny ability that I promptly gave up any notion of ever making it as a successful racing driver. A lap or two of Donington with Emerson in a Granada press car was a tyre-squealing hoot, and a full half dozen at Brands with Jacky Ickx in Pete Lyons'

Only the Series 4 Seven has strayed radically from the original Seven shape. This 1972 twin-cam-powered Series 4 poses with a 1982 Silver Jubilee Caterham, which remains virtually true to the shape of the Lotus Series 3 Super Seven.

Corvette was an unforgettable treat, but Ronnie in an Elan was demonic, all heel-and-toe and armfuls of opposite lock, yet with finger-tip control of the wheel.

These were times when one virtually lived at race tracks, preparing the promotional material during the week and spending the practice and race days distributing it, gathering more data and generally 'being the good news' at the circuits, whether it was a Grand Prix or Player's-sponsored event like an F3 or Formula Atlantic round. In the programme of supporting events, racing Sevens were still around, if not a particularly common sight. Drivers like Barry Flegg and Tim Goss were composing the Lotus Seven's swansong, and of course, nobody except perhaps Graham Nearn had a clue that the Seven would blossom anew. In the early 1970s the Seven's legacy was more prominent in Clubman's cars, like Noel Stanbury's

Andy Diamond-built, Reliant-engined Gryphon, Barry Foley's St Bruno Rough-cutter, and the hordes of Mallock U2s, which looked like low-slung Sevens sprouting aerofoils.

My other books for Crowood, on Morgan, Jensen and TVR, have concentrated on the production side of the cars. The Caterham is not put together in quite the same way as these, but I have tried to show how its various structural components are manufactured, and how the whole package comes together at Caterham's Dartford factory.

Apart from Graham Nearn of course, who was selling the cars as Lotuses before he began making them as Caterhams, there is one man who transcends both Lotus and Caterham nomenclature. He is Don Gadd, chassis development engineer at Lotus in the late 1950s and early 1960s, and long-time development director at Arch Motors. I think his presence and involvement with the Seven exemplifies the continuity from Lotus to Caterham. In the process of writing this book, I encountered several people who were inextricably linked with the cars, such as Peter Brand, still at Lotus, and who built them almost single-handed during the

1960s. The specification has evolved significantly to keep pace with – and indeed keep ahead of – performance and legislative trends, but body design has not altered fundamentally. There are slight changes to the radii of the rear wheel-arches and the height of the headlights, but Super Sevens appear fundamentally the same as they were twenty-five years ago. In fact the only component which would fit an original Lotus 7 is the handbrake lever.

It is a fascinating saga, all the more so because the cars appeal so directly to one's appetite for the driving experience, and equally because their construction is sufficiently basic and logical for a mechanical novice to comprehend. Is it an everyday car, though? Well of course it can be, provided you can cope with the privations of a convertible in an unpredictable climate. If you need to ferry your family around, it would have to be your second car. But it is not the sort of machine which bears objective scrutiny. In the course of researching this book I was lent several Super Sevens to drive, and I can honestly say that I was hooked. If only I can achieve a similar effect on the bank manager. Now, if he were to have a test drive . . .

During the course of writing this book, Tipler drove a number of Sevens, including this Rover K-series 1400 twin-cam, and found himself hooked.

1   Humble Beginnings

The Seven must be the best car Lotus ever produced. In the Lotus annals there are a number of cars of pure engineering genius, and conceptually, the Seven is one of them; on paper, the majority are faster. There are many that, in their day, were certainly more beautiful, but none was more inspired than the simple Seven. This car should be viewed as Colin Chapman's greatest achievement, because it espouses – still – his ideals for an affordable sports-racer. It makes few, if any, compromises, yet it is equally at home on the road as on the track; and it can be built by a mechanical novice, and a relatively impecunious one at that.

One of Chapman's most quoted statements, and one worth repeating here, is 'The Seven was a car I dreamed about as a schoolboy, and when I got the chance to build it, it was the most basic, lightest, high performance car we could come up with – a student's car, if you like – a four-wheeled

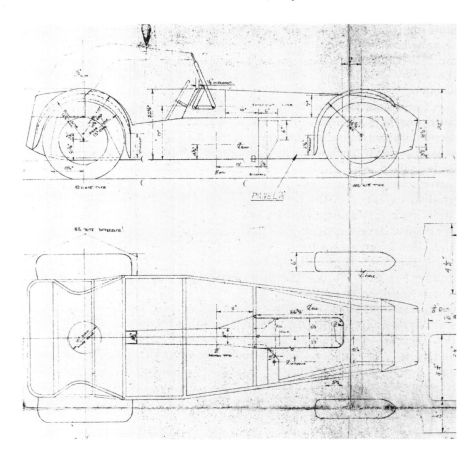

Blueprint of the Lotus Seven, said to have been drawn by Colin Chapman himself, with various amendments dating from 26 September 1957 to 30 April 1959.

A Series 1 Seven on the Motor Sport stand prior to the Earls Court show, October 1959, alongside a Lotus Mk 16 Formula 2 car and an F1 Cooper.

motorbike.' He is also on record as saying, somewhat dismissively, that 'There wasn't much to it really. It was all well known stuff, the sort of thing you could dash off in a weekend.'

A fair amount of water was to flow under the bridge before the Seven could appear, but an inexorable trend in Chapman's career and creations can be seen towards the Seven and its launch in 1957. In the event, the Seven's introduction was a low-key affair, because final specification of the production car was undecided: Edward Lewis had swapped his Mk 6 special for the 'prototype' Seven, which had Mk 12 Formula 2 front suspension and the Eleven's de Dion rear end and inboard disc brakes, plus 1,100cc Climax power, all of which was deemed too radical for the regular enthusiast customer. The cheaper and thus staider spec, live axle, drum-braked, Ford Pop-engined car would go into production, and while the chassis was re-engineered accordingly, only the Elite basked in the Earls Court limelight. Potential buyers had to take a trip to Tottenham Lane if they wanted to see the Seven.

CHAPMAN'S EARLY CAREER

Before tracing the Seven's development, we should really look at Colin Chapman's early career. He took a structural engineering degree course at University College, London, in 1945. His student income was supplemented by dealing in secondhand cars, but petrol rationing prompted him to give this up and modify an unsold 1930 Austin 7 into a sports special. These early years are well documented and make fascinating reading, notably in books by Ian H. Smith, Jabby Crombac and Doug Nye, but a short account is in order here as a means of demonstrating the intellectual and mechanical evolution of Chapman specials into the Lotus Seven. Thirty-seven years after its launch, the Seven is still a cult car, doing the same job it set out to do when Chapman introduced it.

The best bet for an impecunious enthusiast in the post-war years of strict rationing was to build a special and take to the muddy farm tracks on which trialling took place. And it is remarkable that an entire decade later, Lotus saw fit to take a stand at the

Do-It-Yourself Exhibition showing just how long the make-do ethos held sway. Those were the days of Formica and Fablon, of plywood and chipboard, and it was respectable enough for up-and-coming celebrities, including Graham Hill, to visit the Lotus stand.

TRIALS WITHOUT TRIBULATIONS

Chapman's first effort at a trials car in 1948, retrospectively named the Lotus Mk 1, was essentially an Austin Seven. While at University College, London, Chapman and his friend Colin Dare dealt in secondhand cars, helped by the fact that the Warren Street dealers' mecca was very close by; but when the basic petrol ration was suddenly withdrawn in October 1947, Chapman was left with a stock of cars that he had to sell off at a loss. The last one was a fabric-bodied Austin 7, and it was dismantled and clad in alloy-bonded plywood which gave it greater rigidity. It was designed while Chapman was at London University and followed the principles of aircraft construction, as Chapman was a member of the university air squadron. Much time was spent mulling over technical treatises at the Institute of Mechanical Engineers' library in a quest to discover what stresses cars were subjected to, and what had to be done to counteract them. His early cars began to embody some of the principles he absorbed. Not many car designers took these things as seriously as Chapman, and the Seven has to be viewed in this light.

He extended the rear of the Mk 1 body to accommodate passengers or trialling ballast. The Austin 7 special was assembled in a lock-up garage belonging to the father of girlfriend Hazel Williams, and was registered OX 9292, a Lotus Mk 1, early in 1948. Chapman, partnered by Hazel, campaigned it successfully in the mud and ruts of trials

competitions as far afield as Cheshire from 1948. Perhaps Chapman's most notable discovery was that inverting the rear leaf springs cured the Austin 7's propensity to oversteer. He also created an independent front end by splitting the front axle beam and pivoting it in the centre, thus ensuring the wheels were vertical during cornering.

LOTUS MK 2

While doing his National Service in the RAF, Chapman learned to fly in a Harvard two-seat trainer, and this was to stand him in great stead in later life as he commuted from home base to Grand Prix circuit. In his spare time he built the Mk 2 Lotus, which was another Austin 7 chassis clad in a rudimentary cigar-tube body – as many specials were at the time, including Trevor Wilkinson's first TVRs. It was a more sporty-looking device than the Mk 1 and, six years on, featured as the honeymoon car in a Boulting Brothers' comedy called *Brothers-in-Law* starring Ian Carmichael and Nicholas Parsons, very popular when I was at school. Beneath the skin, the Mk 2's main chassis members were boxed in, and tubular braces replaced the existing cross-members. Chapman's Mk 2 used a Ford 8 engine, replaced later with a Ford 10 unit, and an Austin 7 rear axle was retained. He arrived at a 4.55:1 final drive by pairing up an unmatched 42-tooth crown wheel with a 9-tooth pinion, filling the diff with metal polish and driving it for fifty miles (80km). The bearings were shot, but the crown wheel and pinion now meshed perfectly.

Wheels were also Ford pressed steel because they allowed the use of fatter tyres. Whereas the venerable Ford 8 engine was adapted to take a four-speed Austin gearbox, the second engine required no such refinement. It was virtually brand new, obtained from a burned-out Ford 10, and the manner

The versatile Mk 2 Lotus LJH 702, which excelled as a trials car in 1949 and took Chapman into circuit racing in 1950, also featured as a honeymoon car in the 1957 film Brothers-in-Law. Clearly in need of restoration, it surfaced again at the 1990 Lotus Seven International meeting.

of its acquisition is a measure of Chapman's resourcefulness in times of penury, a quality which would stand him in good stead throughout his life. It seems he bought the wreck from the insurance company for £30, having arranged for a shady dealer to buy the shell for £35, plus all-important log-book, but less engine and gearbox. A middle-man acted as breaker, removed the drivetrain for a fiver and passed on the remains to the dealer. Chapman thus got himself a free engine for the Mk 2.

After a year as a construction engineer with a steel-erection company in London, he joined British Aluminium on 17 April 1950 as a construction engineer. Road-going transport at the time was a rare Austin 7 aluminium saloon, later passed on to the Costins, first Mike then Frank, having clocked up over 100,000 miles (160,930km).

The 750 Motor Club had been founded in 1938 for owners of the 750cc Austin 7 to indulge in some sporting motoring. The basic car was a plodder, but the Ulster, Speedy and Nippy derivatives lived up to their names. In 1950 Holly Birkett established the 'unblown' 750 Formula for Austin 7s to go club racing, and Chapman was sufficiently impressed to base his next creation, and its successors, on the 750 Motor Club's formula.

Virtually every weekend Chapman and Hazel or another friend were involved in a motor club trial or rally, or had entered some 750 Formula club event in this car, and successes were many. But after his first proper race, the Eight Club's meeting at Silverstone on 3 June, where he beat Dudley Gahagan's Type 37 Bugatti to the chequered flag, he became more interested in building a car that could beat all comers on the road, rather than the unpredictable terrain of a trials course. So the Mk 2 was sold through a *Motor Sport* advert to Mike Lawson, who continued to be successful with it.

Colin Chapman became friends with 750 Motor Club members Nigel and Michael Allen, and both brothers played an important part in creating the early Lotus models. Here Colin and Michael deliberate over the front suspension set-up of the Mk 3 racing car on the drawing-board, propped up on a hub, at the Alexandra Park workshop.

CIRCUIT RACER

In 1951 Chapman made a move away from trialling to the circuits with his next creation: this was the equally austere and spindly Mk 3. The basis for this car was a 1930 Austin 7, bought for £15 and gutted, its chassis side-members boxed in and the cross-members replaced with 14-gauge tubular beams.

He became friendly with the Allen brothers, 750 Motor Club members who lived in nearby Wood Green, and had reasonable workshop facilities. They were fired by Chapman's enthusiasm into going for a pair of cars similar to the Mk 3 Lotus, and were closely involved in the gestation of the seminally important Mk 6.

The Mk 3 was superseded by the Mk 4,

ostensibly a trials machine, and the Mk 5, which was never completed, but was intended to be a circuit racer. Thus the Mk 6, the direct ancestor of our subject, was up and running in 1953. Chapman's strategy for selling his cars always depended on race successes to produce publicity and inspire potential buyers, and sufficient interest had been generated by his prowess at the wheel of his earlier creations for him to consider putting the concept into production. This is just what happened with the Mk 6.

It was also the start of the kit-car manufacturing industry, in which Chapman was to be a front runner for a decade at least. Customers came to Chapman for their own Mk 6, and he soon devised the scheme of selling them in component form. This wasn't a new idea, having been pioneered by Derek

Buckler in Reading. The Buckler chassis was a complex multi-tubular spaceframe, accepting suspension systems as sophisticated as you cared to make them, and the regular Buckler body was Healey-esque. Buckler boasted 130mph (210km/h) performance with a Coventry Climax 1500 engine fitted. Indeed, a host of specials – Rochdale, Ashley, Warwick, to name but three – sprang up in the 1950s, usually based on a rudimentary Ford Popular chassis and running gear, and clothed in aluminium or, more commonly, fibreglass bodies. These were of varying degrees of competence and aesthetic attraction, and were often modelled on well established sporting marques. Frequently used for club racing, or at least to look the part, they were relatively commonplace in the classified ads of *Motor Sport* during the late 1950s; there was also a degree of interchangeability, in that you might find a Buckler chassis with an Ashley body, and so on. The original TVR Grantura of 1956 was fundamentally two Rochdale front ends joined together.

The kit car was very much the norm, rather than considered something a bit out of the ordinary as it is nowadays. Survivors from the 1950s can be counted on one hand, namely Marcos, Ginetta, TVR and the Seven in Caterham guise. The beauty of a kit car was that you could own something with sporting lines, vaguely like a Ferrari perhaps; and more significantly, you didn't have to pay purchase tax on it, which automatically knocked the price down by a quarter.

Having two 'companies' from which one could dispense components – these being the wherewithal to create a complete car – was the ideal basis for a kit-car operation. Naturally Chapman was alive to the possibilities of financial failure, and by setting up a number of subsidiaries he avoided any single one having the monopoly; if one went down, he could keep going with another. Thus the Seven was built by Lotus Components Ltd, who constructed racing cars for sale, and whose other purpose was to market Sevens in kit form. By 1959 this aspect of the business was run by Nobby Clarke, who unfortunately died in 1962.

TOTTENHAM LANE BECKONS

A modest revenue was gleaned from selling tuning equipment to members of the 750 Motor Club, but it certainly wasn't sufficient to maintain a motor business of the kind Chapman had in mind. Many of us have to thank our parents for setting us up in one way or another, and Chapman was no exception: thus, home was in Barnet, but his workshop and drawing office was a former stable behind his father Stan Kennedy-Chapman's Railway Arms Hotel at 7 Tottenham Lane, Hornsey in residential London N8. This was a step up from his fiancée Hazel's father's garage where the Mk 1 was built.

In February 1953 Hazel, as co-director, brought with her the princely sum of £25 – a good month's wages then – which formed the basis of Lotus' working capital. Colin promptly spent it on setting up the Lotus Engineering Company. The couple were married in October the following year at Northaw church, and moved to Monken Hadley, north of Barnet.

Post university, Chapman had served an apprenticeship at the de Havilland aircraft factory at Hatfield, and his day job was as a structural engineer at British Aluminium. His personal transport was a Lotus Mk 6, which meant he was apt to arrive for work soaked to the skin. These were heady times in aviation with the frontiers being thrust back all the time, and Chapman and his circle were similarly inspired. Three de Havilland design engineers, Mike Costin, Mac Macintosh and Peter Ross, frequently joined Chapman and his associate Mike Allen in their hectic nocturnal work, and were instrumental in honing the chassis development. Macintosh was responsible for designing the early tubular spaceframes, and Ross, an alloys expert, did the castings. They were often joined by merchant banker Peter Kirwan-Taylor, an accounts wizard as far as Lotus was concerned and originally a Lotus customer who fitted his own body to a Mk 6 chassis, and made the initial drawings for the Elite styling. Significant advances in the svelte Elite body were made by John Frayling, who worked with another first class design engineer, Ron Hickman; Ron eventually took over from Costin. Later on, Frayling worked at Maximar Mouldings at Pulborough, where he was responsible for first the Elite and then the Elan body; he would also style the flared wings first seen on the Seven A America.

LE MANS SUCCESS

By 1955 Chapman was sufficiently confident of his prospects to go into full time production, and together with Frank Costin, Lotus became a fully paid-up member of the Society of Motor Manufacturers and Traders. This allowed the company to take a stand at the 1955 Motor Show, a stand which quite by chance was situated opposite the tea room rather than upstairs in the gallery with the accessories. This was the threshold of fame, and the Mk 9 chassis on display created a lot of interest. Chapman had realized his dream of racing at Le Mans that year, despite being disqualified for rejoining the race backwards after an excursion; it was the year of Pierre Levegh's devastating accident, and the organizers were justifiably sensitive.

The level and quality of Lotus racing activity during the mid-fifties should never be underestimated. Lotus Elevens in particular were prominent in sports car events, with rising stars like Graham Hill, Alan Stacey, Peter Ashdown and Innes Ireland battling it out with the establishment – Mike Hawthorn, Ivor Bueb and Archie Scott Brown, and indeed Chapman himself, all driving Elevens. At Le Mans in 1957, one 750cc and three 1,100cc Elevens crossed the line virtually side by side to scoop the Index of Performance award: some achievement indeed after twenty-four hours of racing.

The Lotus partners also set up a subsidiary called Racing Engines Ltd to provide race tuning and preparation, and around this time Chapman established Team Lotus, to run alongside Lotus Engineering; this was staffed mostly by his race-fan friends, who did what they did for the thrill of being involved with an up-and-coming outfit building racing cars. These were happy-go-lucky times when people were more carefree, and perhaps sailed somewhat close to the wind with their legal dealings. There were few other rewards, which was always the case until the arrival of big-time sponsorship, instigated in the UK by Chapman himself, of course; I know how they must have felt, having myself taken a drop in salary just to be involved in the sport in the early seventies.

THE LOTUS MK 6

The forerunner of the Seven, logically the Mk 6, dates from 1952. The Mk 6 was the first proper Lotus, having a chassis built by Lotus' sub-contractors the Progress Chassis Company, owned by John Teychenne, one of Chapman's circle of friends and operating from garage workshops at Edmonton, relatively close to Chapman's own. Their methods were typical of the small engineering company setting up in the make-do-and-mend climate of postwar austerity. The original chassis jig was made out of an angle-iron bed-frame, and suspension and other bracketry fashioned

Dynamism of a Lotus Mk 6 racer, Brands Hatch, 30 June 1957.

from whatever light-gauge steel was around. The aluminium panelling which clad the chassis was fabricated by another small firm – soon to be based in the same complex – called Williams and Pritchard. The rudimentary bodywork consisted of side and rear panels, rear wings, bonnet, nosecone and cycle-wing mudguards. Chassis design was a matter of trial and error, and the spaceframe developed according to what fitted comfortably and what was lightest, sometimes fabricated from whatever was at hand. Very often the layout was assembled before its design was committed to paper on the drawing board.

The Lotus chassis broke new ground in Britain, because it was the first proper tri-angulated spaceframe, unlike regular sports-bodied cars – such as AC or Aston Martin – which were usually based on a ladder platform, stout but crude by comparison, with additional framework to support the body. A notable exception was Jaguar's D-type of 1954, which used a monocoque centre section. In basic terms, the Mk 6 chassis was composed of lengths of 1in (25mm) and 1⅞in (47mm) diameter circular- and square-section tubing welded together in lengths and diagonals and braced at crucial stress points. The Mk 6 chassis had the

advantage of being not only light – at just 55lb (24.9kg) – but it coped admirably well with the bending and torsional stresses generated at racing speeds: all loads in a spaceframe are in tension and compression. The spaceframe hailed from the rarefied and exalted portals of the Italian coach-building *carrozzerie*, where the likes of Pinin Farina (not yet *Pininfarina*) clad spaceframed exotics like the Cisitalia 202 in trendy aluminium panelling. As today, the floor and side panels of the Lotus were in aluminium, and the scuttle and undertray were riveted to the chassis rails, which gave additional stiffness. The Mk 6 set the stage for every subsequent Lotus chassis up to the revolutionary (in Formula 1) Lotus 25 monocoque of 1962.

Stock Block

The philosophy right from the start was to use a stock Ford engine. The chosen motor – also coveted by Sydney Allard for one of his cars – was that of the Consul, which promised reliability, economy and longevity because of its efficient oil supply and large bearings; something of a contrast with the Climax engine, which always used a lot of oil because it had originally been designed as a war-time fire pump unit, to be run at

Devious deals were sometimes done to obtain better engines for the early cars, and the 1,172cc Ford 10 unit was favourite, but for the Mk 3 car a heavily reworked 750cc Austin 7 engine was chosen; here Colin Chapman and Nigel Allen prepare a new acquisition.

maximum revs from cold. But because the Consul's 1,508cc engine was so new, no dealers had a spare to sell, and despite correspondence between Stan Chapman and Ford chairman Sir Patrick Hennessy, the manufacturers wouldn't sell one to him. What a difference a decade makes. So the ever resourceful Chapman assembled one out of individual components, sourced by doing the rounds of Ford dealers in the Greater London area. Michael Allen did much of the assembly work, reducing the stroke to bring the cubic capacity down to 1,499cc, which brought the car into a different class of racing.

The Mk 6 chassis came with mounting points for five engines: the 1,172cc Ford 10, the bigger 1,500cc Consul engine as well as the exalted Coventry Climax, and 1,466cc MG TF units. The Lotus brochure for 1954 also details the cars' successes and lists the sporting options available, which ranged from lightweight wheels fitted with Dunlop racing tyres to close ratio gears and an 'upholstery kit'.

Angles of Suspension

The Mk 6 suspension was similar to Chapman's earlier projects, with the split-front swing axle preferred to the standard Ford beam axle, which gave a hard ride and was inclined to tramp. Other independent systems tended to affect the camber of the outer wheel in cornering, a phenomenon usually countered by running a greater slip angle. This had the undesirable effect of slowing a car quite dramatically in a bend as greater roll resistance was set up. With the swing axle, the front wheels could be kept relatively upright in a corner, provided the roll centre was low enough. Extraordinary camber angles were achieved at the front as the Mk 6 understeered through corners, but the system did the job. The steering rack was located behind the front axle line, and the arrangement produced what was known as the 'Ackermann effect', so that when cornering, the outer wheel performed a bigger arc than its inner companion.

The Lotus system was fabricated from

modified Ford parts: the beam axle was sliced in half, and plates welded over the ends. A pair of bushes fitted here, pivoted on a bracket fixed to the lower front chassis cross-member. A pair of radius arms was made by splitting the V-shaped Ford tie rod, and separate track rods incorporated a slave arm. With the track rod divided and working on a central slave arm, the steering box and column were turned through ninety degrees and mounted by the base-plate; a track rod then ran from the slave arm to the arm of the steering box.

The 'standard' Mk 6 used a Ford 10 back axle with shortened propshaft and torque tube. It was located laterally by a Panhard rod, and suspension front and rear was completed by coil springs and Woodhead Monroe dampers. Brakes were regular Ford fitment, and consisted of cable-operated 10 x 1¼in Girling drums, a perfectly adequate arrangement for cars powered by the regular Prefect motor. All these adaptations and modifications gradually filtered through to customers who built their cars as kits.

What the customer got was the body–chassis unit, including wings, cowl, and bonnet, two seat squabs, an engine – normally a Ford E93A Prefect, unless otherwise specified – plus Ford Prefect suspension components, fuel tank, radiator, instrumentation, plus lights and weather equipment. The formula was as standardized as possible for 'volume' production, which was how Chapman saw most profit being generated. His philosophy was to have more enthusiasts driving cheap sports cars rather than entering the province of the exclusive. However, deviations in the form of specially tuned cars were frequent and priced accordingly.

The concept of the car you could drive on the road as well as enter for club races extended to the well behind the seats, in which a very small child could supposedly be accommodated, along with folded hood and luggage. A bracket could also be mounted on the rear panel to affix a spare wheel. The child and/or luggage cubby-hole could be fitted with a lid if required (although presumably not if the infant was on board). For just short runs, I found it best to strap both my children, aged two and four, into the passenger seat of one of the Caterhams I borrowed (the dog was somewhere in there too).

Headlights were normally positioned behind the suspension uprights, a little higher than the nosecone; competition drivers, however, fitted theirs behind the radiator grille. Indeed, the early racing Mk 6s sported elegantly rounded, faired-in rear wings.

The prototype Lotus Mk 6 attracted much interest at the MG Car Club meeting at Silverstone, 5 July 1952. Michael Allen finished second in the novices' handicap, after a tussle with Peter Gammon's MG TC; Gammon was later to fit his overbored, alloy Laystall-headed 1,497cc MG engine and close ratio gearbox in a Mk 6 of his own. This was UPE 9, probably the most famous Mk 6 of all and for the last twenty-four years residing in the tender custody of Graham Nearn, who restored it – with Len Pritchard beating out the body panels – and who kept everything as was, except for fitting Spax dampers and 145SR x 15 radials. UPE 9 ran on skinny Elektron cast magnesium alloy, split-rim wheels, far more sophisticated than Chapman could provide. The car appeared in 1992 in the hands of Brands Hatch HPC instructor John Lyon, having been refettled by Seven restoration expert Tony Weale.

Chapman drove the prototype Mk 6 in the Silverstone relay event, in which they were placed second after making contact with the oil drums lining Woodcote bend. It promised much, but was subsequently wrecked en route to the *Daily Mail* 100 miles international race meeting at Boreham aerodrome (for three decades Ford's competition HQ and test track), through no fault of driver Nigel

A Mk 6 resplendent in polished aluminium bodywork waits its turn for a crack at the Prescott hill climb in 1954. Rear tyres are Dunlop racing pattern, but has the spare been removed for lightness?

Allen; in practice for this event, he had spun the car repeatedly at the same bend and deranged it somewhat.

In the wake of its demise, and with no tangible assets apart from his day job, Chapman nonetheless elected to put everything into setting up the Lotus Engineering Company. This sounded more glamorous than the reality, which at the time left the retiring Michael Allen with just the remains of the wrecked Mk 6 prototype. The Chapmans were sole directors, but such was Colin's determination that Mk 6 production really began in earnest at this point. Chapman built eight Mk 6s virtually single-handed, taking a fortnight to build one car, working mostly at night. Williams and Pritchard had moved to Tottenham Lane, and produced panels by day.

At weekends, Chapman was more often than not at a race track and it seems that the company's fortunes were assured at a race meeting at Crystal Palace on 19 September 1953, when Chapman held off the leading 1½ litre contenders in a Ford 10-engined Mk 6, described by *Motor* magazine as 'preposterously fast'. In the wake of this performance, customers formed a queue at Tottenham

Lane, and during the next four years over 100 Mk 6s were sold, with some cars going to the United States, Canada and Australia. Here I will refer you to two authors, Ian H. Smith and Jabby Crombac, both of whom raced Mk 6s; obviously their books give a fuller and greatly entertaining picture of the scene then.

Williams and Pritchard

Panelling was done by Williams and Pritchard, a firm with origins in the coach-building traditions of Hooper, Mulliner, Park Ward and so on, which is a far cry from the rudimentary if practical cladding of the Lotus Mk 6. Bodywork consisted of four wings (early ones had the full, rounded spat-clad variety at the rear), nosecone, scuttle, chassis and engine bay sides and rear panel, bonnet cover and propshaft tunnel. Apart from the wings, these are pretty much the components used in dressing today's Caterham. They were practical men, for besides helping design the stressed sections, they were instrumental in locating the panels with simple and easily removable Dzus fasteners.

Charlie Williams and Len Pritchard had served their apprenticeships pre-war in this apparently exalted stratum of artisan-craftsmen. They panelled Spitfires during World War II, after which they set up in Edmonton, north London, mostly doing crash repairs. Johnny Teychenne had them panel a trials car for him, and was pleased enough with the result to introduce Colin Chapman who wanted something similar. Thus began an association that unquestionably produced some of the best sports car styling ever: the Lotus Mark 8, the Eleven, Marks 15 and 16, and if form follows function, their sister the Lotus Seven. Other Williams and Pritchard projects included Mks 6 and 7 Lola sports racing cars, the Lister Jaguar, Costin Amigo, Gordon-Keeble, the Ian Walker Racing Elan GT, and fairings for Mike Hailwood and John Surtees' racing motorcycles.

Williams and Pritchard turned panel beating into an art form, and with the advent of the Elite, became somewhat reluctantly involved with the grp process. This medium was still in its infancy in the mid-fifties, so prototypes were made in aluminium, from which fibreglass moulds were taken; it was felt that the aluminium panels were more accurate. Indeed, Williams and Pritchard panelled every prototype up to and including the Elan. They moved subsequently to Hornsey, then Hammersmith, and back to Edmonton, and although Charlie Williams died in 1969, Len Pritchard maintained the business producing a variety of exotics, including Eleven bodies and the Lynx D-type prototype, until he retired in 1987, set on completing his own unfinished Lotus Mk 6.

NOT THE LOTUS SEVEN

The Mark 7 was originally scheduled to be a one-off commission for the Clairmonte brothers, but the specification was confused, and

the chassis was actually completed by the customers, who fitted it with either an Alta or an ERA engine. The next project for 1954 was the Mk 8, a sports racer with an all-enveloping body designed by de Havilland aerodynamicist Frank Costin, brother of Mike. The following year, Mike Costin concentrated on building and preparing engines, under the auspices of Lotus Racing Engines.

The workshop was getting extremely crowded by now. Both Costin and Chapman had taken the major step of leaving their regular jobs to go into Lotus Engineering full-time. Their output included the Marks 9 and 10, and with approximately 100 units of the Mk 6 built, it was time to concentrate on the Eleven. (We find Chapman drops the prefix 'Mark' after the Mk 10). The Eleven was as much of a milestone as the Mk 6 because of the more finely tuned chassis configuration and suspension set-up. The product of much research by Chapman and Macintosh, the Eleven's spaceframe was made of 1in (25mm)-diameter 18- and 20-gauge steel, with ¾in (19mm)-diameter secondary tubes. The ensemble was triangulated to achieve the desired rigidity, and the suspension was by wishbones and dampers at the front.

In 1957 the ambitious Chapman took over the Williams and Pritchard body building premises – as they in turn moved to larger workshops in Hammersmith – and moved in the Lotus racing workshop. Having demonstrated the potential of the Mk 9, and realized it with the class-winning Eleven at Le Mans, he was already the toast of the motor racing fraternity. Such was his standing that he was hired by the major British Formula 1 teams, Vanwall to design the cars' suspension, and BRM to design a chassis. The first single-seater Lotus – the Mk 12 Formula 2 car – owed more to the Cooper Bristol or 250F Maserati in terms of its looks, but the Mk 16 actually looked like a small-scale Vanwall, though far more elegant.

2 Enter the Seven

Not many Mk 6s were produced after 1955 as Lotus concentrated on the more sophisticated Mks 8, 9, 10 and Eleven. It had been assumed in some quarters that there was no further interest in producing a basic Clubman's car for the enthusiast, so the advent of just such a car in 1957 was greeted with mild surprise. Predictably, there was method in Chapman's timing; apart from the fact that he had always intended to produce a car corresponding to the Seven specification, he was also looking for a money-spinner to tide things over while the technologically advanced Elite progressed through its gestation period. Being closely based on the Mk 6 concept and the Eleven chassis, all the elements were in place to go ahead straightaway.

The Lotus Seven was announced at the Earls Court Show, 1957. In many ways it was very similar to the Mk 6, except for the front wishbone suspension which was borrowed from the Mk 12 Formula 2 car, and also featured on the Elite. At the rear was a mass production live axle located by twin parallel trailing arms and a diagonal strut brace, with coil springs and dampers. Much ground had been covered in the interim years between the development of the Mk 6 and the introduction of the Seven, and the Seven's chassis frame was a rationalization of the Eleven's, clearly lacking the sports racer's curvaceous, all-enveloping bodywork.

The Seven's introduction also had as much to do with honouring a promise as it had to do with satisfying growing enthusiast interest in the Mk 6. Chapman had been mightily impressed by Edward Lewis's de Dion suspended Mk 6 sprint and hill climb car, and

made Lewis an offer of replacing it with a special based on the Eleven. Although Lewis's Mk 6 was sold quite swiftly to a foreign customer, the replacement did not appear for almost another year. Lewis was lent a variety of works' cars to tide him over. The Climax-engined prototype Seven first appeared at the Brighton speed trial in September 1957, and such was its potential that he almost managed to drive it off the promenade and into the sea. The following week saw him win the 1,100cc class at the Prescott hill climb, and the Seven was on its way. The specification of the standard car was rather less exotic, however.

SEVEN SPEC

The first Sevens, priced at £587, were powered by the ubiquitous 40bhp Ford 1,172cc engine coupled to a single dry plate clutch and three-speed Ford gearbox. Steering was by the Burman worm-and-nut system, and road wheels were 15in bolt-on disc type, shod with 5.20 x 15 tyres, unlike the Mk 6 that usually had bigger boots at the rear. Brakes were hydraulic twin-leading shoe drums in cast iron, 9 x 1¾in at the front and 8 x 1¼in at the rear. There was a horizontally mounted handbrake under the passenger-side scuttle, acting on the rear brakes, and both front and rear were served by a combined hydraulic fluid reservoir and master cylinder. For racing, tiny perspex flyscreens could be substituted for the windscreen, and the height of the car was just 27½in from ground to scuttle top. Wheelbase was 88in and track front and rear was 47in.

An immaculate Series 1 Seven A fronts a line-up of modern Caterhams outside the head office. Wire spoke wheels were 15in, from the TR2.

The 1,172cc 'autothermic' sidevalve engine with its steel inserts always had problems with rings breaking, and the trick was to fit a set of Hepsleeve pistons and a Wilment overhead valve conversion; Cord piston rings that adjusted according to bore wear were an alternative. The firm of Aquaplane at Oulton Broad, Suffolk, specialized in hydroplane engines, and their alloy heads and flywheels were sensational. Aquaplane double valve springs and modified Sunbeam Talbot 90 inlet valves, plus polished ports, worked wonders. In broad terms, Chapman was influenced by Ford component design. Items were cheap to put into production, such as the MacPherson strut and integral roll bar.

Fitting radius arms can be tricky; you can get three on but the fourth is difficult. However, the Series 1's top radius arms were curved to go over the axle on bump, and being curved, they could be twisted, and this made them easier to assemble. There was a BMC Nash Metropolitan back axle, as used in the Elite, and this BMC axle had separate nose-pieces so there was a choice of ratios. The

Rear suspension upright and back axle of the Series 1 Seven: this also reveals the location of the diagonal link and curved upper radius arm, plus routing of the brake pipes.

axle was located by a side A-frame bracket, located by a fixing welded to the differential case. Early bushes used to wear, and had to be modified. Even so, the axle used to 'pant' or flex around this pivot point on its rubber mountings, and would crack. Chunky triangular bars were eventually welded to the axle as well, to counteract flexing.

As in the Mk 6, the earlier, massive E93A torque tube had to be shortened. Likewise, the valve guides in this engine had to be modified before the mushroom-based valves could be removed; the subsequent 100E unit was far easier to work on. There were regular deliveries from Perrys, the local Ford dealership.

CHRONOLOGICAL DISORDER

The number seven is considered lucky by some; Stirling Moss always tried to race under that number. But Lotus numerology was not chronological because Chapman became preoccupied with the Frank Costin-designed aerodynamic sports racers, the Mks 8, 9, and 10. The 'Seven' nomenclature was reserved for the follow-up to the Mk 6, which Chapman always believed he could improve upon, and to which, visually at least, it would be more closely related. Like the Eleven, the Seven's number was also always spelled out.

The Seven came out at a time when people without a conventional engineering background could challenge the motor industry establishment; as a structural engineer, Chapman's experience designing girder bridges taught him something about the triangulations involved in chassis design. But it always seemed to me that Lotuses were close to the edge – my own Elan was certainly more often wrong than right, as was the JPS Plus 2 Elan we ran around in – and it has to do with Chapman's passion for racing. There is much less accounting for safety in the

design of a racing car, where the philosophy is that if nothing breaks, it must be over-engineered; thus the ideal racing car is one that wins the race and then falls apart. I was told once that Lotus is an acronym for 'Lots of Trouble, Usually Serious', which was maybe said only partly in jest.

Even so, the Seven was the car for club racing enthusiasts to take to the circuits, and the cycle-wing, cigar-tube configuration was rather more practical for the amateur protagonist, being easier on the pocket to repair if shunted. As we shall see, the nosecone, front and rear mudguards and wings were eventually to be made of glass-fibre for lightness and economy.

EXPANSION AT HORNSEY

By 1958 there was a new office building at Hornsey, initially incorporating the showroom downstairs; however, windows were soon painted over and desks installed, whereupon it became the sales office. Chapman and Fred Bushell were to be found upstairs, Peter Warr and Colin Bennett sat below. Behind the sales office was the machine shop, occupied by Len Terry, Jon Mowatt, Bob Aris, Ian Jones – formerly designer draughtsman at Vanwall – and Nobby Clarke. Jim Endruweit, John Lambert and Bob Martin worked in the adjacent development shop. In the early days, anything could happen; for instance, the local policeman used to drop in at 2.00 a.m., take off his coat and do a bit of work.

On the other side of an access road to a British Railways freight depot yard was the production shop, under Roy Badcock, where the Sevens were assembled. Here the solution to moving overweight toolboxes around was to pull them on dog leads. Chassis would be left leaning against scaffolding in the access road, and were sometimes damaged by careless delivery lorries. Cars belonging to errant parkers were removed with trolley jacks and dispatched down Tottenham Lane.

SUPPORTIVE SEVEN

The following year it was the proceeds from the sales of the Seven that kept Lotus afloat, because despite a full order book, the Elite was not yet in production; Lotus lacked the capacity to build it at the cramped premises of 7 Tottenham Lane, and it was produced at Edmonton where the Team Lotus stable was based. It was shown at Earls Court where it caused a considerable stir, for here, ostensibly, was Lotus's move into the real world of production sports cars; the notion was largely buoyed up by Chapman's boundless enthusiasm which caught the public imagination as much as it inspired his small workforce. The next five years' profits were ploughed back into developing the Elite and funding the move to a new factory at Cheshunt, Hertfordshire. The firm now started to become more organized, with an influx of administrative personnel; however, there was a certain loss of intimacy.

Meanwhile, Lotus's competition activity included racing the single-seater F2 Lotus 12, driven in the 1958 Grands Prix at Monaco, Zandvoort and Spa by Cliff Allison and Graham Hill; and the miniature Vanwall, the 16, which was raced at Rheims, Silverstone and the Nurburgring. It was generally felt that the inconsistent result – only Allison finished in the points – was directly related to Chapman's obsession with paring components down to the barest minimum to save weight. While the Seven and Eleven, and the Mk 15 sports cars were being produced, besides the Elite, the Lotus factory was quite stretched; this was another reason why Chapman set up Lotus Components to build the Seven and customers' sports racing cars.

THE FIRST SEVENS

Chassis number 407 was the factory development car, with imprecise Standard 8 worm-and-nut steering. Number 402 had a de Dion back axle; it was first sold to Paul Fletcher, and subsequently the Chequered Flag garage; later it was bought by New Zealander Warren King. The other factory prototype chassis went to Jack Richards for use as a hill climb car; this had de Dion rear suspension, Climax engine and disc brakes. The owner of 403, the very first Seven sold to the public, was Brian Luff, then a seventeen-year-old serving an apprenticeship at Thornycroft.

Having saved up for a Mk 6, Luff was asked by Chapman if he would take a Seven instead as the Mk 6 was no longer in production. He acquired it on a kind of hire purchase arrangement, paying by instalments as and when the factory could supply the parts to build it. 'This staged delivery meant that every part of the car could be prepared to an embarrassingly high standard,' said Luff. The 100E engine was emeried to a smooth finish and painted Post Office red. Its Aquaplane head and other bare metal parts were polished with Autosolve by a number of willing hands. The body was painted a similar colour using a converted vacuum cleaner. The hood and rack-and-pinion steering were fitted by the factory, and it was registered UOW 429, a Bournemouth number. The Lotus sales manager Colin Bennett was sufficiently impressed to feature it in a very early Lotus sales brochure, in return for which Brian was given a spare wheel, then an optional extra. Only later did he discover that its rightful place was in the boot of a Ford Consul, and it was useless as far as the Seven was concerned.

Luff went on to work for Lotus from 1958 to 1970, during which time he progressed from the post of project engineer to chief engineer, to manager of the vehicle engineering

Brian Luff in UOW 429 stays ahead of an Eleven at Brands Hatch's Bottom Bend. The Seven's 100E engine was painted Post Office red, and the Aquaplane head was polished aluminium.

division. He had developed a passion for Lotus as a schoolboy, enthralled by reports of duels with Bucklers, gleaned from *Autosport* during illicit readings at newsagents. Some of his friends had pre-war Morgan 4-4s, Singer Le Mans and a pre-war Alfa Romeo – cheap then, and in need of work – and they mixed with 750 Motor Club people at the emergent British tracks at Brands, Snetterton, Castle Combe and Goodwood; he remembers Blandford hill climb being popular too. When they went racing, he and his mechanic friend Jon Smith wore Thornycroft overalls, and other competitors presumed them to be enjoying factory sponsorship. 'There was no call for fashionable clothes in those days,' recalls Luff. 'We were used to economizing having just come out of rationing.'

Another aspect of the long delivery time for the full complement of parts for the car meant that Luff knew more than most people how to make them fit together, and it was as much on the strength of this as his

Thornycroft training which got him a job as assistant to technical director Mike Costin at Lotus. There was little advantage in staff discounts in those early days, so Luff's second Seven was made up from a scrapped chassis. Aided and abetted by Trevor Shann from the Lotus service department, it was repaired by Frank Coltman of Progress who made the spaceframes, and repanelled by Williams and Pritchard. As project engineer on the Elan, Luff secured a development 105E motor, Elan gearbox, instrumentation, wheels and trim, and the emergent Seven was also painted with the vacuum cleaner; the registration LOT 7 was obtained from a 50cc BSA moped for £5.00. However, Luff found the joys of company Elan motoring far preferable to the privations of Seven ownership, and the car was quickly sold. Said Luff:

I was only superficially involved with the evolution of the Seven; there was never any intensive effort on development until the Series 4, and that was a retrograde step in engineering terms because the car evolved mainly due to parts becoming scarce or obsolete, or when a choice of engines was possible. There was always a supply and cost problem, and the chief buyer, John Standen, could always get components cheaper.

Chapman's main interest was the racing cars; he wasn't interested in the Sevens. My biggest scare was when I drove the first Seven with 13in wheels, and the hubs had loads of spacers, with only a couple of threads holding the wheels on!

Now living in rural Norfolk, Brian Luff has been involved with a number of vehicle projects, including Gilbern and Clan in the 1970s.

MONEY EARNER

When Colin Chapman handed over the metaphorical keys to Graham Nearn, he would have lost no sleep over his creation. He wasn't like that, never dwelling much on the past and always keen to move on to the next project; besides which, the Seven had almost always represented no more than a reliable source of income for the company. Hardly any trace of the model remains at Hethel, although there are a handful of people still working there who were contemporaries of the Seven. This is not the fault of GM or Bugatti; it is simply that Chapman passed on literally everything to Caterham in 1973. Ironically the Seven, as a Lotus and Caterham product, has outlasted all other Lotus models by eighteen years; the Esprit was only launched in 1975, and is a youngster by comparison.

THE CHESHUNT FACTORY

In 1959 Lotus was poised to enter the big league. Its Mk 18 was a year away from giv-

ing the company its first Grand Prix victory, in the hands of Stirling Moss (driving Rob Walker's car) at Monaco, a success which would make the general public sit up and take notice, and Lotus would get more orders on the strength of reflected glory. It was also on the threshold of the motor manufacturing 'establishment': the new plant at Cheshunt was officially opened on 14 October 1959 by the local MP in a ceremony attended by trade, press and other Lotus well-wishers. There were two blocks, the main one devoted to building the Elite, and the other to race preparation, experimental and servicing work, and significantly, sports car production, including the Seven. Some hundred units had been produced during the model's first two years.

Elite production was increased by the expedient of having bodies made at Filton by the Bristol Aircraft Company, who were specialists in glass-fibre injection moulding. With eight Elites in production at any given time, output from the Cheshunt factory was five cars a week, when the price was £1,949. By the end of 1959, the Elite was all but invincible in production sports car racing, with Graham Warner (of the Chequered Flag garage), Peter Lumsden, David Buxton and Edward Lewis, and indeed, the great Jim Clark in the Border Reivers' car, usually in front on both the domestic and European scenes; one of the main challengers was Chris Lawrence in his famous Morgan Plus 4.

Between producing the last Mk 6 and the first Seven, Chapman had logged two years' hard-won racing experience, and the fruits of the streamliners were carried over into the Seven. The chassis of the Series 1 was more akin to the Eleven than the Mk 6, although smaller section 18-gauge tubing was used – 1in (25mm) or ¾in (19mm) mostly – and there were fewer triangulations, a weight-saving rationalization which was made up for by the riveting of all the alloy panels to

LOTUS SEVEN SERIES 1 (1957–60)

(Super Seven C produced from December 1958, basic Seven known as F from October 1959. Seven S1 America introduced October 1959)

Price

Basic Seven F, fully built less extras – £1,036 7s 0d including purchase tax; £536 in kit form
Super Seven C – £892; or fully built, £1,546 5s 4d
Seven America – £511 in kit form, less extras; $2,795 in USA

Layout and Chassis

Two-seat sports car with multi-tubular triangulated spaceframe chassis (1in and ¾in square and round 18-gauge), aluminium panels, nosecone, wings and mudguards. Seven America had clamshell-style fibreglass front wings

Engine

Type	
Seven F:	Ford Prefect 100E
Super Seven C:	Coventry Climax FWA
Seven America:	Austin Healey Sprite
Block material	
Seven F and	
Seven America:	Cast iron
Super Seven C:	Aluminium alloy
Head material	
Seven F and	
Seven America:	Cast iron; modified options, e.g Aquaplane
Super Seven C:	Aluminium alloy, single overhead cam, four-branch exhaust manifold
Cylinders	4 in-line
Cooling	Water; electric fan on US imports
Bore and stroke	
Seven F:	65.3 x 92.5mm
Super Seven C:	72.4 x 66.6mm
Seven America:	2.48 x 3mm
Capacity	
Seven F:	1,172cc
Super Seven C:	1,098cc
Seven America:	948cc

Valves	8; sidevalve in Seven F, ohv in Seven America and Super Seven C
Compression ratio	
Seven F:	8.5:1
Super Seven C:	9.8:1
Seven America:	8.3:1
Carburettors	Seven F: single Solex or twin SU
Super Seven C:	twin SU H2
Seven America:	twin SU
Max. power (DIN)	
Seven F:	40 @ 4,500rpm
Super Seven C:	75bhp @ 6,250rpm
Seven America:	40bhp @ 5,000rpm
Max. torque	
Seven F:	58lb/ft @ 2,600rpm
Seven America:	50lb/ft @ 2,500rpm
Fuel capacity	7 gallons (32 litres)

Transmission

Gearbox	
Seven F:	Ford 3-speed; internals optional, e.g. Buckler C-type. Standard ratios: 3.664, 2.007, 1:1, reverse 4.79:1
Super Seven C:	Austin A30 4-speed. Ratios: 4.08, 2.58, 1.66, 1:1, reverse 5.17:1
Seven America:	Austin Healey Sprite 4-speed. Ratios: 3.63, 2.37, 1.41, 1.00, reverse 4.66
Final drive	BMC Nash Metropolitan hypoid
Final drive ratio	
Seven F and	
Seven America:	4.875:1
Super Seven C:	4.55:1

Suspension and Steering

Front	Independent, by lower wishbones and upper arms incorporating anti-roll bar, combined coil spring and damper units

Rear	Live axle located by twin parallel radius arms, diagonal Panhard rod, coil springs and dampers	**Dimensions (in/mm)**	
		Track	
		Front	47/1,194
Steering	Initially Burman worm-and-nut, replaced by Elite (BMC) rack-and-pinion. Super Seven's column adjustable for length, three-spoke alloy leather-rim wheel	Rear	47/1,194
		Wheelbase	88/2,235
		Overall length	129/3,277
		Overall width	
		Seven F and	
		Super Seven C:	53/1,346
		Seven America:	55/1,397
Tyres		Overall height	27.5/699 to top of scuttle, 44/1,118 with hood erect
Seven F and			
Seven America:	5.20 x 15; pressures 18psi front, 22 psi rear	Ground clearance	5in/12cm
		Unladen weight	
Super Seven C:	4.50 x 15 front, 5.00 x 15 rear, 4.50 x 15 spare	Seven F:	1,008lb (with 5 gallons of fuel)/457kg (with 23 litres of fuel)
Wheels			
Seven F and		Super Seven C:	924lb/419kg
Seven America:	Bolt-on 15in pressed steel disc; wire spokes; Lotus 'wobbly web' optional	Seven America:	960lb/435kg
		Performance	
		Top speed	
Super Seven C:	Knock-on 15in splined hub wire spoke	Seven F:	81mph/130km/h
		Super Seven C:	104mph/167km/h
Brakes		Seven America:	83mph/134km/h
Type	Hydraulic; front, Girling drums with twin leading shoes; rear, Girling drums	0–60mph	
		Seven F:	17.8sec
		Super Seven C:	9.2sec
		Seven America:	12.1sec
		Fuel consumption	
Size		Seven F:	35.6mpg/7.9l/100km
Seven F and		Super Seven C:	30mpg/9.4l/100km
Super Seven C:	Front, 9in x 1.75in; rear, 8in x 1.25in	Seven America:	30mpg/9.4l/100km
Seven America:	8in x 1.25in		

the frame; this now included transmission tunnel and side panels instead of just scuttle and undertray as in the Mk 6. Where components were attached by bolts or rivets, the Seven chassis used square-section tubing, and from 1965 the frames were made by Arch Motors, just as they are for Caterham today. However, for a time – until 1962 – the panelling continued to be produced by Williams and Pritchard.

The Seven is a shining example of the axiom that form follows function, with hardly a curved panel to be seen, and corresponding to the most basic tenets of a cheap competition car. The most obvious differences between Mks 6 and Seven are the Seven's sloping nose and its squared-off rear end which superseded the Mk 6's rounded rump. This provided marginally greater cargo-carrying capacity, and the wings or

Newly built Series 2 Downton conversion car at Cheshunt, still equipped with cycle-wing front mudguards, and Lucas fog and spot headlight arrangement – on dip, the spotlight simply went off. Aluminium front mudguards were fixed and did not turn with the wheels, and despite the subsequent introduction of flared 'clamshell' wings, cycle wings in fibreglass were available until 1964.

mudguards were now separate entities. The front mudguards continued to be the pointed cycle-wing type, carrying torpedo sidelights, and the by now familiar egg-crate grille was also carried over. In the cockpit, the instrument binnacle of the Mk 6 was simplified to a flat dash panel; this, like the nosecone, was secured with Dzus fasteners, while four over-centre stays held the bonnet down. To top up the radiator header tank meant removing the nosecone. The Series 1 fuel tank was held in place by nothing more sophisticated than elasticated straps, which had the dubious benefit of making for easy access, but a propensity to shake loose when in motion;

this facility extended to many other components, and continued to be the case with the Elan S4 I ran more than a decade later.

ELITE SUSPENSION

The Seven inherited a modified version of the Elite's double wishbone set-up, which was derived from the Mk 12 Formula 2 racing car. Because of the Seven's narrower track, only the top arms (which formed a wishbone with the anti-roll bar), trunnions and uprights fitted, and the lower wishbones were specially fabricated. These provided the

Front suspension assembly awaits the anti-roll bar, and nearside upright and hub assembly is yet to be fitted.

mounting points for the coil springs and Armstrong damper units and uprights, which were linked to the upper arm by a ball joint; all chassis pick-up points used rubber bushes.

Initially, steering gear was of the Burman worm-and-nut variety, and brought up to date with an Elite-style rack-and-pinion system shortly after production got under way; this gave two-and-a-half turns lock to lock. The basic car – the Seven F – was endowed with a hugely unglamorous Wilmot Breedon ivory plastic steering wheel of which the American *Sports Cars Illustrated* magazine commented that 'it couldn't be any larger, or even a skinny driver couldn't get in the car . . .' followed by the damning statement '. . . and if you weigh much more than 180lb [82kg], you might as well forget it . . .' They also described getting into a Seven as 'climbing into a frozen sleeping bag with a wooden leg'. The Seven C or Super Seven fared better in this respect, with a leather rim version. Whatever the wheel looked like, the Series 1 driver was always confronted with the steering column between his feet, making it necessary to curl his toe around it to get at

the clutch. In any case the pedals were tiny, making it difficult for anyone with more than a size nine shoe to cover just one pedal. It made heel-and-toe changes easy, provided the right pedals were danced on.

Instrumentation was, predictably, minimal: it included speedo, oil pressure, water temperature, ammeter and an optional rev-counter, located in front of the passenger. There was no fuel gauge; not until the Series 3 appeared in 1968 could Seven owners be certain of how much fuel they had left. The handbrake was located under the dash on the passenger side, and had to be pulled towards the cockpit like an oar; its handgrip was bent upwards to clear the transmission tunnel.

At first the Series 2's live rear axle was located by twin trailing arms, attached to the chassis inside the wheel-arch, and a diagonal member located the differential to the rear of the chassis. Coil springs and dampers echoed the frontal arrangement, and like the front set-up, all joints were rubber bushed. A measure of Chapman's business acumen can be gauged by the fact that the majority of Sevens made before 1968 used Triumph Mayflower and Standard 10 Companion

Instruments and gauges were minimal, but nonetheless generously distributed across the Series 1 dashboard. Like any real sports car, the tacho was directly ahead of the driver, while the speedo was positioned to reassure the passenger – or not.

View of the underside of the A-frame supporting the rear axle. Early bushes were prone to wear as the axle flexed around the pivot point, and the axle itself could even crack.

back axles; clearly he bought in bulk, and at an advantageous price presumably, because both these models were defunct by 1959. And therein lay the problem, too, because in its original incarnation, the poor old axle had only been expected to trundle sedately around in a saloon car. Now, however, it was required to transmit considerably more power, from engines ranging from the 1,172cc Ford to the 75bhp Coventry Climax, often at racing speeds; as a result it was thoroughly over-stressed, leading to blown seals and worse. The solution was to brace it with a sturdy A-frame from a bushed mounting welded to the differential casing, combined with a radius arm on either side.

Cast-iron drum brakes were fitted front and rear, of 8in diameter and 1¼in wide, with twin leading shoes at the front, and the handbrake acting on the rear. Road wheels were 15in pressed steel on skinny 4in rims, with a spare mounted on the back panel and

bound on with a leather strap. Thus the style was set for basic Lotus motoring for the next three decades and more. A basic Series 1 cost £587, roughly the equivalent of a respectable annual salary then: which shows what good value a Caterham is today.

Colin Chapman was always keener on the next project; once a model was up and running, it had to be refined, and variations on the Series 1 theme quickly followed. The Super 7 was an export version with a high compression head, twin SUs, and a four-branch exhaust. A rev-counter and spare wheel were thrown in at no extra charge. The Seven A used the 948cc BMC A-Series engine, which was slightly more sophisticated than the sidevalve Ford unit, and drove through a four-speed gearbox. It needed ingenuity to get the carburettor dash pot to fit under the bonnet: one way was to machine its top off, shorten the needle and the pot itself, and put it back together again.

The Series 1 Seven A came out in October 1959 and used the 950cc BMC A-series engine with twin SU carbs, normally found in the Austin Healey Sprite. It particularly appealed to US customers, since there was an established BMC dealer network for servicing.

The side exhaust has been a feature of certain Seven models, and the Series 1 car was no exception. The twin SU carburettors on the BMC A-series engine had to have their dash-pots shortened to fit under the Seven's bonnet.

The Series 2 car was slightly dearer at £611. A variation on the A-Series-engined car was the up-market Seven A America, featuring fibreglass wings and a full weather kit including hood, canvas doors, carpets, plus rev-counter, cooling fan and spare wheel, for a final price of $2,897.

Lastly, the S1 series was topped by the £700 Super Seven, or Seven C indicating Coventry Climax power. The potent little 1,097cc device drove through the BMC four-speed box, and lighter wire spoke wheels were fitted.

The flared 'clamshell' wings of the Seven America would be adopted for other Sevens, and contemporary feeling was that they were a 'vast improvement over the cycle wing type', although the view from the cockpit was described as 'vintage'. Nevertheless, they were a major step forward in civilizing the car, whose earlier cycle-wing mudguards were fixed so that they didn't turn in unison with the steered wheels.

There is probably no one who knows as much about the Lotus Seven as Peter Brand. A native of Cheshunt, Peter joined Lotus at Hornsey in May 1959; today he is chief inspector at Hethel, making him the longest serving employee still with the company. Formerly in the Fleet Air Arm, and then a technician with Handley Page making Victor bombers, Brand answered an advert for fitters in his local paper, and although it was well known that Lotus was soon to move to Hertfordshire, he began at 7 Tottenham Lane. Peter recalls the conditions as being exceedingly cramped, and whenever the weather was fine, work carried on outdoors:

At Hornsey, Series 1 Sevens were made alongside Elevens, 17s and other racers; in fact at first I found it hard to cope with the different terminology of the motor business, as opposed to the more precise vocabulary of the aircraft industry. At Lotus in those days you had to be able to 'cut, shut and weld',

Introduced at the Detroit Show in 1960, the Seven America was built with flared 'clamshell' front wings in fibreglass (originally designed by Chapman in 1957) because legislation did not permit the cycle-wing type. Lucas 7in (177mm) sealed beam headlights could also be dipped, while sidelight and indicator units had twin filament bulbs. The Seven America was also equipped with indicators, wipers, better instrumentation and revised spare wheel carrier. The rear wings were also in grp, and were somewhat smaller than those of the Series 1 model. Moulds were made by Albert Adams, who was largely responsible for the development of composites at Lotus.

and it was a lot cruder work than making jet aeroplanes.

The relief felt at the move to the spacious, purpose-built premises on a green-field site at Cheshunt was tempered by the loss of company character. No longer would the odd policeman turn up at night to lend a hand; no more could just a single employee be left at his job when everyone else had packed up; and where once people used to clock off, and then go straight back to work, now legislation forbade it.

That was a commonplace practice if we had to get a car ready for a customer to race the next day. Still, wages went up, from 4s 10d an hour at Hornsey to 5s 1d an hour at Cheshunt. We still had to work a forty-seven hour week though, which included Saturday morning.

Peter Brand recalls:

It was us and them at Cheshunt, and there were two separate buildings: one where Lotus road cars were built, and ours, Lotus Components, where we made Sevens and the racing cars sold to customers – as opposed to Team Lotus cars. So you had Formula Juniors, 18s, 19s, 23s and Formula 1 stuff, as well as racing Lotus Cortinas and Elans, being put together in one building. Much of the Seven production took place on the first floor, effectively up in the roof space

The Seven shop was on the mezzanine floor of the Lotus Components block at Cheshunt, and cars were lowered out of a hoist through the doors at the far end. Taken in 1963, the picture shows Don Fibbens at the bench and Peter Brand fitting a nosecone. To the left are storage racks, and right is a partly assembled car for export and the stores; components for kits arrived in cardboard boxes, bottom centre.

in fact. There was no machine shop at Cheshunt; the only machine there was a centre lathe, with a couple of bench drills. Opposite the factory across Delamere Road was a company called Heldrew Engineering, who used to do the bulk of Lotus' machining and make the mag wheels. And not far away was HD Collins, which did spinnings, and they still produce a bezel for Caterham for the back panel into which the recessed filler goes.

DAMPERS

Lotus used to deal with Armstrong Engineering because Chapman had a good relationship with the firm, and their engineer used to call to sort out damper problems. Nowadays, Caterhams are fitted with Bilstein units.

It was always considered important to put 'mileage' on factory cars, and if a journey had to be made, a Seven, an Elite or Elan – especially the Elan prototypes – would be taken to increase its mileage and thus build up a picture of reliability. Very often this was

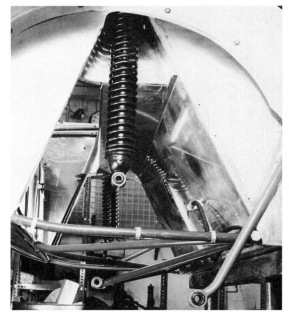

A view of the rear suspension's anatomy before the live axle is fitted, showing spring damper units, A-frame, radius arms and chassis tubes. The aluminium undertray of the Series 1 cars was absent, allowing better access to this area.

done by the works drivers, who had different preferences; for instance, Clark preferred a very stiff anti-roll bar, whereas Ireland wouldn't want that at all. Feedback was therefore somewhat varied. But if anyone ever had a query on a particular car, if Peter was given the chassis number then he would know what engine it had, what colour it was and when it was made. He stayed with Sevens for seven years, and describes the methodology:

We were doing a lot of our own aluminium panel work then, and making a lot of our own running gear. Lotus had three panellers working on Sevens, and also making fuel tanks. Williams and Pritchard were making Elevens and 15s mostly by the time I joined, building kits mainly, but occasionally there were fully built cars for export; it took sixty hours to build a 'home delivery' car. We did everything, including cutting out and making the trim, and

covering it in red vinyl; no two were ever the same, and this remained the case in other areas for some time, too. For instance, there was no tool for bending brake pipes; it was done by hand, and you could tell who had built a car by the way the brake pipes were bent.

Originally the screen pillars had been fitted by eye, which affected the rake of the screen and consequent fit of the hood. This was eventually settled when templates were made for the gap between rear dampers and screen. Because of the unpredictable alignment of the chassis' back rail, the sticks of the hood frame were bent over the fitter's knee; it wasn't worth bothering with a jig.

Apart from the regular Climax, E93A and BMC-engined cars, a lot went out without engines for customers who wanted to fit their own power-plant; this could be something a bit exotic like a Bristol unit. The letters and

Clutch and brake fluid reservoirs mounted on a support bracket above the pedal box, with chassis plate behind. Brake pipes were all bent by hand.

The Seven's Standard 10 rear axle has the A-frame bracket welded on, with four U-bolts either side for the suspension mountings, plus a breather tube fixed by a Jubilee clip, intended to stop oil blowing out under pressure. The script MS3 4.11 indicates that this is destined for a Cosworth or Classic-engined car.

figures MS3 411 were painted on the axle to identify which engine and drivetrain were to be mated up, in this case a Cosworth or Classic engine; the number 4.5 indicated that the car would be running a 105E motor. The regular axle was prone to blow its oil seal, so a breather tube was fixed to it by means of a Jubilee clip to cure the problem.

'People knew the Series 2 was in the offing,' said Peter Brand. 'We were playing around with fibreglass wings designed by John Frayling and made by Albert Adams, who was into composites.' They experimented with self-coloured grp, putting pigment in with the resin, but colour separation was a problem in the early days; reds and yellows in particular came out streaky. The flared wings, first fitted on the cars for the States, were admired by a lot of people, and adopted for general Seven production. The main advantage in practical terms was that less mud was distributed over the rest of the car than with cycle-wing mudguards.

Another feature that changed with the US model and was announced on UK cars at the 1961 Earls Court Show, was the adoption of the 7in (175mm) Lucas sealed beam headlights that could dip in the conventional way. The arrangement for the Series 1 and early Series 2 was a chromed spot and fog either side, the driving light on the near-side, and when dip was required, the driver flicked a toggle switch and the off-side light went out. However, this was not an ideal situation, and it was phased out by legislation.

The sidelights mounted on top of the clamshell wings had twin filament bulbs fitted so they could double as indicators. As more prominent illumination became desirable, rear lights were sourced from the Sprite caravan. The battery moved from the luggage boot to the top of the pedal box, and an electric fan was mounted in the cowl ahead of the radiator. The first Series 2 was chassis SB 1000, and used a Lotus factory registration number 7 TPE. It was a red car, pictured in Graham Arnold's *Lotus Super Seven Profile* – wrongly captioned as a Series 1 in fact – and at some point was fashioned with a boat-tail body. It appears to have ended up in New Zealand via the USA.

By the middle of 1960, with Cheshunt fully operational, the Seven had a rationalized chassis – produced by Universal Radiators now, and sent for panelling to Alert Motor Works – and the cars were called Series 2s. Whereas the Series 1 spaceframe was derived from the Eleven, the Series 2 was designed to match the body shape. Under racing loads, however, the

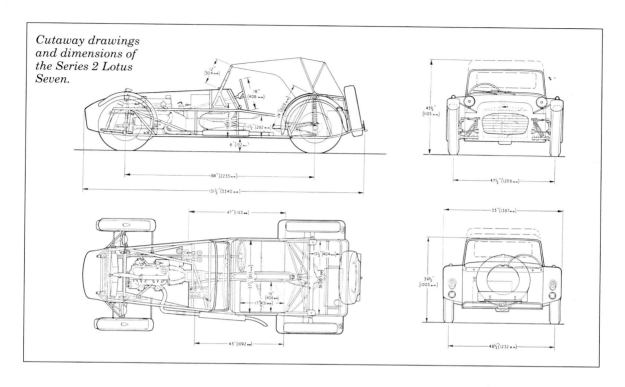

Cutaway drawings and dimensions of the Series 2 Lotus Seven.

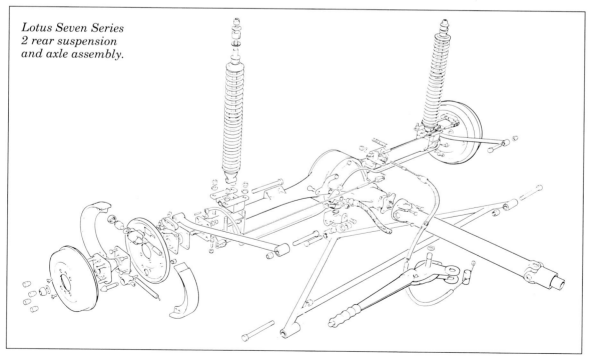

Lotus Seven Series 2 rear suspension and axle assembly.

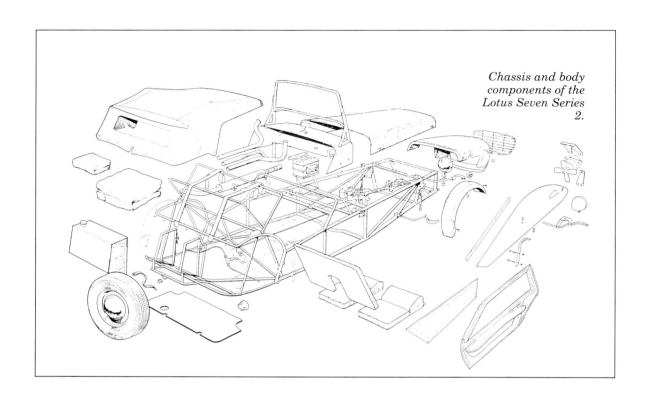

Chassis and body components of the Lotus Seven Series 2.

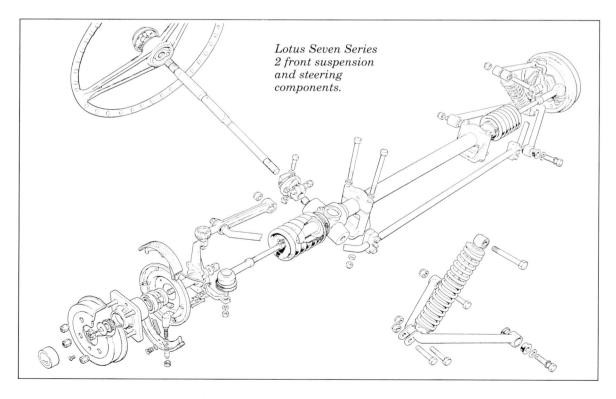

Lotus Seven Series 2 front suspension and steering components.

simplified chassis proved to be weaker than that of its Series 1 predecessor.

BARGAIN BASEMENT SEVENS

Although Seven production hardly stood still, competition cars took priority. There were no fewer than ten variations on the S2 theme, with the good old Ford 100E sidevalve engine powering the Seven F, now at the extraordinarily low price of £399. According to Peter Brand, a number of cars were unsold and gathering dust in a field, so the price was reduced by £100, and they went like hot cakes. A year later, the base model was using the 997cc push-rod 105E Anglia engine and four-speed gearbox, fitted with a single Weber carb or twin SUs; the DIY man could buy one for £499. The most common faults committed by home builders were to fit the lower wishbones upside down, which produced an ungainly 9in (225mm) ride height

instead of 6in (150mm), and the anti-roll bar could also be inverted erroneously. Customers were therefore encouraged to bring their cars back for a post-build check-over. Another common mistake was that the dowel to stop steering column movement was often overlooked, even discarded; one customer's steering column was coupled to the rack by a mere 2mm of spline, and the factory refitted it there and then rather than allow him to drive home again.

Alongside the Anglia-engined Seven in 1961, there was the 1,340cc Classic-engined option, which gave 84bhp. In retrospect, Peter Brand considers this unit to be the best balanced engine for the Seven. In the mid-sixties I ran a 'Fatty' Anglia with a Classic engine and single downdraught Weber, looking the part on its lowered suspension and Lotus Cortina wheels – my first car in fact – and it showed 100mph (160km/h) on its Classic-sourced speedo. The 1340-engined Seven, or Super Seven as it was known, was a different matter, however, as it had a

Ford engines sat further forwards in the Seven chassis. This 997cc unit has twin Webers and Cosworth head, and the car is a fog- and spot-light model.

43

LOTUS SEVEN SERIES 2 (1960–8)

Price
Kit form – £587 in 1960, £499 in 1961, £645 in 1962; £868 15s 0d fully built.

Layout and Chassis
Two-seat sports car with (simplified) multi-tubular triangulated spaceframe chassis, aluminium panels; nosecone, front and rear wings in glass-fibre

Engine

Type	
Seven:	Ford Anglia 105E
Super Seven from 1961:	Cosworth-Ford Classic 109E
Super Seven from 1962:	Ford Cortina 116E
Block material	Cast iron
Head material	Cast iron
Cylinders	4 in-line
Cooling	Water, electric fan standard from 1962

Bore and stroke	
105E:	80.96 x 48.4mm
109E:	80.96 x 65mm
116E:	80.96 x 72.7mm

Capacity	
105E:	997cc
109E:	1,340cc
116E:	1,498cc
Valves	8 ohv

Compression ratio	
105E:	8.9:1
109E:	9.5:1
116E:	8.3:1

Carburettors	
105E:	Twin SU H2; pair twin-choke Weber 40DCOE on Cosworth version
109E:	Two twin-choke Weber 40DCOE
116E:	Single Weber 40DCOE; pair twin-choke Webers on Cosworth version

Max. power (DIN)	
105E:	39bhp @ 5,000rpm
109E:	85bhp @ 6,000rpm
116E:	66bhp @ 4,600rpm; Cosworth: 95bhp @ 6,000rpm

Max. torque	
109E:	80lb/ft @ 4,000rpm
Fuel capacity	8 gallons (36 litres)

Transmission

Gearbox	
105E:	4-speed Ford Anglia
109E:	4-speed Ford Classic
116E:	4-speed Ford Cortina GT; Hardy Spicer propshaft

Ratios	
116E:	15.81, 9.34, 5.50, 3.90: 1, reverse

Final drive	
105E:	Hypoid, Standard Companion axle 4.55:1
109E:	Standard-Triumph axle 4.1:1
116E:	Standard-Triumph axle 3.90:1

Suspension and Steering

Front	Independent by lower tubular wishbones, forged upper arms located by anti-roll bar, combined coil spring and Armstrong damper units
Rear	Live axle, controlled by A-frame, radius arms, coil springs and Armstrong damper units
Steering	Triumph Herald uprights, Alford and Alder rack-and-pinion with steering column at shallower angle
Tyres	5.20 x 13 or 4.20 x 13 Dunlop C41 or India C46 Autoway
Wheels	13in pressed steel
Rim width	4in or 4.5inJ

Brakes			109E:	966lb/438kg
Type			116E:	1,036lb/470kg
105E and 109E:	Girling hydraulic drum		Ground clearance	
116E:	Girling disc front,		105E:	6.5in/16.5cm
	hydraulic drum rear		109E:	4in/10cm
Size			116E:	6in/15cm
105E and 109E:	8in front, 7in rear		**Performance**	
116E:	9.5in disc front, 7in x		Top speed	
	1.25in drum rear		105E:	89mph/143km/h
			109E:	103.6mph/166.7km/h
Dimensions (in/mm)			116E Cosworth:	103.4/166.3km/h
Track			0–60mph	
Front	51.5/1,308		105E:	12.2sec
Rear	50.8/1,290		109E:	7.6sec
Wheelbase	90/2,286		116E Cosworth:	7.7sec
Overall length	131.25/3,334		Fuel consumption	
Overall width	57.5/1,461		105E:	25mpg/11.3l/100km
Overall height	43/1,092 to top of hood		109E:	22.9mpg/12.3l/100km
Unladen weight			116E:	24.8mpg/11.4l/100km
105E:	952lb/432kg			

Cosworth head, high-lift cam and twin Webers, plus four-branch manifold. Resplendent with polished alloy rocker cover – racing-spec engines were painted red – there would have been little to touch it on the road then, especially not for £599. US racers could get a limited edition of the 109E-engined Seven for competing in the Sports Car Club of America (SCCA) series. Use of the 1,340cc unit was advocated by Mike

When the Cosworth-tuned 109E engine was fitted as standard, the car became known as the Super Seven once more. Here the 1961 Motor Show model – an export version – stands in the Cheshunt forecourt, with shop foreman Eric Howgill and electrician-fitter Richard Champion at left.

Costin and pioneered by Warren King, employed at the time in the Lotus accounts department, and King was also responsible for prompting another quantum leap in the Seven's inventory with a pair of sidescreens hinged onto the windscreen pillars. Wet weather Seven motoring never looked back. Along with a heater, rev-counter and electric cooling fan, the sidescreens gradually became standard issue instead of merely options.

As the Ford Motor Company increased the capacity of its engines, the Seven kept pace with them, in much the same way as Morgan was doing at the time with its 4/4 model. In 1962 the Super Seven 1500 came out, using the five-bearing 116E Cortina unit and gearbox, with single Weber. The remote gear shift

was from the Herald, adapted with an aluminium wedge to raise the angle of its mounting. The gear lever was bent to clear the dashboard, just as the handbrake lever was bent to clear the transmission tunnel. Power output was 66bhp, and for the first time front brakes were Girling discs, and the spec extended to tonneau and sidescreens. It was yours for £585.

The Seven A continued to be available, now with the BMC 1,098cc engine option, for which extra bracket work was required on the frame, and it used single or twin SUs, four-branch exhaust manifold, driving through a Sprite four-speed gearbox. US customers could still get their 'luxury' version. There was also a Cosworth version of the Super Seven 1500 which used twin Webers,

Peter Brand works on the twin 40 DCOE Webers fitted to this Cosworth 1500 Series 2 model. The swirl pot serves the bigger radiator, which is shrouded to catch more air.

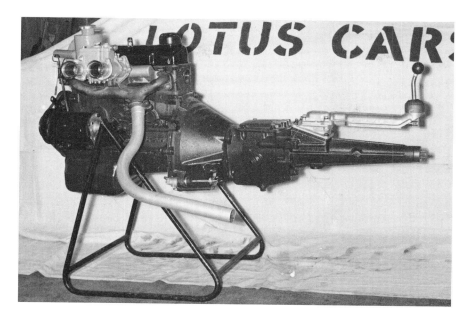

A standard 1500 Ford engine with single Weber on show. The Herald remote shift is mounted on a triangular plate to obtain a horizontal fitting.

a high-lift cam and four-branch manifold to boost power to 95bhp. There was much interest in developing a dry sump lubrication system at this time, and Peter Brand designed one using other Lotus competition parts.

When founder employee Nobby Clarke died in 1962, sales manager Peter Warr became general manager of Lotus Components. Although I knew he had raced a Seven, I must admit I was unaware of this when I encountered him in his role as Lotus' F1 team manager in the early seventies, when he was decidedly cool and authoritative; and yet, I recall, never short of his sense of humour. He must have needed it, too,

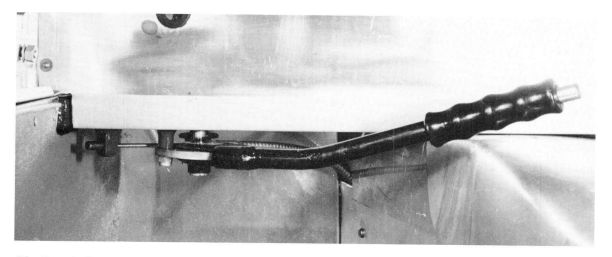

The Seven's fly-off handbrake is located under the passenger-side dashboard, and bent to clear the scuttle and transmission tunnel. In practice, few people use it.

In the early days the engines were fitted by hand, progressing to three-legged hoists before production moved upstairs at Cheshunt; here, Peter Brand uses the power hoist to lower a standard 1500 unit into a Series 2 chassis. The engine mounts lie ready on the scuttle.

he eventually managed to persuade Colin of the advantage of bronze-welded chassis tubes over fusion welding; the bronze-welding method is more accurate because there is minimal tube distortion, they are easier to repair, and the strength and integrity of the join are not affected. Arch Motors specialized in this technique, and under the guidance of Bob Robinson, they began to supply Lotus, and have done so ever since.

Production of the Seven was always erratic, and it also depended on the number of orders for racing cars, for these took priority. Sometimes it was two a week if the cars were to be fully built, and nine or ten if orders for kits were being satisfied. Peter Brand was continuously employed on Sevens but, he says, 'I was sometimes alone working on Sevens, and sometimes there were three or

when coping with the frustrations of delivery day (Friday) when it was discovered someone's kit had gone out but parts had been left behind, or the wrong chassis dispatched. The notion of reverting to the Lotus Mk 6 practice of selling just the chassis and Lotus-made parts, and telling the customer to source the rest himself, was briefly considered as a means of side-stepping such difficulties and the problems with component supply.

The next major change in Seven evolution was the switch to Arch Motors for supply of chassis. Don Gadd, now development director at Arch Motors, had been development engineer at Lotus from 1958 to 1964 – his wife Sheila was Chapman's secretary – and

Ready for action: a Series 2 kit with Ford Cosworth engine and all components laid out in the London garage of owner Ted Wilson in 1963.

The Series 2 Super Seven 1500 with new vinyl hood, now featuring rear three-quarter windows. The nosecone is in fibreglass rather than aluminium, and has a less drooping profile. Hubcaps are embossed with the Lotus logo.

four of us; the most was five.' Brand trained John Robinson at Cheshunt to be his understudy, and John subsequently held the record for assembling a Seven in the quickest time, managing four hours in a publicity stunt organized by Graham Nearn at a Hethel open day in 1968. But it was later revealed that the vehicle had been put together previously and then dismantled again, to ensure it would go together all right during the actual demonstration.

RECORD BUILD TIME

Peter Brand's time for putting together a kit car was nine or ten hours, when twelve hours was the average. This was attained after the production department came up with an anti-roll bar machined to fit correctly, which knocked a couple of hours off the build time. Assembly time for a complete car was by now thirty hours, but Brand managed a fully built one in twenty-two hours. That included

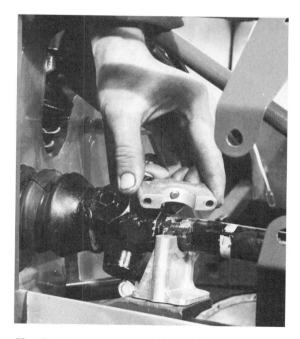

Hand of the master: Peter Brand fits the housing containing the aluminium dowel which prevents fore and aft steering column movement.

testing, but not painting; the cars went off to the paint shop and were painted with lights off and wings akimbo, to ensure paint reached right into the joins. The ancillaries were refitted and tightened up after painting.

But, says Brand with a twinkle in his eye,

> I did each one differently, perhaps starting one off with the chassis, and another by assembling bits on the bench. It was partly to avoid the boredom of doing the same thing over and over again, and partly so John Robinson couldn't follow my method and beat my time. We raced each other to see who could build one fastest, and it also made for added interest to see whose car won on the circuit. It was nice to know that you'd actually built a race winner. That way the customer also got a better car made.

Robinson, whose nickname was 'Tweak', was later to transfer to Team Lotus in the JPS days as an F1 mechanic; later he left to work on the offshore oil rigs.

The factory could always be relied upon to produce something a bit extra if required, and one such customer was Keith Hamblin. A Series 2 car known as the 7/20 (or Seven-and-a-half), was built up to Eleven spec around a written-off S1 chassis, with independent rear suspension and disc brakes all round, plus the added sophistication of these being inboard at the rear. Lotus project engineer Hugh Haskell – who sadly died in 1994 – fitted a 997cc Cosworth-Ford unit, and it proved a potent racing machine; at various times it was driven by Wendy Hamblin, Clive Lacey and Natalie Goodwin. Chapman himself drove it in the 750 Motor Club's Birkett Six-Hours relay at Silverstone in 1962. On the strength of this, four similar spec cars were built.

One notable customer at this time was Martin Lilley, who owned the TVR Car Company from 1965 to 1980; he was considered to have one of the quickest Sevens around. A Series 2 car was designed by Bill Wells, who nowadays makes wooden gear knobs; it was built by Peter Brand for the 1965 Racing Car Show, and exhibited as a Clubman's racer. It was sufficiently different to be given its own Lotus type number: the 3/7, or 'Three-Seven'. Powered by a Cosworth version of the 116E Cortina engine, producing 125bhp, it featured an independent rear end, Elite diff and inboard discs at the rear, set off by mag-alloy wheels of the Wobbly Web variety. It was sold to John Berry who put it to good use in the Clubman's category, winning the title three years running; however, no further examples were made. Berry's car was sold to Tim Goss.

HETHEL CALLS

Having been shop supervisor, Peter Brand was elevated to the post of chief inspector. He was the only qualified tester at Lotus outside Team Lotus itself. Therefore he drove everything which came out of Lotus Components. At Cheshunt, a 20-mile (32km) route was devised around the local countryside, and complaints from neighbours were usually only forthcoming when unsilenced F1 cars were started in the small hours; this would happen if a car was due to race imminently. In fact the Lotus factory was there first, but residents weren't necessarily sympathetic. Hethel of course is blessed with its own test track, and Peter recalls driving the 7X, campaigned with great success by Tim Goss. 'It was a Formula 3 car in disguise,' said Peter. 'It was a fabulous car to drive, brilliantly responsive.' That was in 1969, the year Peter Brand posted the record for the largest number of Lotus cars destroyed in one accident: testing a Formula Ford, he ploughed off into a line of seven Elans, happily without personal injury. All were write-offs, and the insurance company could not understand why so many cars were in such proximity to the test track – and you have to see their point.

Along with a number of employees, Peter Brand had not been over-keen on the prospect of a move to far-flung Norfolk, and in fact a few, including Warr, elected not to go. Yet more were relocated, though later they returned to the suburbs. The move was made for several reasons: one was that Lotus had simply outgrown the relatively confined Cheshunt factory, and Chapman's future aspirations demanded greater capacity; relations with residents were strained at times by nocturnal testing; and Hethel's potential as a test track and airfield were greatly influential. Twenty years or so earlier, the site had been the province of the B24 bomber.

The move took place during October 1966, organized by an initially reluctant Mike Warner, then group purchasing manager. With Lotus Components' operations based at one end of the vast hangar which constituted the factory, and Lotus Cars' production line at the other, the company was set to press ahead with its 'lurch' upmarket. This was bad news for Seven fans, for the burgeoning Elan Plus 2 and Europa models were uppermost in the minds not only of Chapman but most of the company; it needed someone with a vested interest in selling Sevens to give Lotus a nudge: enter Graham Nearn, with an order for twenty Series 2s, and the line continued. By now, 1,362 Series 2s had been built, the majority of which were Super Seven 1500s.

At Hethel, some Seven panelling was still made by Alert, but the bulk of the business went to JW Eve & Son of Norwich. Nosecones and wings were produced by Williams and Pritchard, Ivory Plastics near St Albans, and Barnham Broom Fibreglass not far from Hethel. Yellow, red and green were the main colours. It seems curious that, given the

The Lotus Components division at Hethel in 1969, with Seven S3s in build at left rear, beside a 47 Europa. A Formula Ford 61 wedge contrasts with a Mk 12 in the foreground, as a pair of Type 59 F3 cars are assembled. Team Lotus was located behind the back wall, and stores were out of shot, to the left.

nature of Lotus products, the company's production structure didn't cater for manufacturing Seven extremities.

THE ARCHETYPAL LOTUS SEVEN

The Series 3 cars were built between 1968 and 1970, with production totalling some 350 units, roughly 200 of which were sold in 1969. There had been a division of responsibilities within Lotus, and the Series 3 was developed by Lotus Components, and marketed, like later Series 2 cars, exclusively by Caterham Car Sales, as can be traced in their ads which were almost invariably on the first page of *Motor Sport* magazine. Graham Nearn was very much instrumental in getting Lotus to fit the Elan's twin-cam engine in the Seven, by proving it could be done and showing up at the factory in the donor car to demonstrate the fact. He also showed that it would be cheaper to use than the ubiquitous Holbay-tuned Cortina unit – the same engine as used in Formula Ford – because it was produced by Lotus themselves.

The main difference between Series 2 and Series 3 cars was the adoption of the Ford Escort Mexico rear axle, which gave a wider track, prompting the fitment of wider wings and allowing 5½J Lotus Cortina wheels to be used; the propshaft and front hubs were revised, there was Triumph Herald rack-and-pinion steering gear, revamped dash, eight-gallon (36-litre) fuel tank and, as considerations of race safety now included seat-belts, the Seven got these too. The rear of the chassis was subsequently strengthened as well. There were four main derivations of the Series 3: in basic form it was known as the Economy model and used the Ford 225E engine from the 1300 GT Escort, coupled to the 116E Cortina gearbox; this was sufficient to develop 68bhp. The same engine in 1,600cc guise, out of the Cortina, and equipped with crossflow head, downdraught twin-choke Weber carb and four-branch manifold, produced 84bhp; the S3 running this motor was called the Standard model, and was priced at £775. While the 1300 was frugal, the 1600 was entirely adequate as regards performance, and it was reliable too; running the optional 3.7:1 diff, it was as quick as the 1,500cc Cosworth which preceded it.

The Series 3 was introduced in 1968, and this restored example is fitted with Cosmic alloy wheels, a popular, and cheap, after-market wheel at the time.

A Series 3 fitted with Ford crossflow 1,600cc Holbay engine and twin Webers.

SUPER SEVEN SS

On a far more exalted level was the Seven SS, or Super Seven Twin-Cam, powered by the famed Lotus 1,600cc twin-cam. In basic form this was good for 90bhp; with Holbay modi-

fications and a pair of twin Webers, it pushed out 125bhp. The Super Seven cost £1,250, but the figure quoted for the very swish, Lotus Components-built Seven S was £1,600 from Hethel. For this you got the Holbay modified twin-cam, plus a fully trimmed and

The 125bhp twin-cam-engined SS on the Lotus stand at the 1969 Earls Court show, where thirteen orders were taken – and officially only that many were ever produced. Front indicators are beside the nosecone instead of under the headlamp brackets.

LOTUS SEVEN SERIES 3 (1968–70)
CATERHAM SUPER SEVEN S3 (1974-81)

Price

1600 – £775 in kit form
SS twin-cam – £1,250 in kit form (officially only
13 units made)
One-off Holbay S show car (TNG 7G) – £1,525
Caterham Super Seven S3 – £2,196 in kit form,
1975; £5,638, 1980

Layout and Chassis

Two-seat sports car with multi-tubular
triangulated spaceframe chassis, modified to
accept new rear axle; aluminium panels;
nosecone, wider front and rear wings in glass-
fibre. SS twin-cam had additional chassis
triangulations in side panels plus a number of
minor stylistic variations. Caterham S3 to
similar spec with engine variations until 'long
cockpit' model introduced in 1981. Bonnet and
nosecone raised to accommodate casting on 'Big
Valve' engine

Engine

Type	
1300:	Ford Escort GT
1600:	Ford 225E Cortina
Holbay S:	Modified Ford 225E (flowed head, polished ports, using Holbay R120 high-lift cam etc.; dry-sump lubrication system optional)
SS:	Lotus-Ford Holbay-tuned twin-cam; chain-driven camshafts; (based on Ford 1500 block; Lotus Special Equipment and 'Big Valve' versions introduced later)
Caterham S3:	Ford 1600GT; Lotus-Ford Big Valve twin-cam (as for Lotus Elan Sprint); Vegantune VGA (based on Ford 225E block, belt-driven camshafts)
Block material	Cast iron
Head material	
1300, 1600GT, S and VGA:	Cast iron
SS and Caterham S3 twin-cams:	Cast aluminium
Cylinders	4 in-line
Cooling	Water, electric fan
Bore and stroke	
1300:	80.96 x 62.99mm
1600 and S and Caterham S3:	80.96 x 77.62mm
SS and Caterham S3:	82.6 x 72.8mm
Caterham S3 with Vegantune VGA:	80.96 x 77.62mm
Capacity	
1300:	1,297cc
1600 and S and Caterham S3 with Vegantune VGA:	1,598cc
SS twin-cam and Caterham S3:	1,558cc
Valves	8 ohv
Compression ratio	
1600:	9.1
SS:	9.5:1
Caterham S3 Big Valve twin-cam:	10.5:1
Caterham S3 Vegantune VGA:	10:1
Carburettors	
1300 and 1600:	Single twin-choke downdraught Weber 28DCD
S and SS:	Two twin-choke sidedraught 40DCOE Webers
Caterham S3 twin-cam and Vegantune VGA:	Two twin-choke Dell'Orto
Max power (DIN)	
1300:	72bhp @ 6,500rpm
1600:	84bhp @ 6,500rpm
S:	120bhp @ 7,000rpm
SS:	115bhp @ 7,000rpm
Caterham S3 Big Valve twin-cam:	126bhp @ 6,500rpm
Caterham S3 Vegantune VGA:	130bhp @ 6,500rpm

Max. torque	
1600:	108lb/ft @ 4,000rpm
SS:	116lb/ft @ 4,500rpm
Caterham S3 Big	
Valve twin-cam:	113lb/ft @ 5,500rpm
Fuel capacity	8 gallons (36 litres)

Transmission

Gearbox	Ford 116E Cortina
Ratios	2.97, 2.01, 1.40, 1.0:1; reverse 3.32:1
Final drive	
1600:	3.7:1 Ford Escort Mexico
SS:	3.9:1 Ford Escort Mexico with Hewland limited slip diff, 8in Borg and Beck clutch
Caterham S3:	3.89:1 Ford Escort RS2000 (replaced by Morris Ital in 1980)

Suspension and Steering

Front	Independent by lower tubular wishbones, forged upper arms located by anti-roll bar, coil spring and Armstrong damper units; hubs changed to accommodate Ford and Brand Lotus wheels
Rear	Live axle, controlled by A-frame, radius arms, coil springs and Armstrong dampers
Steering	Rack-and-pinion; turning circle 29ft 6in (9m), 2.7 turns lock-to-lock
Tyres	165 x 13 Dunlop SP Sport, 195/70 x 13 Goodyear Rally Special or G800
Wheels	
Lotus S3:	Pressed steel 5.5J Ford, or cast-alloy Brand Lotus or Dunlop 5.5J
Caterham S3:	Brand Lotus, Goodyear or KN Jupiter alloy

Rim width	5.5in

Brakes

Type	Girling discs front, drums rear
Size	9in discs front, 8in drums rear, 1.5in wide shoes

Dimensions (in/mm)

Track	
Front	49/1,245
Rear	52/1,321
Wheelbase	89/2,261
Overall length	133/3,378
Overall width	61/1,549
Overall height	37/940
Unladen weight	
1600:	1,204lb/546kg
SS:	1,258lb (with 4 gallons of fuel)/571kg (with 18 litres of fuel)
Caterham S3:	1,162lb/527kg
Ground clearance	
Lotus S3:	3in/7.5cm
Caterham S3:	4in/10cm

Performance

Top speed	
1600:	101.2mph/162.8km/h
S:	107mph/172km/h
SS:	103mph/166km/h
Caterham S3	Big Valve twin-cam: 114mph/183km/h
0–60mph	
1600:	8.8sec
S:	7.4sec
SS:	7.1sec
Caterham S3	Big Valve twin-cam: 6.2sec
Fuel consumption	
1600:	26mpg/10.9l/100km
S:	18.3mpg/15.5l/100km
SS:	19.2mpg/14.7l/100km
Caterham S3:	28.3mpg/10l/100km

upholstered cockpit. Several SSs were sold after the model was shown at the 1969 Racing Car Show.

The SS represented the swan song of the Series 3 cars, immediately prior to the advent of the Series 4, and they were given an extra touch of exclusivity by the factory. The rear lights were recessed into the wings, headlight brackets were lower, the grille slats were different, and the dashboard was in anodized aluminium, with rocker switches instead of flick switches; dials were black, and indicators were on a stalk to the right of the steering column. Lotus's world championship winner's logo was displayed on the flank. The other badge was Twin-Cam SS, and the prototype had a similar badge in red. Cockpit upholstery differed from the standard car.

The twin-cam-engined Series 3 SS (for Super Seven) is the most valuable of all the Lotus models, as only thirteen were built. The price new was £1,250, as compared with a normal Series 3 at £775. The twin-cam unit was first seen at the 1969 Earls Court Show. The car ought to have taken an award for the best presented coachwork at the motor show, but its bonnet was cut in half to display the Holbay twin-cam, and was deemed ineligible. Key staff including Mike Warner, Peter

Brand, Alan Barrett and Peter Lucas were highly annoyed, having worked well into the small hours to get it ready. But pre-show and pre-race 'all-nighters' were very much the norm then, as now – as I can confirm, having been around the JPS team in the early seventies, and having observed TVR's Cerbera launch at the 1993 Earls Court Show.

The one-off Holbay S car, TNG 7G, with tuned Holbay 1600 motor, was some £300 dearer still. This was also on the Lotus stand at the 1969 Earls Court Motor Show, painted in Rolls Royce regal red. It now belongs to

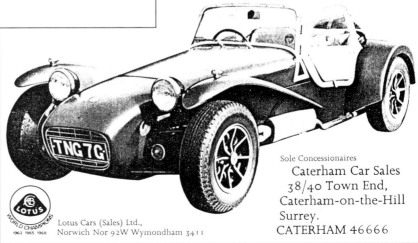

The Ultimate Lotus 7

66 From its deceivingly graceful and flexible behaviour in traffic to its startling performance and Grand Prix handling and cornering capabilities on road or circuit, driving this rorty road-going racer is an experience not to be missed in a lifetime, whatever cars you've driven before 99

Sole Concessionaires
Caterham Car Sales
38/40 Town End,
Caterham-on-the-Hill
Surrey.
CATERHAM 46666

Lotus Cars (Sales) Ltd.,
Norwich Nor 92W Wymondham 3411

The one-off Holbay S model.

Vincent Haydon, the Salisbury-based Lotus specialist, and is being restored. Its original log-book bears the signature of John Miles, Lotus test driver at the time and soon-to-be Team Lotus F1 pilot.

A further one-off which can be seen as a prototype Series 4 car, since its chassis was fundamentally the same, was the Seven X, built for club racer Tim Goss. Fitted with the Holbay engine, independent rear suspension and discs all round, it took Goss to the top of the 1970 Clubman's Championship.

Dropping a twin-cam engine into a Seven was not simply a matter of welding on different engine mounts. It had been discovered that there were limits to the amount of power the regular chassis could handle, and owners who had already played with super-powerful engines and increasingly effective tyres, found there was chassis distortion. Lotus' chief draughtsman Peter Lucas redrew the chassis with extra tubes and tri-angulations in the engine bay and side areas, and made the stressed outer panels of sheet steel instead of aluminium. Predictably the weight of the car increased, and equally unsurprising were *Autocar*'s disappointing test results: 103mph (165km/h) maximum and 0–60mph (0–100km/h) in 7.1secs. At 125bhp it was only 5bhp up on the Seven S, although mid-range power and tractability were better. Nevertheless, the way was paved for the Series 4.

THE UGLY DUCKLING

It is difficult not to have an opinion about the Series 4: you either like it or you don't, and I incline towards the former, being an aesthetics man rather than a technical expert. My opinion was rocked when I caught sight of a Series 4 tub at Arch Motors, however, for its basic form contained none of the satisfying structural aesthetics of the spaceframe chassis: just slab sides and square-frame tubing. But whatever your view, the Series 4 has to be seen as a creature of its time. The Series 3 was doing very nicely, and then in 1970 it was decided to pitch for the fun-car market as well, occupied by beach buggies, Mini Mokes and, also in 1970, the Bond Bug.

The Series 4 Seven managed to fit into this category by virtue of its less sporting specification and the fact that its previously stark aluminium body was now clad in an angular glass-fibre shell, which from certain angles could match the pod of a beach buggy. The headlights were more faired in, with niches cut in the bonnet to make them more snug, the indicators were on top of the integral wings, with the sidelights hiding in the extremities. The one-piece bonnet hinged forwards to reveal the 1,600cc Ford 225E motor, or the twin-cam in the Super Seven. The rear wings tapered in a way which conceded a connection with race-derived aerodynamics, and a roll-over bar was prominent. Actually, aerodynamics and Sevens are virtually total strangers, since the Seven's cd figure is estimated to be a barn door-like 0.70. This is why it runs out of steam rather sooner than a car wearing an all-enveloping body. The Series 4 made no serious attempt at bettering that, although the brand new Caterham 21 completely redresses the balance.

Both the Series 4 Seven and the typical beach buggy were showy, provided noisy, wind-swept motoring and paid lip service to the late sixties ideals of no-cares freedom. Perfect for the Kings Road. But as far as the S4 was concerned, that doesn't do it justice because taken away from the precedent set by the S3, it was an excellent sports car, if prone to rattles; although there is no getting away from the view that its specification was retrograde.

The S4 was based on a traditional ladder chassis of round- and square-section tubes. The sides, front suspension bay and scuttle were of sheet steel panels, which were then covered with the glass-fibre body. As we shall see later, this has sounded the death-knell for many Series 4 cars through corrosion set up by moisture being trapped between the steel and the fibreglass.

The double pressed-steel wishbone front suspension set-up was derived from the mid-engined Europa, conveniently sourced in-house, with the rear axle still the Escort unit, located by leading and trailing arms and an A-bracket, plus coil springs and dampers all round. Contemporary Dunlop alloy wheels were generally fitted. The short-coming in this arrangement was that the axle casing of the S4 was, in effect, acting as a torsion bar, and with the Watts linkage on either side, the suspension could only work with the axle twisting. This resulted in numerous fractures as transmission nose-pieces blew. One remedy was to assemble the axle with Hermetite to counter the leaks.

The Standard model cost £895 in 1970, and the Super Seven was £100 more. You need to be a driver of considerable ability to establish that the S4 is inferior to the S3, and roughly a thousand customers were sufficiently impressed to buy Series 4s between 1970 and 1973, so it should in no way be dismissed as a failure.

In 1970, Lotus Components metamorphosed into Lotus Racing; this was closed down in 1971, and Lotus Cars carried on production. But the imposition of Value Added Tax (VAT) in 1973 shattered the burgeoning kit-car industry, and prompted Chapman to call a halt; in May 1973 he handed over the whole Seven assembly line, including jigs, moulds and existing stocks, to Graham Nearn at Caterham Car Sales. Caterham persevered with the S4 for a year, and thanks to requests from enthusiasts, began to remanufacture the Series 3 car.

A number of factors came together to seal the Seven's fate as a Lotus model. Tighter safety certification laws were looming large in the States, and this would have forced Lotus to upgrade the Series 4 spec to meet them. Then there was Chapman's inexorable drive towards a more exalted niche in the market place, which saw the Elite, Eclat and Esprit enter production; this meant a move completely away from 'down-market' kit cars to fully automated production lines. With Britain's recent entry into the EEC 'Common Market', and the introduction of VAT in place of the old purchase tax, which applied to cars whichever way they were sold, the end of the line was in sight for the Seven at Hethel.

3 The Odd Man Out

When the Europa came out in 1967 with its 1,470cc Renault 16 engine, we all approved of it, but wondered why a twin-cam engine had not been used. The works racers were the twin-cam 47 variants, but for road-going Europas with Lotus power we had to wait until 1971 and the facelifted 74. But what people had failed to appreciate was that Chapman's original idea was for simple kit-build Europas to replace the Seven. Back in 1964 he had Lotus Developments build a prototype 46, based on a John Frayling design, and it ended up looking so attractive and promising a proposition that he decided it had to be built by Lotus Cars rather than Components.

Happily for Lotus Components, the Seven Series 2 was a steady seller, which Components needed to lean on when racing car sales were poor. Unlike smaller concerns which could withstand the hard times, Lotus Components was part of the grand scheme of Group Lotus and had to pay its way. This included stumping up for overheads it did not actually use, like company planes, though the burden could be eased by reducing Components' financial commitment to the parent. One proposition was to move the operation to another building just outside the main Hethel complex, over the road in Potash Lane, the original rather unprepossessing workshops to which the grp operation had come when it left Cheshunt.

There were job cuts, too. Yet despite the fact that Warner was returning to Lotus after a six months' stint with the firm making Brand Lotus wheels, the figures for the cars themselves did not look too good: where the Elan made a profit, the Seven made a loss

of around £100 per unit. Clearly, there was a need to rationalize production costs, or else price the car out of existence. The most expensive component of the traditional Seven was its chassis, bought from Arch for £55 in the mid-sixties. As labour costs rose, so did the price of such a labour-intensive and time-consuming article. The Elan's backbone chassis might have provided a plausible alternative to the spaceframe, but that model was scheduled for the axe. Serious measures were called for.

Chapman's interest in the Seven had waned to practically zero, and given that Mike Warner had convinced him that the S3 was no longer financially viable and the job could be done more cheaply and efficiently with a ladder chassis and steel and glass-fibre panels, there is no wonder Lotus Components went ahead with the Series 4. So, what seems illogical to us today, bearing in mind how good the S3 and subsequent Caterhams were, appeared quite a sensible move in 1970. They even attempted to distance it from the Seven by giving it the Lotus type number 60. But was it such an undesirable vehicle, one unworthy of the badge?

No other Seven was produced in such relatively high volumes. Nearly 600 were built in two years, at a rate of fifteen units a week, and Warner had his sights set on as many as 2,000 a year. To sell this many meant breaking into new overseas markets, with all the legislative traumas that implied. It also required the Seven to appeal to sports car buyers who would normally go for something a little more middle of the road, so the Series 4 would need to offer more in the way of creature comforts. Indeed, with its self-

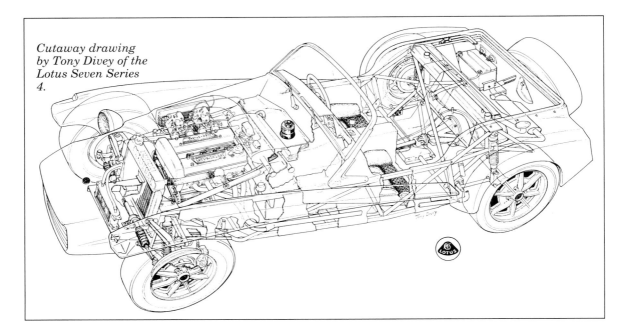

Cutaway drawing by Tony Divey of the Lotus Seven Series 4.

consciously fashionable grp styling aiming fair and square at the increasingly prosperous 'youth' market – that is to say, anyone under twenty-five – the S4 was clearly the Lotus entry-level car: once hooked, the young Series 4 owner would be on the Lotus ladder and a potential purchaser of more exotic models; 'Lotus Motoring Begins Here' ran the slogan on the windscreen sticker.

Group Lotus was not exactly on the up when the S4 was launched at Geneva in March 1970; it was confronting serious financial problems, even though Rindt was destined to be World Champion, and all the attendant publicity surrounding the Lotus 72 was unquestionably good for sales. By the end of the year, Lotus Components had become Lotus Racing Ltd, and thanks to sales of the Series 4, this arm of the company was showing well; which was more than can be said of Lotus Cars, where sales of the Elan Sprint were boosted with a power hike and Players' Gold Leaf colour scheme.

DEMISE OF LOTUS RACING

A year later though, Chapman decided he didn't want to build racing cars for customers any longer – Jabby Crombac suggests in his book on Chapman that his obsession was veering towards boat-building at the time (fulfilled in 1973) – and indeed, what started off as a promising season, with Lotus racing cars available for all the major single-seater Formulae at home and in the States, ended with many disappointments; 1971 was the first year since 1959 that Team Lotus had been without an F1 victory. Also Chapman discovered that fifty-four three-year-old Lotus 61 Formula Fords remained unsold, largely because the rival Merlyn was proving the more successful car.

Everyone was aware, too, of the impending introduction of VAT on all products, whether these were sold in component form or otherwise, which would spell the end of the British kit-car industry in 1973. Furthermore, US safety legislation could easily have meant

Eminent 1970s motoring journalists examine the Seven Series 4 Clubman on the Lotus stand at the 1971 London Racing Car Show. Meant to replicate the 7X prototype, panels were in stressed aluminium with Type 41 F3 front suspension, albeit with a de Dion set-up at the back. Closure of Lotus Components scotched this project as a customer car.

expensive modifications having to be made to the S4. By the end of 1973, the only car in production at Lotus Cars was the Europa. The best route as far as Chapman was concerned was to sell off Lotus Racing, the prospect of which prompted Warner to resign. Maybe the decision had already been mooted in April 1970, and perhaps it was this which caused Warner to walk out of a Lotus board meeting immediately prior to the press launch of the Series 4 at the Grosvenor House Hotel; this incident left Chapman and Arnold, somewhat bemused, to handle the launch with impromptu speeches. Then in March 1971 Chapman and Fred Bushell flew to California for talks with US dealer Kjell Qvale (who had just bought Jensen Motors), ostensibly for supplying Lotus type 907 engines for the Jensen Healey; however, this may have been misinterpreted by Warner as the prelude for a sell-out. Even so, the call for an impromptu stock check a week after the California trip made Warner put two and two

together, and after a blazing row with Chapman, he walked out.

Chapman's lack of patience with people and with projects that he felt were not going his way is well known; he did not suffer fools gladly or any other way. I remember during my JPS stint at Grands Prix, that during his pre- and post-race briefings with Peterson, Fittipaldi and Warr, if Chapman was fired up, the JPS 'Travco' motor-home was a particularly uncomfortable place to be; unless you had a useful contribution to make, it was better to make yourself scarce. So for someone in Warner's position, being the object of Chapman's anger must have been extremely unpleasant.

Warner's place was taken by John Standen, purchasing director and veteran of the Hornsey days; but after Warner went for good, Lotus Racing more or less fizzled out, and production of the still profitable S4 was transferred to use up spare capacity in the main factory. Team Lotus, or John Player

LOTUS SEVEN SERIES 4 (1970–2)
CATERHAM SEVEN S4 (1973–4)

Price
1600 GT – £895 in kit form
Twin-Cam – £1,245 in kit form, less extras, e.g.
heater, £17, roll-over bar, £15, magnesium alloy
wheels, £42, tonneau cover £10
Caterham Series 4 – £1,487

Layout and Chassis
Simplified round- and square-section tubular
spaceframe chassis, with stressed steel panels
wrapped and spot-welded to sides, scuttle, front
suspension bay, and forming front cross
member. Two seats. Separate self-coloured
fibreglass body, produced in four sections and
bolted to chassis; forward-hinged bonnet,
redesigned hood with no rear three-quarter
windows, but sliding perspex panels in
sidescreens. Caterham S4 identical but without
Lotus badge.

Engine
Type	
1300:	Ford Escort 225E
1600GT:	Ford Cortina 225E (also available as Holbay Clubman)
Twin-Cam:	Lotus-Ford ('Big Valve' head available for late models)
Block material	Cast iron
Head material	
1300 and 1600GT:	Cast iron
Twin-Cam:	Aluminium, chain-driven camshafts
Cylinders	4 in-line
Cooling	Water, engine-driven fan
Bore and stroke	
1300:	80.96 x 62.99m
1600:	80.96 x 77.62mm
Twin-Cam:	82.6mm x 72.8mm
Capacity	
1300:	1,297cc
1600:	1,598cc
Twin-Cam:	1,558cc
Valves	8

Compression ratio	
1600:	9:1
Twin-Cam:	9.5:1
Carburettors	
1300 and 1600:	Single Downdraught Weber 28DCD
Twin-Cam:	Twin Weber 40DCOE
Max. power (DIN)	
1300:	72bhp @ 6,500rpm
1600:	84bhp @ 6,500rpm
Twin-Cam:	115bhp @ 7,000rpm ('Big Valve' and Holbay-tuned versions: 125bhp)
Max torque	
1600:	108lb/ft @ 4,000rpm
Twin-Cam:	116lb/ft @ 4,500rpm
Fuel capacity	7.5 gallons (34 litres)

Transmission
Gearbox:	Ford Corsair 2000E
Ratios:	2.97, 2.01, 1.40, 1.00, reverse, 3.32:1
Final drive:	3.77:1

Suspension and Steering
Front	Double wishbones ex-Lotus Europa, separate anti-roll bar, coil spring and damper units
Rear	Ford Escort axle controlled by quadruple Watts linkage, A-frame on off-side, coil spring and damper units
Steering	Burman rack-and-pinion, collapsible Triumph column, 2.75 turns lock-to-lock
Tyres	165 x 13HR Dunlop Sport, 165 x 13SR Goodyear, pressures 24psi front and rear
Wheels	Brand Lotus forged alloy, or Ford pressed steel
Rim width	5.5inJ

Brakes			Unladen weight	
Type	Discs front, drums rear. Elan-style 'umbrella' handbrake lever		1600:	1,200lb/544kg
			Twin-Cam:	1,310lb/594kg
Size	9in discs, 9in drums			
			Performance	
Dimensions (in/mm)			Top speed	
Track			1600:	101.2mph/162.8km/h
Front	50/1,270		Twin-Cam:	105.5mph/169.7km/h
Rear	52.5/1,334		0–60mph	
Wheelbase	90/2,286		1600:	8.8sec
Overall length	144.5/3,670		Twin-Cam:	7.7sec
Overall width	60.5/1,537		Fuel consumption	
Overall height	43.5/1,105		1600:	26.3mpg/10.8l/100km
			Twin-Cam:	19mpg/14.9l/100km

Team Lotus as it became known in 1972, moved into the vacant Lotus Racing premises. In July 1971 the decision was taken to stop making the S4, although sufficient stocks of chassis remained to keep it going until October 1972. Graham Nearn had been waiting in the wings for precisely this eventuality, and the way was now clear for him to take on S4 production at Caterham Hill.

The stage was set for Caterham's involvement back in 1967, when Nearn approached Lotus' sales director Graham Arnold with a view to becoming sole distributor of Sevens. That of course was what happened, and Nearn was a regular visitor to Hethel, running the Seven stand at the Racing Car Show, and being generally on the ball with Seven matters. So, when it became clear that Warner planned to shift some 2,000 S4s a year, Nearn was somewhat incredulous. Regular Lotus dealers were already having a hard time selling Elans, and in any case were under pressure from Lotus Sales to sell the more up-market cars – although sales of the Plus 2 Elan and the twin-cam Europa largely pulled Lotus Cars out of the mire in 1971. Lotus Sales was amenable to Lotus Racing setting up its own dealer network, which

Caterham acquiesced to, as clearly it was a tall order for Caterham to sell the entire production. Six outlets were appointed, on the condition that they took fifteen S4s a year. Part of the inter-Lotus deal involved Lotus Racing taking back more than a hundred Formula Ford 61s, and they were facelifted and marketed as Lotus 61Ms – and amazingly sixty or so were sold. It was the leftovers which Chapman discovered in a hangar that proved the final straw in his mind. They were stood on their noses against a wall and were known as the 'wall-flowers', because no one wanted to dance with them.

The Series 4 also has the distinction of being built in both camps, as it were, at Hethel and at Caterham; equally, it was the model present at the symbolic Pub Lotus handover. When the deal was done, everything to do with Sevens was dispatched from Hethel to Caterham, for Chapman was never sentimental about such things. Enough components arrived at Caterham for a further thirty-eight Series 4s to be built, at the rate of about one car a week.

DESIGN OF THE SERIES 4

The two men responsible for designing the Series 4 were Peter Lucas and Alan Barrett, and work was under way in 1969. It took just twelve months to get it up and running, and the Series 4 was launched in March 1970. Much of the groundwork was done lapping the Hethel test track for hour after hour with a bare chassis, protected from the elements by a windscreen, seat-belts and roll-over bar. Eventually Peter Lucas rationalized the frame by having round- and square-section tubes supporting a simple spaceframe, strengthened with sheet steel panels. These were wrapped around the lower side-rail and spot-welded underneath and along the sides to give the chassis torsional rigidity, and they also created the scuttle and front suspension bay, with a folded section of sheet steel as a box-section front cross-member. I saw a bare chassis at Arch Motors, and although the tubing was actually the same inch square 18-gauge as the S3, I was struck by the relative crudeness of its steel panelling, compared with the elegance of a pure spaceframe. The other problem that this design threw up was that the glass-fibre body was also the undertray, so the steel chassis was in effect sitting in a plastic bath, and any water that got in wasted no time in setting up corrosion on the chassis tubes and side panels. Over the years, many have rotted away for this reason.

There was a degree of similarity with the Elan, which also counted on its bodyshell to add stiffness. Indeed, Lucas had also contemplated utilizing the Elan's backbone chassis as the basis for the S4 Seven; it was considerably cheaper, at £27 in 1969, compared with the £55 that Components was paying Arch Motors for an S3 spaceframe. A widened Lotus 61 Formula Ford chassis was also considered, and despite its rear-engined layout, the latter is not as fanciful as it might at first seem. To create a Seven, it would have been turned back to front.

More significantly, the wedge-shaped lines of this 1969 Formula Fordster were drawn by Alan Barrett, and unquestionably influenced his thinking when he penned the Series 4 Seven. The Lotus 61 is pre-dated by the 4WD gas-turbine 56 Indianapolis car of 1968, and if you look hard enough at the Europa you can discern characteristics broadly in keeping with the Series 4 Seven. Other stylists, notably Giorgetto Giugiaro, were drawing wedge-shaped cars at the time, and the Italian's major contribution to the Esprit is well known. What Barrett succeeded in doing was to amalgamate the traditional elements of the Seven with contemporary styling cues. These were largely drawn from his other creations, then the latest shapes on the race track, trend-setters in their own right; so in fact the S4 was ahead of the game.

Although Warner had a fairly free hand within Lotus Components, and the prototype was made behind an artificial wall, there was no question that Chapman knew all about the S4's genesis, since he was always on top of everything going on in the factory as well as at Team, and would frequently make his own personal contribution to a project. That Components was working with a development budget reputed to be in the region of £30,000 would also have ensured Chapman knew absolutely what was afoot. Barrett had come up with a quarter-scale model of the proposed Series 4, incorporating alternative designs for the front and rear wings on either side. One was pretty much how we see the Series 4 today, while the other was like the regular Series 3 at the back. At a board meeting involving Barrett, Lucas and Warner, Chapman indicated he preferred Barrett's rear wing treatment, but doubted it would work in a full-size model. In order to tip the balance, Barrett was at pains to make 'his' side more desirable than the old styling,

Details of the fibreglass-bodied Series 4, showing sidelights and indicators housed in the wings, and headlights snug in scallops beside the bonnet. The bonnet bulge is superfluous since this car has a Lotus twin-cam engine; it would be needed for a standard Ford crossflow unit with downdraught carb, however.

and spent much more time and energy on that aspect of the mock-up. Chapman realized what he was up to, but gave his approval, and the creation of the moulds was put into effect in March 1969.

The trendy outer skin was made of self-coloured grp, and rather belied the austerity of the chassis. The cockpit, transmission tunnel, console, dash and front scuttle formed a sort of dual bath-tub which was bonded to the outer skin, then bolted to the chassis at strategic points via housings bonded into the fibreglass shell. Chassis and fittings were made by Arch Motors, and bear the prefix AM, while some were made locally by Griston Engineering (of GRD fame) and prefixed GE. Completed chassis were dispatched ten at a time from Arch Motors' factory.

The S4's distinctive flared front wings were much longer and straighter in shape than their clamshell forebears; the extended moulding, going right back to the rear wing, protected the unwary from exhaust burns,

and the indicators on top of the front inner edge, plus recessed sidelights on the outer edge, were neat touches. Similarly, the headlights now protruded from shallow niches on the forward-hinging bonnet. Some earlier Series 4s had their front indicators down alongside the nosecone, with a secondary 'blip' on the wing. A raised air intake for the downdraught Weber was prominent on the bonnet, while the aperture for the radiator air intake was starkly rectangular, compared with the neater, more rounded-off shape of its predecessors.

The intention was for the Series 4 to be made on a flow line principle. It was no longer the province of the defunct Lotus Components, or its successor Lotus Racing; whereas earlier Sevens were built by individual fitters, S4s were assembled on a line where two people did specific jobs, and there were six separate stages in its assembly. Thus the individual builders tended to lack interest in the vehicle they were working on. Times were changing, and Lotus was

Access to the Lotus 'Big Valve' twin-cam in this Series 4 is less easy with the forward-hinging bonnet than it is with the lift-off aluminium bonnet models. The engine is a tight fit in the Series 4, and the air cleaner for the twin Webers is a monster.

beginning to employ a different kind of fitter – not so much of an enthusiast.

The fibreglass bodies were made in-house, not surprising perhaps bearing in mind the composition of Lotus' regular product. The bodies were composed of four basic sections: back end and sides, incorporating rear wings and dashboard, bonnet, and the pair of front wings. Working on the gel-coat principle, the sections were laid-up from the top outwards, starting with the top coat being sprayed into the mould, followed by an undercoat. Then the matting was laid in, and resin liberally brushed in. After the fibreglass had 'gone off', the body sections were removed from the mould and left outside to cure for a couple of days before entering the production cycle. They were attached to the chassis by threaded bobbins bonded into the fibreglass, as in other Lotus grp models. The bonnet was fixed by hinges (prone to corrosion) at the forward end, and Graham Nearn recalls this as being an extremely difficult operation when they were making them at Caterham.

The bodies were not without blemish, however. Former Lotus painter Mike Kelf described how a number were returned to the paint shop for complete resprays: you cannot touch up a gel-coat body, as the pigment is locked into the fibreglass. The paint was not applied to the moulds by the painters, but by the grp fitters, who, whilst expert in their trade, were not necessarily expert painters. The most common reason for a rejection was if the paint ran. It would not show up as a blister on the surface, of course, but as a blemish within the fibreglass. It could also be said that as a bottom-of-the-range car, the Series 4 did not receive the same degree of care in-build as the Elans and Europas. Colour range for the S4 was yellow, orange, lime green – all garishly trendy colours at the time, even for Porsches – and the more traditional red, white and blue.

There were other difficulties in assembly. With a left-hand drive car, the steering column. had to pass through the complex piping of the four-branch exhaust manifold. The hood was a departure from accepted Seven practice, with a more completely enveloping canopy made specially for the S4 by Weathershield. It lacked the valuable rear three-quarter side windows, but had no shortage of poppers, and was thought at the time to be an improvement on the old design. The S4 sidescreens were also hinged on the windscreen, but the design was sufficiently different for them not to stay pushed against the bonnet when opened. Their saving grace was their sliding plastic windows.

Hood fit was inconsistent, because Weathershield were making them up on a buck. The problem was caused by the angle of the screen pillar, naturally crucial, and Peter Brand and three others were dispatched to Weathershield's Birmingham factory to sort it out. 'Don't come back till it fits,' was the command from Mike Warner. The Lotus fitters were away four days.

Peter Brand recalls that the Series 4 was a different concept from the models it replaced. 'It was heavier, and had lost its classic looks, which meant it had also lost something of the Seven's character,' he said. Brand tested virtually everything Lotus produced, racer or production car, and he believes it handled better than the Series 3. 'It was less skittish, but that took some of the fun out of it. High-powered twin-cam versions had a reputation for lifting their inside

rear wheel on cornering, and also for axle tramp under hard acceleration. Its shape grew on you; it was considered a better looking car than the Series 3 at the time. And it was probably more refined and more comfortable.'

With the demise of Lotus Racing, Alan Barrett departed to set up his own design company, and actually supplied Series 4 bodies and Europa shells for a while. Other racing car designs followed, as well as a striking successor to the Invader for Gilbern, still-born when the company crashed. Barrett's last act before heading off to Cyprus to grow oranges was to build himself the ultimate Series 4. He had accumulated the wherewithal, having stockpiled virtually all the necessary components during the car's production period. Those he didn't have, like sidescreens and bonnet catches, he was sufficiently well versed to make himself. Barrett's Series 4 is fitted with a hardtop too, one of only twelve factory-produced items; it attaches to the car by just two bolts at the rear and a pair of windscreen clips. He also switched the original – leaking – glass back window for a hinged pane.

The Series 4 cockpit is one-piece glass-fibre moulding, so is quite austere. The driver has full instrumentation and toggle switch controls. The tube at left is for a (non-standard) map-reading light.

Barrett's Seven is a Rolls-Royce among Sevens, having velour trim and plush carpets in the cockpit and boot, and a matt black fascia. Other modifications include a tunnel-mounted handbrake, Triumph Spitfire competition uprights and bigger Triumph discs at the front. Wider rear wings cover 185/70 section G800s, and the twin-cam engine was rebuilt by Argo cars.

If any one area of the Series 4 looks dated today, it is the interior. The seats were fixed in place, as you find with Marcos today, and the pedals could be adjusted to the appropriate driving position, which ended up being semi-recumbent. The seats were the only areas to be upholstered, and the fascia was plain body colour. Dials and console-mounted rocker switches were as you might expect for 1970, but eminently clear and well laid out. Now there was a built-in roll-over hoop. Basic and simple sums it up.

Not a lot changed in the power-train from the Series 3. The base model Series 4 used the 1300 Escort GT motor, an alarming side issue of which was that the oil pan on this engine was at the back of the sump where it fouled a chassis rail; the simple expedient was to remove the offending chassis tube. The 84bhp 1600 Cortina GT lump which was also available was not affected in this way,

and the top model got the Lotus twin-cam. The really hot one was Holbay-tuned to give 125bhp. All Series 4s used the Corsair 3000E four-speed gearbox, in conjunction with an Escort rear axle. Although it had a live rear axle, that old Seven *bête noire*, the cracked differential, was a thing of the past with a triangulated arm (A-bracket) to locate it laterally on the offside. There was a pair of forward-facing radius arms – heavily bushed Watts linkages – which was quite a strange arrangement, plus a pair of coil springs and dampers.

Up front were double wishbones in pressed steel, sourced from the Europa, plus coil springs and dampers. Brakes were cast-iron Ford parts-bin drums at the rear, and 8½in discs with Girling trailing callipers at the front. A Burman rack-and-pinion system, giving 2¾ turns lock to lock, replaced the Triumph set-up, although the collapsible steering column was Triumph-sourced. A separate anti-roll bar picked up the bottom of the front shock absorbers. Wheels were pressed steel Lotus Cortina 5½J, with the Brand Lotus pattern optional; beyond doubt, the alloys suited the styling better and lifted the Series 4's image, as the pressed steel versions somehow made it all too reminiscent of a beach buggy.

4 The Caterham Story

The Caterham story starts in 1959 when co-owner Ian H. Smith, author and Lotus *aficionado*, set up on Caterham Hill as a Lotus Centre. His partner Graham Nearn summarized the company's evolution like this:

> Caterham Cars started in 1959, when there was an old garage at the back and petrol pumps at the front. Subsequently I sold the petrol station to Esso, and five years ago bought some land on the side, knocked the house in half and did the development round the back here. And in 1987 we moved down to Dartford.
>
> I grew up with the Seven. I was a young man when it came out, and it was thought of as a good little open two-seater which you could race if you felt like it; I thought of the Seven as the ultimate sports car, and I did a bit of racing for two or three seasons. Another of its virtues was that it was easy to maintain.
>
> There were a number of us here when we started out. One was Ian Smith, who wrote the first definitive book on Lotus. Chapman was just starting to appoint agents, and we were new, young and enthusiastic, and it was a natural thing to do. Later on we took on TVR and Marcos, and we had Gilbern for a while. The Caterham Cars advert was always to be found inside the cover of *Motor Sport* – and life was much easier, as that was the only serious British monthly you

Graham Nearn, pictured in a Vauxhall-engined car outside Caterham's Dartford plant. He has maintained the Seven legend for thirty-five years, nurturing sales all through the 1960s, and taking over manufacture of the cars from Lotus in 1973.

could get. It was straightforward to target your advertising then, whereas today you have to say 'no' to everybody!

Graham pointed out that economic recessions are by no means a modern phenomenon.

> In 1962–3 we had a recession, and Chapman started selling the cars direct from the factory because they needed the cash, and cut his dealers out. I just carried on buying and selling secondhand ones, and renovating anything that needed it. Lotus was pretty casual about spares, and we got a good name for giving good service and spares, and over a period of time we became established as the place to come to for Lotus Sevens.

This is absolutely the case, verified by Caterham's adverts in *Motor Sport*. It is therefore curious that Caterham's letterhead featured an Austin Healey Sprite, even in 1970; although the stationery also said 'Sole "Lotus Seven" concessionaires', however.

Graham became curious about the prospects for the Seven:

> I spoke to Chapman at the 1966 Racing Car Show and asked him what he was doing with the Seven, and he replied that he wasn't sure if he was going to drop it or not – he didn't really know. He wasn't fully convinced there was still a demand for it. [Lotus had just relocated to Hethel, of course, and Chapman was probably still feeling his way a bit.] At first they wouldn't commit themselves, but I had a word with David Lazenby who was running Lotus Components at the time, because they hadn't started building it again. Indeed, they were more concerned with building the Lotus 51 Formula Fords for the new category, introduced in 1967. They also made all the Team Lotus cars right up to Formula 1, and Lazenby said if we could sell them, they would build them.

There were enough parts in stock to put together twenty Series 2 cars, including a number of 1,500cc Ford motors – one is

A pair of young women enjoying an early Series 1, courtesy of Caterham Cars. The windscreen sticker promotes the first annual Racing Car Show, January 1960 – and where did they get those hubcaps?

reminded of the recent revival of the Elan, in the wake of the Bugatti take-over – and Caterham bought the lot. Nearn's gesture was enough to convince Chapman to continue. The cars were still built as kits, sold by Caterham and assembled by the customer. It was ever thus with the Seven. Said Graham:

Chapman pioneered the concept of buying your car in kit form to avoid what was then purchase tax. If you bought the car in parts there was no tax; only a completed car had to have tax paid on it. So you bought two lots of parts, engine and gearbox from Lotus' Racing Engines, and the rest of it from Lotus Components: two ostensibly separate sources, all in spare parts, and therefore not taxable. It was strictly monitored by customs to make sure some garages were not building them; penalties were potentially very heavy if you were caught.

Caterham collected the kits; indeed, Nearn went in person to check the parts were all there. That *modus operandi* took Caterham through to 1968 when Lazenby left Lotus to set up Hawk Formula Fords, and Mike Warner appeared on the scene.

CATCH THE BUZZ

Graham Nearn continues the story:

The history of the Seven flows up and down with the economy. Towards the end of the 1960s we were coming out of a recession, and everything began to buzz again. The *Prisoner* series gave Seven sales a big lift, of course. Warner arrived as the new boy and had to make sense of everything, and that included the casual relationship with the man who takes them away and flogs them; for various reasons Warner decided to rationalize the whole thing and modernize the Seven concept, and that was how the Series 4 car came about. Much money was spent on research and development, which he couldn't hide forever.

Then in the early 1970s things began to go wrong with the economy again, and the chickens came home to roost on all the Series 4's development costs; so he got booted out, and Lotus staff took over the bits and assembled what was there in the main factory, and that was the point at which I started pressing Chapman to see if we could take the whole thing over.

As we know, Mike Warner had a stock of virtually obsolete Formula Fords stored away in a nearby hangar, and Chapman wanted to get rid of them. So he sent John Berry down to Caterham to sell them. Nearn's response was that he would take the Formula Fords on the condition that he could have the entire Seven package. At first Chapman was reluctant; 'But,' said Nearn, 'he was always keen to move on, never dwelt on the past, and eventually Bushell and I thrashed out a deal. As well as the Formula Fords, Caterham got all the spare parts for the Seven, besides the goodwill that went with them.'

'It was a logical thing for us to do,' continued Graham, 'as we had a reputation as the Seven Centre; and from retailer we became the manufacturer as well. So everything came here to Caterham.' I asked him if it was a bit of a scramble, finding space for all the moulds and assembly equipment. 'There was a new development coming along, and I rented a number of lock-ups and an old boatyard around the corner to keep everything in,' he replied. 'There was a lot of junk too, but we slowly worked our way through it.'

There is no doubt that Graham Nearn put himself on the line taking over production of the Seven, for the sports car market was far from secure in the early seventies, what with a severe recession brought on by oil crises, the three-day week and the demise of traditional sports cars such as those made by Triumph, MG and Jensen. Taking on such a big operation was a brave move, especially considering he was moving it into little more

Graham Nearn has his own distinctive number plate on the Series 3 twin-cam Lotus Super Seven SS which starred at the 1969 Motor Show.

than a lock-up garage; though perhaps it was not dissimilar to Lotus at 7 Tottenham Lane, and indeed it has been said that Nearn models himself on Chapman.

Seven House maybe sounds a little grandiose; it was, in fact, just an Edwardian two-up two-down which from a decorative point of view had seen better days. Graham

Nearn's office was here, reached up rickety stairs, with the sales office at the rear of the showroom; like the stores, this bore all the signs of a life other than that which its builders had intended. Water was inclined to flow through the workshop, and from pre-1973 days until 1987, chassis fresh from Huntingdon were leaned up against a

The Caterham workshops at Town End were somewhat cramped, as this 1976 photo shows. The bonnet at centre right is destined for a car with a 1600 Kent engine; the hole is to accommodate the downdraught carb's air filter.

One of the first Caterham-built Series 3 Super Sevens, with Lotus twin-cam motor.

chicken-wire fence, and there they stood in the elements until they were needed.

Return of the Magnificent Seven

The car was to be known as the Super Seven – and indeed, all Caterhams are Super Sevens, whatever engine option is fitted – and although Chapman would obviously not countenance the use of his logo on the car, he permitted Lotus to be associated with the spares side. 'We used the Lotus twin-cam engine,' said Graham, 'so the association with Lotus continued. The name Caterham wasn't one I would actually have chosen for it; it just became universally accepted.'

Although Caterham carried on with the fibreglass-bodied Series 4 car, there was a major stumbling block in that its side-screens, made by Weathershield, were in short supply, and the windscreen surround was a special piece of extruded aluminium, all specially designed for the Series 4. Weathershield ran out of them and demanded a large sum of money – £50,000 – before they would create another batch. 'They wanted a guaranteed order and money up front,' said Graham. 'Basically it was not an economical car to build, which is ironic really, in view of the fact that the Series 3 was stopped because its aluminium panels were thought to be too dear. Our production rate then was about one car a week, and suppliers weren't geared up to service small-volume orders like ours.'

It was an impossible situation, and Nearn, who never much cared for the S4 in any case, put the word out that he had enough components to build eight or nine of the Series 3 cars. 'That sparked it off,' said Graham. 'The phone never stopped ringing. It was easier for us to build, and it was the right thing for us to do. At that point we were the same sort of size Lotus were when they were at Hornsey.'

At that time Caterham also had a showroom at 142 Finchley Road in Hampstead; the main workshop was on Caterham Hill, and also tackled accident repairs. This side of the business paid for the manufacturing of the Super Seven, which was a very low-key affair to start with, and Nearn and his staff were very much learning the game. Component supply was dire: they were the 'new boys', and parts manufacturers

Caterham staff and showroom at Town End prior to the building of the new development, featuring from left, Graham Nearn, Roy Crane, Jez Coates, Neil Whitford, David Wakefield, Clive Roberts, Johnny Johnstone, John Payne, Reg Price, Ian Cowdery, Peter Cooper, Isobel Forster, and Alex Davids.

invariably prefer to satisfy existing customers and leave the smaller orders until last. Strikes and industrial unrest were rife, and an event like a dock strike would give suppliers the excuse to deliver late. Orders for the cars came in, but Caterham were unable to commit themselves on delivery times; they had to keep throughput deliberately slow, because otherwise cars would be left unfinished, and the scene thoroughly confused.

Nearn considers that the situation changed for the better in 1979, and he points out, 'It is no coincidence that that was when Margaret Thatcher came in, and 1979 to 1981 is when we turned the corner again.

Though politicians can take the blame or credit for it, even so it's just the ebb and flow of the economy, I believe.' Just as importantly, the rise of the Caterham operation during the 1980s was due to the thorough groundwork put in during the previous decade, and now the firm's profile has risen to the point where major manufacturers including Vauxhall, Rover and Ford and the various tyre companies approach Caterham in order to try to persuade them to use their products because they want the kudos of being associated with a builder of dynamic sports cars. And naturally, the offers of the Rover K-series engine and Vauxhall twin-cam unit were seized upon.

Cooper's Relish

Peter Cooper, formerly Caterham service manager and now a partner in Redline Components, an approved service agency, filled in a little background on the early years of Caterham production.

When Caterham took over production of the Seven, initially with the Series 4, there was a string of people overseeing production. Dave Merritt from Bell and Colvill was the first one, then they brought in Johnny Johnstone as production manager; he still does a bit of sub-assembly work for the company. When they realized the S4 wasn't going to be a commercial success and resurrected the Series 3 in 1974, that's where I came in, doing construction work. Ron Davis and myself built the first Series 3, and we didn't have the best of conditions; the main workshop was a coachworks doing general accident repairs at the time, and that was eventually turned into the main assembly area. The Series 4 Caterhams had been built three or four at a time in a Banbury prefab hut. But it had a big valve twin-cam engine and went quite well.

Chassis-wise, the Caterham remained in that format until 1981, and the Vegantune engine was introduced because of the demise of the Lotus twin-cam. Smaller changes included the reintroduction of crossflow engines as opposed to just twin-cams.

CHRONOLOGY OF DEVELOPMENTS

The upturn in Caterham Cars' fortunes was the signal for revisions to the specification. First was a move from the historic Escort and Ital live back axles to a de Dion layout. With the demise of the Lotus twin-cam, the Ford-based engines carried on with the belt-driven Cosworth BDR and 1600 Sprint.

In 1981 came the revamp by new development engineer Clive Roberts. Possibly the most fundamental change made here, to the Caterham body at any rate, was the lengthening of the cockpit by 2.5in (63mm). This made for a much more comfortable driving position for the taller driver, and for the first

When supplies of the Lotus twin-cam engine dried up, Caterham introduced the 1,597cc Ford Kent engine. The 110bhp Sprint version, with modified cylinder head, high-lift cam and twin Webers, is fitted in this Silver Jubilee car.

time, the seating position was also adjustable. Clive Roberts, now (in 1995) on secondment from Lotus at General Motors' Electric Vehicle Project – known as Impact – explained why some of the changes were made to the Caterham specification. For instance, the adoption of the Morris Ital rear axle was forced on them by the demise of the rear-drive Escort RS2000, which had bigger brakes and longer diff (4.1:1 and 3.89:1 in 1300 guise, or 3.64:1 in 1700 Ital and 1800 Marina) than the more humble Escorts.

'It didn't take much study to suggest the Ital unit, because there was no sensible alternative,' he said. As they examined its virtues more closely, it became clear that not only was it significantly lighter, it was usefully wider, filling the rear wings with tyre. It also came with wheel studs on a 3.75in (95mm) pitch circle, the same as the Spitfire front suspension originally had. 'This saved the hassle of sourcing and modifying front hubs to match the Ford Escort rear axle,' Roberts pointed out. 'The Ital brakes were manually adjusted, simpler to maintain than the supposedly auto-adjusting Escort units,' he continued. It was also available with a slightly shorter final drive ratio (3.64), which suited the car better for road use, although a wide range of ratios was available for racing. What could not have been foreseen was that the differential was physically smaller than the RS2000 unit, and this became crucial when Caterham conceived the long cockpit chassis. It enabled them to narrow the tunnel around the diff and create more passenger width. And moreover, the Ital axle was cheaper.

It wasn't all good news, however. The Ital axle had a lower torque capacity, although Roberts and Price calculated that it would not be a problem as the Seven would spin its wheels before it could transmit a damaging level of torque; this proved to be true, although the initial batch of Ital units tended to whine after prolonged hard use. Caterham started fitting baffles to retain the oil around the gears under hard cornering, and while this undoubtedly helped matters, Roberts believes they were prone to develop mechanical noises if not carefully run in. Another minus factor – theoretical rather than actual – was that braking efficiency dropped by going from 9in RS2000 units to 8in Ital ones. In practice, however, this was more than compensated for by the ability to keep the Ital units well adjusted, and there was always the option of fitting higher output rear linings and larger wheel cylinders. Roberts says that he always preferred the brake feel of the Ital axle, and that overall, it was a good move technically and commercially. In contemporary Seven club circles, Graham Sykes is a leading transmissions man and a fount of knowledge on rebuilding and modifying Ital axles.

Suspension System

Suspension improvements have been in two major stages. Around 1983 it was realized that the Ital rear axle would soon be history, and as more and more manufacturers went front-wheel drive, this time there would be no obvious replacement. Then at the launch of the Ford Sierra, Clive Roberts noticed the aluminium casing of the rear-drive diff, with plenty of handy mounting points. He asked Ford for one, realizing that it could form the nucleus for the projected fully independent rear suspension system, although there were daunting considerations attached to this, such as complexity and mass, not to mention additional costs.

Said Roberts: 'Reg walked in one day and pointed out that a de Dion system had many advantages. Structurally, the chassis would need fewer changes; component costs would be lower; development and durability would be simpler, and there was a good precedent in the Lotus Eleven.' Indeed, Edward Lewis's Mk 6 Special had a de Dion

Caterham Development Engineers Clive Roberts and Reg Price (in car) warming up Dave Bettinson's ModSports Seven in the Brands Hatch paddock, 1978.

rear end. The upshot was that the de Dion set-up received general agreement, and Reg and Clive began to build a car, with Roberts doing the detailed drawings and Price making the parts. 'From Reg's original idea, the general layout pretty much decided itself,' said Roberts.

The new set-up was very good from day one, and development was limited mainly to detail changes like setting driveshaft lengths and angles, and link clearances. In gaining some extra chassis stiffness, they made some geometry changes which were not possible with the live axle. Somewhat ironically, changing to Sierra rear hubs took the Caterham back to Ford hubs at the front again. Although the de Dion car wasn't immediately faster than the best live axle cars on the race circuit, it did have a significant traction advantage, and from that point on was destined for production.

At this point, Clive Roberts left Caterham to work in the current engineering department at Lotus on Esprit and Excel development, becoming development engineer on the Elan project in March 1987. Having seen the car through rigorous testing, Clive went to GM in April 1991.

In 1985 the live axle was sidelined, except for bottom-of-the-range models, by the introduction of the de Dion system. The rear wheels are driven by shortened Ford Sierra driveshafts, from the chassis-mounted Sierra final drive unit, and linked by a de Dion tube. The de Dion tube is located fore and aft by a pair of radius arms at either end of it. These work in conjunction with a lower, centrally mounted A-bracket, which provides lateral location. For the first time, the Seven came with a rear anti-roll bar, which could be adjusted to suit desired handling characteristics.

When you improve one facet of a design, you very often expose weaknesses in another, and so it was with the de Dion set-up. Now the front suspension looked jaded, and understandably so, since apart from the digression of the S4, it had not altered since the Series 2 car. The original cost-saving expedient of using the backward facing arms of the front anti-roll bar as the forward components of the top wishbones held a couple of adverse legacies. The rubber bushes between roll bar and wishbones were obviously compressed during roll, producing a delay before the roll bar started doing its job.

The arrangement also apparently altered the castor angle significantly; as the roll bar flexed, the ends pulled the hub carriers forward on bump and rebound, affecting castor angle by 1.25 degrees in 6 degrees.

The simple solution was to introduce a new, one-piece wishbone, to which a new anti-roll bar, four times stiffer than before, was now attached, with spring and damper rates revised as a result of racing and testing with manufacturers Bilstein. The advantage of running such a stiff anti-roll bar is that it allows suspension travel if the car strikes a bump during cornering, while maintaining a rollfree posture.

Turbo Seven

As with many Seven innovations, the chief inspiration for this project came from Reg Price. Because of perpetual crises surrounding the supply of Lotus twin-cam engines in the late 1970s, Price and Clive Roberts started looking at turbocharging a motor they could readily get their hands on: the Ford Kent engine. You have to remember that this was when fitting turbos to production cars was fashionable, yet not quite the accepted way to go. Although the turbo was an old concept in itself, pioneered by First World War bi-planes to get them ever higher and out of the range of gunfire from the ground, only a handful of manufacturers had bothered fitting turbos on production engines. GM's early 1960s Chevy Corvair was the first, and largely ignored, then BMW's 2002TiK was prominent in the 1969 European Touring Car series; the car it spawned, the BMW 2002 Turbo, was only produced during 1973. It was slow to catch on. Only four production cars in 1977 were using turbochargers: the Saab 99, Porsche 911 (type 930), and the TVR 3000M. The turbocharged Lotus Esprit S3 was introduced in 1980.

Caterham's first Turbo Seven was built in 1979; it featured the well-known Garrett AiResearch T3 turbo, allied to various Saab components including the wastegate. This was made to be adjustable, and after a couple of days the Seven was soon pushing out 150bhp on the John Nicholson/McLaren test bed. Roberts recalls that it was 'Fearsomely quick, especially when the crude control systems failed and allowed enormous spontaneous overboost.'

Turbo Seven BPK 207T achieved considerable notoriety. On one occasion it caught fire at 90mph (145km/h) in the outside lane of the M1, and on another, David Wakefield and Reg Price were to be seen attacking it in the Silverstone paddock, armed with nothing more sophisticated than a screwdriver, in order to improve the air circulation in the footwells; turbos run exceedingly hot, of course.

In the event, it proved little more than a workshop curiosity, as Caterham did not have the resources necessary to develop it into a production car. In 1981, the company was approached by David Lazenby, former chief mechanic at Team Lotus, and manager of Lotus Components when John Player & Sons came on the scene. Lazenby was representing Pace Products, and offered Caterham a turbo package available for the XR2. It was installed on a yellow Seven, GPL 39V, but Price and Roberts were distinctly disappointed; they felt they could do better themselves, and were put off by the aftermarket nature of the product.

The episode coincided with Wakefield's decision to circumvent the twin-cam shortage by building the 1600 Sprint with its twin Webers. These were traditionally the carbs to have, although Dell'Ortos were standard fitment on the Lotus twin-cam, and indeed, my Elan S4 had twin Strombergs. 'Personally, I was happy to forget about turbos, and press on with the Sprint, which was exactly what the car needed,' said Roberts. The 1700 Super Sprint, developed later by Peter Cooper, was one of the best engines ever fitted in a Seven. Clive Roberts summed it up: 'It had plenty of grunt in the right places, made nice noises, was reliable, and was much lighter than a twin-cam or BDA.'

SUPPLIERS

On the whole, suppliers are reliable in the mid-1990s. Occasionally there are battles over prices. There are something like 150 major suppliers and sub-contractors providing input to the Caterham. Caterham Cars employs just fifty-four people, but the key sub-contractors such as Arch Motors and Oxted Trimming Company employ a further hundred or so between them.

The decision was taken to relocate the production side, and Graham was keen to buy premises outright rather than to rent somewhere. The chosen location at Dartford is initially somewhat puzzling; however, the management had quite exhaustively scoured most of Kent and Surrey to find somewhere, and the closest suitable site was Dartford, down among the sprawling quasi-industrial estate hinterland which borders the Thames estuary. It lacks the suburban charms of hilly green-belt Caterham, and indeed the romanticism surrounding the character of the original operation: twenty years is a long time in the motor industry. But the new plant serves its purpose. There was a need for space and availability, and doubtless the area is cheaper than bourgeois Caterham. Besides, customers can still come to see their car being built, and in what are almost clinically clean surroundings.

WIND OF CHANGE

The move took place at the beginning of October 1987, and as luck would have it, the majority of stock and equipment had gone before the 'hurricane' swept by on 15 October: this was the notorious storm which devastated much of southern England; situated as they were on top of the hill, the Caterham premises were badly damaged, with the roofs of the showroom and workshop torn off. Had the move not been effectively made already, it is likely that they would have had to close down for a lengthy period to rebuild. In fact the process which the hurricane had started was completed by the bulldozers, as during the following two-year period to May 1989 the site was razed to the ground: Seven House and its showroom was demolished, and replaced with the present sandy-coloured breeze-block buildings. These are set back from the main road behind an Esso site, although the large sign saying Caterham Cars with the Super Seven logo proclaiming the company's whereabouts is hard to miss next to the filling station. It backs onto a park, with new housing and shopping developments close by.

This is not exactly what Nearn wanted, however, as the local council would not countenance a new showroom, so there is no conventional display space as such. The compromise was to erect a number of small workshop garages with accommodation above, with a 'residents' car park out in front, and the resulting mews-type development is in a way appropriate since it is the company's headquarters. Besides, if you want to buy a Caterham, you go there to do just that, and potential passing trade would be unable to see the showroom anyway. In practice, Graham Nearn rents the property to his own company; the administration office is tucked away in the corner of the L-shaped building, and secondhand Caterhams are displayed in four of the lock-up garages. The remainder of the garages are let as workshops to local craftsmen, and the flats above are also let, to cover the cost of the development.

The relocation and restructuring was not

In 1987 Caterham production was moved some 20 miles (30km) around the M25 to a new factory at Dartford. Here is the main assembly area in 1994, looking towards the administration offices at the top, with the engine-building area at top right.

without its logistical problems, naturally, as the company was growing perhaps four-fold; what used to occupy 26,500 square feet (2,462sq m), now covered 35,000 square feet (3,252sq m). There was also extensive computerization of the business, plus the challenge of spanning thirty miles of Kent countryside between administration centre and factory. In a sense, though, Caterham – and this goes back to Lotus days, too – has always had long tentacles to reach out to its suppliers, with Arch Motors at Huntingdon, and the trimmers at Oxted, with, more recently, the main fibreglass manufacturer at Dartford and the painter at Crayford. Caterham differs from other traditional British manufacturers like Morgan and TVR, in that all components are manufactured by outside contractors instead of being made in-house. The wisdom of this is that less cash is tied up in manufacture and stocks of components, and these elements can be supplied on a 'just-in-time' basis.

Caterham production amounts to twelve cars a week in all forms: kit, component and fully built. The present factory is spacious, and the build process consistent, but no way as pressured as the Metro line at Longbridge, or even the manufacture of Morgans at Malvern or TVRs at Blackpool. The Dartford plant could accommodate more cars, although the capacity for chassis-build at Arch Motors would probably be at full stretch at 1,000 units a year. There may be another advantage in maintaining production at current levels. There is a degree of exclusivity in having a waiting list, the maxim being: Don't over-produce, because it is good for demand; it keeps the market waiting, and thus the product is more desirable. People always want what is not quite attainable.

RELATIONSHIP WITH MORGAN

Journalists are fond of comparing the Caterham with the Morgan, and naturally so, because neither car has changed its basic appearance since its inception. Both makers had a brief foray into fibreglass bodyshells, the Series 4 Seven of course, and Morgan's Plus Four Plus of 1964, of which only twenty-five were actually produced. We will undoubtedly see Caterham go fibreglass again with the 21. But any conceptual similarities are merely skin deep, and the differences between these two marques go much deeper than an adherence to tried and tested principles: Morgan continues to use traditional coachbuilding methods, skilfully and affectionately produced by craftsmen of the old school, installing modern drivetrains and running gear – discounting the 1911 vintage sliding pillar front suspension – in a ladder chassis and ash frame, panelled in steel or aluminium. A sports car it may be, but that was how all cars were built before the advent of unit construction; the Morgan thrives because enough discerning people admire the build qualities and character they produce.

The Seven's continuing success is more clearly justified. It hasn't changed its basic design because it always did what was expected of it. Designed as a racer for the road, it has never strayed from those first principles, and as virtually the first space-frame road car, it has not needed to, apart from the incorporation of revised engine mounts and uprated suspension. In a way, the Seven is more easily compared with TVR's S model, which has its roots in the M-series derivative, the 3000S. A 1978 model,

this may not seem to be old enough to qualify in this mini-debate, but it was TVR's first sports car in a long line of two-seater coupés going back to the Grantura of 1959. TVRs have always been built around a complex tubular-frame chassis – it has been called crude – with race-bred double wishbone suspension front and rear, topped with a glass-fibre body, which in the case of the S, is a curvaceous 1970s design. Therefore TVR possibly makes a more apt comparison with Caterham, especially the new 21.

SILVER JUBILEE

In 1982 Caterham celebrated twenty-five years of Seven production with a Silver Jubilee model. It was finished in silver – naturally, although you could order it in any colour if you wanted to – and this was a Volkswagen colour, with striping on the nosecone, front and rear wings designed by James Whiting. The impressive list of extras included stainless exhaust system, nickel-plated wishbones, and chrome headlights

In 1983 Caterham bought out the Silver Jubilee limited edition model to commemorate twenty-five years of Seven sales. The striking coachlines were designed by James Whiting.

and roll-over bar; the front disc back-plates were also chromed, the interior was in pale grey leather trim with matching carpet and hood, there was a map pocket in the passenger footwell, and the chassis was painted grey. Brake pipes were in braided stainless steel, and the ensemble was finished off with a tinted screen. This all added a cool £1,750 to the basic Sprint price of £4,920.

NEW ENGINES

The Vauxhall engine was installed in production at Caterham before the K-series, although the Rover unit was up and running first; this was because K-series engines were in short supply for Rover's own products – George Simpson said, 'We haven't enough for our own spare parts, let alone to supply our customers.' So the Vauxhall preceded the Rover power-plant by nearly a year.

EVOLUTION

Remarkably, if you were to stand a twenty-year old Caterham against a modern Super Seven, only a few details would give their ages away, as Graham Nearn has insisted that all changes have to be incorporated within the original dimensions of the Series 3 car; even so, apart from the handbrake lever, there is not one single Lotus-compatible component left on the car now. Only the shape is the same; otherwise chassis, engine, gearbox, wishbone design, wings, all are different. There has always been a progressive improvement; even the chassis tubes are thinner, the result of computer-aided design which established that the rails were slightly over-specified. This change came about in 1989, and the honeycomb panelling was introduced in 1990. Pre-1989 cars are sometimes known as 'big tube' Sevens, and are still favoured by some enthusiasts. The

chassis are now universal and can accommodate each one of the three basic engine options, and two tubes are removable.

1991 saw the fitting of a new top double link in the upper wishbone, and the spec also included a new battery location, at last; originally it was at the end of the passenger footwell, which now provides more welcome space, and its interim position was on the side of the engine bay where it was quite inaccessible underneath the carburettors. Over a four-year period further modifications included revised spring rates, stiffer front anti-roll bars, adjustable rear anti-roll bars as standard, plus adjustable front geometry.

State-of-the-art 1994 cars have de Dion rear suspension with five-speed gearbox, and the latest pedal assembly; the pedal box has been enlarged to accommodate size tens, and the pedal positions are adjustable. Moreover the long-legged among us are fully catered for because the off-set of the pedals can be adjusted one against the other. These specific ergonomics are so important for the fullest enjoyment of a car, and it would be nice if the mass-producers could be equally adaptable. The 1994 spec also brought with it a quicker steering rack, and the bottom front wishbones have an additional brace to counteract any tendency towards twisting.

All live axle cars have drum brakes at the rear. These days we are accustomed to all family hacks running around with discs all round, and perhaps view drums as having gone out with the Cortina. But they were always an efficient system if big enough, and the Seven is such a light car that drums at the rear are quite adequate, provided that correct rear cylinders and linings are used to achieve enough rear braking.

FUEL TANKS

Fuel tanks are now aluminium rather than steel, and are actually more useful in the

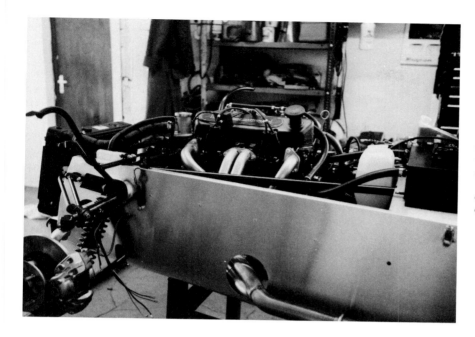

Caterham's 1994 entry-level Classic model uses the 84bhp version of the Ford CVH 1600 engine with a downdraught Weber, while the 100bhp Super Sprint version installed here will have sidedraught Webers, an A2 cam and modified cylinder head.

event of an accident: whereas the panels of a steel tank are stronger than its welds, with the result that these will burst, an aluminium tank will crumple progressively. The 8-gallon (36-litre) tank sits on a platform and is held in place by a couple of straps which tighten down onto it, with felt underneath to stop it getting damaged. One of the traditional shortcomings of the Seven has been the length of time it takes to fill up at the pumps: because of the 90-degree angle for the nozzle, fuel could only be trickled into the tank, otherwise the pump would keep switching off and blowing back. From 1989 the filler hole on Caterhams acquired a smoother angle of approach, and the problem was less acute. It is amusing to reflect that the fuel cap was originally in the top of the tank itself.

BUYING THE SUPER SEVEN

The Caterham is sold in four forms, if you

count the completely finished turn-key LVTA cars. The most basic of all, for the die-hard home builder or the just downright skint, is the starter kit, in which you get a chassis with a de Dion or live axle, source your own engine and gearbox, and buy the parts over an extended period as and when you can afford them.

Your next option is to acquire the Super Seven in full kit form or CKD (complete knock-down), where you buy all the bits and spend between seventy and a hundred hours putting it all together. The chassis is supplied complete with bodywork fitted, plus wiring and brake pipes installed, front uprights fully assembled, and the engine ready for fitting.

Then there is component form which requires twenty hours of work to bring the car to final completion. This gets the cars around full type approval because it is not safety related. The component car is supplied as a rolling chassis, with engine and gearbox installed and running, but without interior trim and without the fuel filler neck fitted, so

CATERHAM SUPER SEVEN CLASSIC (1994–present)
CATERHAM SUPER SEVEN 1700 SUPER SPRINT (1982–present)

Price
1700 Super Sprint (or 1700 Classic SE), live axle 4-speed – £10,995 (1994)
1600 Classic SE, live axle 4-speed – £9,995 (1994)
1600 Classic, live axle 4-speed – £8,450 (1994)

Layout and Chassis
Two-seat sports car with multi-tubular triangulated spaceframe chassis, altered in 1981 to create long-cockpit – seats moved back 2.5in (63mm) for greater interior space, extra bracing to cockpit sides; revised in 1985 to accommodate de Dion rear suspension: the 1700 Super Sprint can also be specified with de Dion set-up. Increased triangulations and cross-bracing with smaller chassis tubes in 1989. Powder-coated. Use of honeycomb sandwich for certain aluminium panels. Nosecone, front and rear wings in glass-fibre.

Engine

Type	Ford Kent pushrod. This is the basis for a range of engines fitted during the 1980s and 1990s, from standard 84bhp GT engine, 100bhp Sprint (using A2 cam, gas-flowed head, four-branch manifold), 135bhp Super Sprint, to a 170bhp Cosworth-Ford RS 1700 BDR unit (incorporating a twin-cam 16-valve head)
Block material	Cast iron
Head material	Cast iron, SOHC
Cylinders	4 in-line
Cooling	Water, engine-driven fan
Bore and stroke	
1600 Classic:	80.96 x 77.62
1700 Super Sprint:	83.27 x 77.62

Capacity	
1600 Classic:	1,598cc
1700 Super Sprint:	1,698cc
Valves	8 ohv
Compression ratio	
1600 Classic:	9:1
1700 Super Sprint:	10.5:1
Carburettors	
1600 Classic:	Single twin-choke Weber 28DCD downdraught
1600 Sprint:	Two twin-choke Weber 40DCOE
1700 Super Sprint:	Two twin-choke Weber 40DCOE
Max. power (DIN)	
1600 Classic:	84bhp @ 6,500rpm
1600 Sprint:	110bhp @ 6,500 rpm
1700 Super Sprint:	135bhp @ 6,000rpm
Max. torque	
1600 Classic:	108lb/ft @ 4,000rpm
1700 Super Sprint:	122lb/ft @ 3,500rpm
Fuel capacity	8 gallons (36 litres)

Transmission

Gearbox	Ford Escort Sport replaced Ford Corsair in 1981; Ford Sierra from 1986 (1600 Classic models supplied with reconditioned units)
Ratios	3.34, 2.01, 1.42, 1.0:1, reverse 3.32:1
Final drive	Ford Sierra, 3.92:1; limited slip diff optional

Suspension and Steering

Front	Independent by adjustable double wishbones (from 1989), anti-roll bar, coil spring and Bilstein telescopic damper units (Classic uses Spax dampers)
Rear	Live axle, controlled by A-frame, radius arms, coil springs and Bilstein dampers (Classic: Spax dampers)

Steering	Rack-and-pinion; 11.5in diameter steering wheel, 2.3 turns lock-to-lock, 33ft (10m) turning circle
Tyres	Classic: 185/70 HR13 Michelin MXT
Super Sprint:	185/60 x 14 Michelin XGTV (185/60 x 13 Yokohama are popular retro-fit)
Wheels	
Classic:	13in Weller pressed steel disc
Classic SE and Super Sprint:	14in aluminium alloy Superlite, KN Jupiter, Caterham 'Prisoner' style. (13in Minilite, 14in Revolution are popular options)
Rim width	5.5inJ or 6inJ

Brakes

Type	
Classic:	Discs front, drums rear
Super Sprint:	Discs all round from 1988; dual circuit split front/rear, with low fluid warning system. Handbrake operates on rear wheels

Size	
Classic:	9 in discs front, 8in drums rear;
Super Sprint:	9in discs all round

Dimensions (in/mm)

Track	
Front	50/1270
Rear	52/1320
Wheelbase	88.5/2250
Overall length	133/3,378
Overall width	62/1,575
Overall height	41/1,041
Unladen weight	
1600 Classic:	1,110lb/503kg
1700 Super Sprint:	1,196lb/542kg
Ground clearance	4.3in/110mm

Performance

Top speed	
1600 Classic:	100mph/161km/h
1700 Super Sprint:	111mph/179km/h
0–60mph	
1600 Classic:	7.7sec
1700 Super Sprint:	5.6sec
Fuel consumption	
1600 Classic:	27mpg/10.5l/100km
1700 Super Sprint:	23.5mpg/12l/100km

that notionally, you cannot get fuel to the front of the car to make it go. It is not too arduous, but there's enough to do to provide twenty hours of work to reach an MoT-worthy car. The customer then registers it himself as an amateur-built car.

MODEL RANGE

A certain amount of mix-'n'-match has always been possible with Sevens, and certain mechanical spec and trim options can be carried over from one model to another. However, the basic range starts with the Classic, a 1,600cc live axle car, rated at 84bhp. A tuned version is available, producing 100bhp thanks to its twin Webers. In spite of the fact that it has been replaced in the Ford range by the Zetec unit, the 1700 Super Sprint cross-flow engine is still available. In practice, Caterham imports the engines direct, although they are supplied through Ford Motor Sport because the lump is still used extensively in racing, particularly in Formula Ford, of course, although

CATERHAM SUPER SEVEN 2000
(1990–present)

Prices
1994: £17,995 in kit form, £19,495 in component form, £20,495 fully built
Race car, complete in kit form – £18,625

Layout and Chassis
Two-seat sports car with multi-tubular triangulated spaceframe chassis, accommodating de Dion rear suspension. Powder-coated. Use of honeycomb sandwich for cockpit area aluminium panels. Nosecone, front and rear wings in glass-fibre

Engine
Type	Vauxhall twin-cam
Block material	Cast iron
Head material	Aluminium alloy
Cylinders	4 in-line
Cooling	Water; engine-driven fan
Bore and stroke	86 x 86mm
Capacity	1,998cc
Valves	16, hydraulic tappets
Compression ratio	10.5:1
Fuel system	Multi-point electronic fuel injection
Max. power (DIN)	165bhp @ 6,000rpm (uncatalysed, running twin Weber 45DCOE carbs: 175bhp.
Max. torque	165lb/ft @ 4,500rpm
Fuel capacity	8 gallons (36 litres), unleaded

Transmission
Gearbox	Ford Sierra XR4i type 9 5-speed
Ratios	3.36, 1.81, 1.26, 1.0, 0.82, reverse 3.87:1
Final drive	3.92:1 Limited slip diff optional from 1994

Suspension and Steering
Front	Independent by adjustable double wishbones, anti-roll bar, coil springs and Bilstein dampers
Rear	De Dion axle, lower A-frame, upper radius arms, adjustable anti-roll bar, coil springs and Bilstein telescopic dampers
Steering	Rack-and-pinion, 2.13 turns lock-to-lock, 30ft (9m) turning circle
Tyres	205/45 VR16 Michelin XGTV
Wheels	16in cast alloy Caterham
Rim width	7inJ

Brakes
Type	Discs front and rear, dual circuit split front/rear with low fluid warning system. Handbrake operates on rear wheels
Size	9in

Dimensions (in/mm)
Track	
Front	50/1270
Rear	52/1320
Wheelbase	88.5/2250
Overall length	133/3380
Overall width	62/1,575
Overall height	43/1093 hood erect
Unladen weight	1,322lb/600kg
Ground clearance	4.3in/110mm

Performance
Top speed	120mph/193km/h
0–60mph	4.8sec

In July 1993 Caterham began building cars powered by the 2-litre, 16-valve Vauxhall twin-cam engine; these were originally called VX models, after the Brands Hatch-based High Performance Course which owners were invited to complete before driving their cars.

the Kent unit was abandoned in 1992. Emissions legislation will mean a premature end to the Super Sprint unit, because of the heroically proportioned twin 40 Webers: to fit a catalytic converter you need fuel injection.

Potentially Caterham's best-seller is the K-series Super Seven, powered by the excellent 16-valve Rover twin-cam engine equipped with multi-point fuel injection and catalytic converter. It produces 110bhp at 6,000rpm.

Caterham's top-of-the-range car is powered by the 2.0-litre, 16-valve Vauxhall twin-cam, a 175bhp car originally known as the VX, after the High Performance Course at Brands Hatch run by well-known racing personality John Lyon, himself a champion in Super Sevens. It used to be part of the deal when ordering one of these cars that you

participated in the VX course, since Caterham felt the car's performance warranted the extra training.

JPE

There is another Caterham. A Seven too far, some might say, for it costs a phenomenal £37,130 (1997). However, what you get with the remarkable JPE – Jonathan Palmer Evolution – is at least an extra £10,000 worth of engine modifications. Needless to say, it is a limited production model, but replicas of the cars which Jonathan runs as his personal promotional vehicles can be bought and assembled to order.

The bright mustard-yellow Super Sevens are distinctive, with their 7-in-a-shield logo in the radiator grille, and their black faring

CATERHAM SUPER SEVEN 1400 K-SERIES (1991–present)

Price
£16,495 fully built, or £13,995 in kit form;
£15,495 in component form (1994)
110bhp Class C race car, complete in kit form –
£13,355
Optional extras include K-series Supersport
engine upgrade – £995; limited slip diff – £493

Layout and Chassis
Two-seat sports car with multi-tubular
triangulated spaceframe chassis,
accommodating de Dion rear suspension.
Increased triangulations and cross-bracing with
smaller chassis tubes in 1989. Powder-coated.
Use of honeycomb sandwich for certain
aluminium panels. Nosecone, front and rear
wings in glass-fibre.

Engine
Type	Rover K-Series MPI
Block material	Aluminium alloy
Head material	Aluminium alloy
Cylinders	4 in-line
Cooling	Water, engine-driven fan
Bore and stroke	73 x 79mm
Capacity	1,397cc
Valves	16, hydraulic tappets, DOHC

Compression ratio
K-Series:	9.5:1
K-Series Supersport:	10:1
Fuel system	Multi-point electronic fuel injection

Max. power (DIN)
K-Series:	110bhp @ 6,000rpm
K-Series Supersport:	130bhp @ 7,400rpm

Max. torque
K-Series:	93lb/ft @ 5,000rpm
K-Series Supersport:	100lb/ft @ 5,000rpm
Fuel capacity	8 gallons (36 litres) unleaded

Transmission
Gearbox
K-Series:	Ford Sierra 5-speed

	Caterham 6-speed

Ratios
K-Series:	3.36, 1.81, 1.26, 1.0, 0.82, reverse 3.87:1
Caterham 6-speed:	3.05, 2.16, 1.64, 1.34, 1.14, 1.0, reverse 3.87:1
Final drive	3.92:1

Suspension and Steering
Front	Adjustable double wishbones, anti-roll bar, coil springs and Bilstein dampers
Rear:	De Dion axle controlled by lower A-frame and upper radius arms, adjustable four-position anti-roll bar, coil springs and Bilstein telescopic dampers
Steering	Rack-and-pinion, 2.75 turns lock-to-lock
Tyres	185/60 x 14 Michelin Pilot or 195VR/50 x 15 Michelin XGTV
Wheels	Caterham *Prisoner* aluminum alloy
Rim width	6inJ

Brakes
Type	Discs front and rear; dual circuit split front/rear with low fluid warning system. Fly-off handbrake operates on rear wheels
Size	228mm

Dimensions
Track
Front	49/1,245
Rear	51/1,295
Wheelbase	87/2,210
Overall length	133/3,378
Overall width	61/1,549
Overall height	41/1,041
Unladen weight	1,269lb/576kg

Performance	
Top speed	
K-Series:	105mph/169km/h
K-Series Supersport:	110mph/177km/h
0–60mph	
K-Series:	6.9sec
K-Series Supersport:	5.9sec
Fuel consumption	
K-Series:	40.9mpg/6.9l/100km
K-Series Supersport:	36.5mpg/7.7l/100km

3.4 seconds – and 100mph (160km/h) in less than 8 seconds. Top speed is 150mph (240km/h), surely making it the fastest Seven ever, and apparently there is very little buffeting. More than 25 JPE cars have been sold, which is perhaps surprising, considering the startling price tag – until you consider it has a full-race 250bhp Swindon-tuned engine, similar in specification to the Cavaliers raced by John Cleland and his co-drivers in the 1992 British Touring Car Championship; the spec extends to aluminium radiator, high spec four-pot calliper brakes with ventilated discs on the front, and Dymag magnesium-alloy wheels. Steering is two turns, lock to lock; seats are in carbon Kevlar, wings and nosecone are in carbon fibre for strength and lightness. Palmer uses these cars very hard in his corporate promotions, which is excellent PR for Caterham.

instead of a windscreen. These are the JPE cars developed in conjunction with ex-Grand Prix ace, McLaren test driver and BBC F1 commentator Dr Jonathan Palmer. The JPE quickly became established as the production car with the fastest 0–60mph (0–100km/h) time, which Palmer achieved in

Former F1 star and now BBC commentator Jonathan Palmer in his sensational JPE at Milbrook test track, where it earned its reputation as the fastest production car to 60mph (110km/h).

TYPE APPROVAL LEGISLATION

Caterham started producing fully built LVTA (Low Volume Type Approval) cars in 1993. Around 250 units are sold each year as fully built turn-key cars. Some LVTA cars are bought by UK customers. The rest are fully built for export and conform to local legislation. The prime export markets are Japan and Germany; legislation here is tight on aspects such as seat-belt anchorages and emissions, but allows more freedom in areas such as lighting. Caterham won full TUV type approval in Germany in 1984, where fully built cars have been sold ever since.

Graham Nearn is chairman of the Specialist Car Manufacturers Group, which is a division of the SMMT. LVTA allows the manufacture of a small number of cars, up to 500 units a year, without having to subject an example to full crash testing, something which all major manufacturers clearly have to comply with. The list of aspects with which they must comply to supply fully built cars is long. It includes seatbelts, emissions, anti-theft devices, glass, fuel input, brakes, noise, rear-view mirrors, external projections, internal fittings, horn, demisting, windscreen wipers, lighting, seating; in fact most things we tend to take for granted. The two models in the current Caterham range with LVTA are the K-series cars and the injected Vauxhall-engined cars. At the time of writing, however, there haven't been many takers, and only a few appear to have filtered onto the scene. The traditional Caterham buyer appears to want to build his own car, and for many, the assembly factor is evidently an important part of ownership. In some quarters, the catalysed, injected cars are perceived to be somewhat emasculated and therefore relatively dull compared with the noisy exhaust and rasping carburettors of the unfettered, traditional version. But their days are numbered and Caterham must embrace the new technology.

The LVTA cars will continue to be offered alongside the kit cars, and there is no reason to suppose that legislation will do away with the home-built models. In a free market economy, people will always be able to buy and drive what they like. Indeed, legislation is quite supportive of kit cars, provided owners comply with the requirements. The chief loophole in circumventing emissions tests is to fit an engine built before 1992, which is not subject to emissions regulations. At the MoT test, emissions monitoring is graded according to a car's age. Vehicles manufactured post 1983 are kept to a certain level, and anything post 1991 is subject to more stringent controls. There is simply a visual check for anything built before 1975, to the extent that if it is belching out blue smoke, it fails, and a kit-built car, regardless of when it was actually built, is subject only to the pre-1975 check.

A disadvantage is the 'Q' registration plate, but that is part and parcel of Seven ownership. At first sight, the number of Q-plated cars is somewhat baffling; the Q signifies what the car contains, that is, secondhand components of an unknown or unspecified age and origin. When ordering a car from Caterham, you don't have to buy it all; you can buy a rolling chassis less engine and gearbox, get it home and fit an engine built to your own specification, and that may be a reconditioned Escort engine which has done 170,000 miles (273,500km) for example. The Q plate warns the after-market that the car may be a 'bitsa'; if a UK-registered car has a J, K or L prefix, for example it indicates the car was supplied by the factory, and that everything was brand new when it first turned a wheel. The paradox is that many Q-plated cars are cheaper than ex-factory registered ones, and yet the running gear may well be to a higher or more exotic specification.

THE FUTURE

The future? I am often asked this question [said Graham]. There's no secret to it. Don't expand too quickly, keep grinding away at it, and try and make this year's car a little better than last year's. A new model is always at the back of our minds, but we get side-tracked by the car we're already building. Demand is such that we can make more money by building more of the car already in production. On the other hand, employing more people to do that just brings greater headaches; the bigger you are, the harder you fall. Also you can't suddenly decide to make another couple of hundred cars, because of the difficulties of co-ordinating extra output when it's required from the sub-contractors – they can't be turned on and off like a tap. We can expand gently, and at the moment we're only just emerging from the recession. Caterham's delivery time is about four to five months, with output running at 600 cars in 1994. That's twelve to fifteen cars a week, about half of which are in kit form. Slightly more than half production is made for export, although the majority of the kits are sold in the UK; very few kits are exported, partly due to the cost of freighting components, and perhaps more fundamentally, because of the reluctance of foreign customers to assemble their own cars. Import restrictions have played their part in the past, and cars have been sold unofficially to the States in kit form as 'spare parts'.

We're a little maverick ourselves [referring to the *Prisoner*]; we run with the herd, recognizing that there are rules which must be obeyed, but are perhaps free with the way we interpret them; although we still stay legal.

Because it is a small company, Caterham has the flexibility to play with the rules like this. Japan is without question Caterham's biggest export market. 'We're spread fairly evenly over Europe,' says Nearn. 'And we're taking a long, hard look at making the car legal in America so we can sell a turn-key

motor car.' Nearn relishes the challenge, and believes in casting his net far and wide. 'I enjoy marketing,' he continued. 'You can always market something if you get it right, and I also believe you can keep on selling it. And I like to sell in different countries, so that if one market slows down for some reason, there will be others which are still flourishing. The whole wide world is never in total recession. I can see Japan easing off a bit' – although any signs of that are not at all clear at the time of writing – 'so I think America is worth going for.'

Said Nearn:

> The rest of the procedure is carried out by assessment; there are no tests for which you get a certificate, as in Europe; you go along and say, this is what we're going to do for the barrier test, and they might say, we'll test it, or they might say prove it. But one way or another you have to have the engineering backup to prove you have tested it correctly. The frontal impact test is the biggest problem: the European test is to measure the steering column intrusion, and the Caterham passes with flying colours because it has a very stiff chassis. For the US test, however, they put a dummy in the car, and the chassis has to be seen to collapse progressively in order to protect the occupant.

Caterham has Leeds University working on the project – at PhD standard – and the concept is to extend the tubes without distorting the look of the car. One way might be by building in a telescope effect, a tube within a tube, and if the authorities can be convinced that the car has been changed, subjecting a car to the test will be avoided. It is always heartening to find a manufacturer working with an academic institution, since both benefit enormously from the research. Graham Nearn believes that rules, particularly those concerning emissions, will be even more stringently applied in 1996, and that it is important to crack the US legislation as soon as possible; by the time you read this, it may be a *fait accompli*. Whatever may happen, he hopes for a sympathetic hearing from the US authorities, with a year or so's grace to overcome any unforeseen problems.

Legislation goes in circles. In Germany, for instance, it was necessary at one time to drop the lights from the standard position; and then the legal requirement changed, and the lights reverted to their regular position. Similarly there was a phase of having to fit a great deal of sound deadening; then this, too, was eventually dropped.

There are other aspects, such as having to fit bumpers, or attend to 'sharp' edges on which pedestrians could injure themselves; also the height of stop-lights – at one time Morgan had to fit a Porsche 928 rear light on a stalk above the spare wheel. Says Graham Nearn:

It's an illusion to think that because you've been successful with one car, you can automatically repeat it with another. It's not that easy; and of course the market is very crowded these days. I would have liked to have taken over production of the original Lotus Elan, but despite the existence of the Evante, the Elan has been dead for twenty years now. We would have needed to have picked it up when Lotus dropped it, and carried on developing it then – it was a great car in its day, but if we began to produce it now, we'd be producing a twenty-year-old car; unlike the Seven which hasn't stood still. It might have been feasible even up until the General Motors take-over, but by that time they weren't hard up, and were set to use the name for the new Elan, which would have confused the issue somewhat. It was always a hope on my part. We could have done something with it, but it didn't happen.

In the course of writing this, the whole future of the Seven was blown wide open by the revelation that Caterham had a new model waiting in the wings. Would the 21 eventually replace the Super Seven? Somehow I doubt it, as the basic concept is rather compromised by that beautiful body.

Company Structure

Caterham Cars is owned by Graham Nearn, with David Wakefield as Finance and Export Director. On the development side, Jez Coates is Technical Director, and Development Engineer is Reg Price; both are backed by a small team of engineers and technicians. Andy Noble is purchasing director, who oversees the stores and parts; there is also a stores manager, Nick O'Brien. Production manager is Tim Ward, Steve Peakin is Service Manager and Simon Nearn is Sales Manager. Most key figures operate from Dartford now, and Graham Nearn is only to be found at the Caterham office on Tuesdays

Jez Coates is technical director, and masterminded the 21 project.

Andy Noble is purchasing director.

and Fridays, spending most of his time at Dartford. His other son Robert Nearn co-drives the 'works' racing Super Seven, having won the Class C series in 1990 and 1991 and the Caterham–Vauxhall Challenge series in 1993. Customer relations manager Paul Kite drives a Vauxhall-engined car under the Arrowstar umbrella.

SIX-SPEED GEARBOX

Caterham perceived that the car's character would be improved with a six-speed gearbox, an extremely popular move among members of the racing fraternity. It was important that the gearbox could replace an existing five-speed Sierra unit, so its dimensions could not change; and getting an extra ratio into a similar size housing threw up the additional demand that it should be able to handle the JPE engine's 200lb/ft of torque.

The exterior castings and assembly were in die-cast aluminium by Flowtech Engineering of Sussex, and the internals – helical gears and needle-roller bearings – were

Robert Nearn drives works Caterhams and handles club liaison.

This 2-litre Vauxhall engine sitting on its portable stand is equipped with twin Weber carbs, resplendent with shiny K & N air filters. To the left sits Caterham's six-speed gearbox, an optional extra which can replace the standard Sierra five-speed unit.

developed in-house. Top gear is direct, more efficient and quieter for cruising. Because fitting the gearbox to finished LVTA cars involves fresh homologation tests for noise and emissions, the six-speeder is at present only offered as an option for kit and component cars. The price is £1351.25, or £1,992 retro-fitted to any de Dion car on a part-exchange basis; the five-speeder is taken back for reconditioning.

SPIN-OFFS

At times, compiling material for this book proved somewhat contentious with regard to the mention of certain replicas and independent specialists, and there were moments of soul-searching in order to retain objectivity and integrity. Nevertheless, such pressures encourage one to look harder at the subject matter, and the end result is, I think, altogether more focused.

This is probably the most acrimonious aspect of the Seven story, and it should be said from the outset that copies or replicas have been in the picture for a long time. The Seven is such a beautifully simple concept that it is no wonder that people have tried to emulate it, nor is it difficult to do so. It has even been done legitimately. In 1973 Lotus granted a licence to Steel Brothers in Christchurch, New Zealand to build Series 4s, as a way of circumventing high import tariffs, and Steels had one of the two sets of Series 4 jigs when Lotus gave up on the Seven. They proceeded to modify the suspension and their fibreglass body builder contributed a more rotund back end to the styling; after some 100 units had been produced, Steels then modified the chassis and switched to the Lotus 2-litre 907 Elite engine. However, despite having beefed up the sidescreens, 1979 safety legislation on car doors took the Steel Series 4 out of commission.

This was the only legitimate competitor to Caterham, as far as the genuine article was concerned, although Lotus had previously supplied Series 3 rolling chassis to an Argentinian producer who equipped them with Fiat 1500 drivetrains. The Spanish Porsche concessionaire produced a small quantity of Series 4 Sevens in 1975, and these used Seat running gear. However, it is often said that imitation is the sincerest form of flattery, and so it is with the Seven. Its continuing success has spawned a host of imitators, some of which have improved on the original format, others have been downright inferior. A few, like Dutton, have strayed far enough away aesthetically to remove themselves from any contest with Caterham. At the time of writing, there are no fewer than twenty-nine companies around the world making vehicles which bear a resemblance to the Seven, at least one in every country in the Western world.

'It's actually a compliment, in a way,' said Graham Nearn, 'providing they're not deliberately passing off their car as a Seven, deliberately setting out to mislead, which has certainly been the case with some companies.' And for reasons not entirely of a protectionist nature, Caterham Cars would like to see off every one of them: clearly, for every copy of a Seven sold, Caterham loses a buyer, and it is a challenge which any businessman would resist. He was once approached on the Caterham stand at the Motor Show and asked for directions to the 'Westerham' stand, and had to turn his back, and you can quite understand his point of view; mercifully he didn't hear another questioner asking whether the Caterham was copied from the Westfield.

The paradox is that, if you remember your *Prisoner*, the whole Seven ethos is about being a 'maverick', which Caterham's rivals obviously are. As far as Graham Nearn is concerned, the real danger is that the high-status reputation of the Lotus and Caterham Sevens could be jeopardized through the inferior manufacturing techniques and shoddy assembly of replicas. The identity and heritage of the true Seven would thus be blemished, and it would be only a short step before the production and sale of kit cars as a whole were called into question. Not only does that amount to commercial suicide, but unless countered by threat of litigation, production of Seven pastiches could get out of hand.

Whether you want to own a copy of a Seven depends not just on whether or not you can afford a Caterham, but on whether you would be happy with something other than the genuine article. It's a bit like having a copy of a Cézanne painting rather than an original. One or two makers have come very close to the Lotus original. I do not propose to go into this in any detail, but as a feature of the Seven's history, it does warrant a mention.

The Westfield saga is most widely remembered, though not well documented. As far as Caterham was concerned, Westfield had to be stopped, mainly because it eventually produced such a good copy – it had gained a good reputation with a copy of the Lotus Eleven sports racing car, back in 1982. A decade ago the Westfield 7 was in fact relatively crude, comparable with early Lotus models perhaps, and it lacked niceties such as a fuel gauge – you shook it to judge how much petrol there was in the tank, and the bonnet catches were prone to come undone at speed, with consequent loss of engine cover. Like an early Lotus, there were no sidescreens and the hood fastenings were imprecise. But then quality and attention to detail improved immeasurably, and Westfield had to be taken seriously. Quite apart from the similarity of the cars, Graham Nearn was concerned about the use of the word 'Seven'. The affair was ultimately settled in 1988, with Westfield consenting to a court order and paying Caterham's costs and damages.

They also surrendered jigs and tools.

From then on, Westfield's stated intention was to make its car in fibreglass, which Caterham could not object to, although naturally it could not endorse it either. A press release issued by Caterham at the time spoke in a reconciliatory way of how the two firms would 'compete on legitimate terms'. Westfield altered the shape of the car sufficiently to differentiate it from the Caterham, and the bodies were indeed in glass-fibre. Thus it looked as if the two companies had agreed to occupy opposite ground in the same market niche, with Caterham at the top and Westfield catering for the buyer with a more modest budget. But now the models have crept closer in price, to the point where they overlap, although both stylistically and mechanically the Westfield and Caterham are relatively different.

Westfield's managing director Chris Smith admits to a degree of naiveté in his original business plan. But things have changed, and he puts it this way: 'If you go into a Renault garage and ask what the difference is between a Clio and a Peugeot 304 – on the face of it very similar designs – you will be told they are as unalike as chalk and cheese. And that's how it is with Caterham and Westfield.' Indeed, other mainstream manufacturers have had similar disagreements: Alfa Romeo was not best pleased when Peugeot came out first with its 405, a Pininfarina design commissioned previously for the Alfa 164. When Peugeot's even more similar 605 appeared, the Milanese company was even less pleased.

Graham Nearn remains stoical:

I don't regard these cars as a threat; in fact they improve market awareness. The amount of publicity all Seven lookalikes get is out of all proportion to their actual significance. I suppose it's down to the Seven's newsworthiness. But if anyone's attempting to pass one off as the real thing, then we go for them, and we've had several successful cases.

It's reverse engineering, in that they copy what we do without putting any *new* technical input into it – and it's often inferior quality, too. And those who jump on the bandwagon usually rip people off as well. However, it's the price of fame, and we have to live with it or revert to the 1970s when we didn't have much business, or competition. I know which I prefer.

Nowadays the two principals, Graham Nearn and Chris Smith, sit on the same SMMT committee on LVTA matters, and an uneasy truce exists. They are both on the same side, as it were. Westfield was actually the first kit-car manufacturer to win LVTA, with Marcos second and Caterham third. In fact Marcos has done better for itself through LVTA than the other two because its potentially up-market Mantula and Mantara models were always held back by a perceived kit-car image. Now they all compete on more level ground with TVR and Morgan, although against a Westfield is its poor residual value. But a pre-litigation Westfield is so like a Seven that it must be tempting to seek one out if funds are not available for a second-hand Caterham. The difference will be about £5,000; but at the end of the day, a Caterham will always get you your money back because it is the genuine article.

5 Chassis Manufacture

ARCH MOTORS

The only place I have been where the din was louder than Arch Motors was the tin shop at Morgan, where they played Radio 1 all the louder to compensate for the racket. The inevitable cacophony of metalworking noises which greets you at Arch Motors is composed of grinders, welders, screaming compressed air tools, rivetters, clanking chassis being shifted, jigs being moved, lathes, hacksaws, drills, the occasional fire alarm being tested, and good old Radio 1 of course; here and there you catch the blue-green flash of welding torches, the white light of cascading sparks

too intense to look at. There is a certain smell of the foundry, too: of burned spelter, red-hot metal, a whiff of acid, all some way removed from the relative clinical cleanliness of Caterham's Dartford factory.

Arch Motors was founded by Bob Robinson in Tottenham in 1958, and initially they did a lot of work for Lola building their 1,100cc sports racing car. Robinson had been involved with motorbike and sidecar racing, selling components to other competitors, but there wasn't enough money in that so he turned to cars. The first Lotus chassis made by Arch was a Lotus 23. At the time, Seven chassis and bodies were made by Progress

General view of the Arch Motors factory, virtually all devoted to Caterham chassis and component manufacture, and like all metal-working premises, a very noisy environment.

Engineering, Alert Engineering and Universal Radiators – on the basis of safety in numbers – with panelling done by Eves of Norwich on chassis made by Progress.

Due largely to Bob Robinson's friendship with Don Gadd, Lotus design engineer at the time, Arch was given the contract to construct Seven chassis for Lotus from 1965 until 1972. They made Seven components and other Lotus parts before 1965, and continued to make them for Caterham when the latter picked up the Seven from 1973. Arch Motors moved to its present site on an industrial park on the outskirts of Huntingdon in 1965, and the single-storey building and layout of production hasn't altered radically in that time. The chassis manufacturing process takes place in compartments, administration offices are at the front, and there are a couple of mezzanines at either end for storage. Inside the factory, first encounter is with the cosy 'sentry-box' office of foreman Bob Hobbs. A veteran of twenty-eight years with Arch, Bob has been foreman since 1978, and, he says, 'I don't know if I like it here yet!'.

Tubes are stored down the left side of the building, with lathes, presses and cutters also mainly down the left-hand side. The acid wash and powder coating is off to the left, with chassis jigs and welding up joints at the centre; panelling takes place at the far end of the building, and suspension components are made to the right. Everyone is industrious and amiable, yet seemingly unhurried, which is deceptive, as you soon realize that work is proceeding at an inexorable pace. They have been producing Seven chassis for so long now it comes as second nature.

Arch has been making Sevens continuously from 1965 to the present day, although Bruce Robinson, Bob's son, who has worked at Arch since 1977, makes an interesting distinction in identifying the Series 4 separately, saying 'We made the Series 4 chassis as well for both Lotus and Caterham

Bob Hobbs has been with Arch Motors for twenty-eight years, and foreman since 1978.

between 1970 and 1973.' They still do make new S4 chassis as accident repairs or restorations, or spares for Caterham.

Bruce Robinson told me that 1989 and 1990 were the busiest years, simply because the market was very buoyant then and sales were good; in some months Caterham were taking orders for seventy cars. 'That was pretty encouraging,' said Bruce, 'although it's dwindled a bit since, it's still very healthy.' They produce around sixty body-chassis units a month at present.

The Caterham chassis is still built on jigs similar to the original pattern; in 1986, a new jig was made to build the de Dion chassis, followed by another in 1991. The present live-axle chassis jig was built in 1982, replacing the original jig used to build the Series 3 Lotus Seven chassis. When an order comes from Caterham, it takes the form of a spec sheet, saying what chassis is required – left-hand drive Vauxhall-engined car for instance – and the Arch fitters build it accordingly. There is a monthly schedule from Caterham, although this is not necessarily what Arch builds, as they have a float of chassis. This means that while the fitters are preparing the components for the month's build, the men doing the panelling can continue with their work. In effect this means having two schedules at once, complicated by the fact that Arch cannot guarantee that whatever they have in their 'float' is going to be needed.

I asked Don Gadd if a customer's specification for a kit order affected how the chassis actually left Arch Motors, or whether everything in the way of ancillaries was taken care of in the packaging at Dartford:

> Yes, the customer's specification does matter, to an extent. The chassis-body units, or CBUs, are more or less all the same, but the order may be for the standard short chassis of the LC – the long cockpit version, still

Arch Motors is co-run by Bruce Robinson, who joined the family firm in 1977.

Ken Clark and Mervyn DeWilde hoist a chassis out of the jig.

*Rectangular-section
tube is cut to length
and appropriate
angle in a hand-
operated cutter.*

Rectangular-section tube is cut to length and appropriate angle in a hand-operated cutter.

with the live axle – or the de Dion axle, with one of the three engine variations fitted. The other considerations are whether it's a racing car, or whether it's a left- or right-hand drive. When it gets to Caterham, they allocate the chassis according to the orders in hand. It's then that the particular options are dealt with, like flared wings or cycle wings, or it may be painted, or left unpainted, by Caterham. The JPE has the panels in the engine bay powder-coated black, just to differentiate it and make it a bit more special. That's done by us, whereas the exteriors are all painted down at Caterham. Of course, you can order a plain chassis-body unit and buy the rest of the kit when funds permit. But you can't get it direct from Arch; you order it direct from Caterham.

Evolutions in the chassis make-up happen from time to time, brought about when engines change, for example. The Vauxhall and K-series engine mounts are similar, although the K-series requires a left-hand mount approximately 3in (76mm) further

back than the Vauxhall unit. The Ford engine bay is similar to the Vauxhall's. With the so-called '94' chassis, engine mounts have been standardized to universal format to accept any engine variation. Previously there could have been as many as eighteen different permutations, including left- and right-hand drive. This isn't as haphazard as it sounds. Caterham has model year chassis, for example 1986, '87, '88, '90, '91 and '94.

With any open-top sports car, the relative flexibility of the untriangulated cockpit area restricts overall torsional rigidity, and Caterham wanted to see if it was possible to refine the spaceframe in other areas. For example, stress analyses carried out on the spaceframe using CAD computers at London's City University, showed quite dramatic possibilities. If an additional, angled, longitudinal tube was incorporated on the left-hand side of the engine bay, torsional stiffness was increased by a remarkable 18 per cent: it now matched the opposite side, but had previously been left out because it interfered with the exhaust manifold. As a result, Arch was able to switch to lighter tubing for both front and rear bays.

These changes have been made over a lengthy period of time by a process of experimentation, and triangulations are revised by moving particular tubes and subjecting the change to torsional tests and finding out what poundage they get per degree of deflection. Nothing more scientific than that. On occasions they refer to a computer, to decide whether the repositioning of various tubes would have any effect torsionally in beam-loading. 'It's more a case of trial and error,' said Bruce, 'making up a special chassis with some changes in it and seeing what effect it has.' By inserting extra tubes in the floor and transmission tunnel, the void of the cockpit was bolstered and overall torsional stiffness increased to some 1,800ft lb/deg; a great deal better than the original Series 1 car, but still some way below a unit-construction car like an MX-5.

There appears to be an equal contribution towards the changes in chassis development: thus Caterham comes up with ideas and

seeks advice from Arch on costs and the best production method. Most recent were those proposed in late 1993, that is, revised bottom wishbone mountings, bushes for the de Dion tube and A-frame; and the facility to fit a JPE fuel tank if required. Arch have also made alterations to private customers' Seven chassis by request, when carrying out restorations or accident repairs; for the most part, these amount to suspension mountings.

Honeycomb Panelling

Many concepts applied to road cars are ultimately derived from racing, and it is fitting that the Super Seven should benefit in this way. A couple of Seven racers, Alex Hawkridge (of Toleman fame) and Barry Lee (world hot-rod champion) were racing in the A-series events, and they started using a bonded composite, installed by Reynard improving side intrusion protection.

From the beginning of 1990, Arch began producing the honeycomb aluminium panels which line the Caterham's cockpit sides and floor. In exactly the same way as in the race

Arch Motors use a myriad of jigs and wooden templates for Caterham panels. Here James Metson uses a router to cut out a section of honeycomb panelling for the passenger-side footwell end-plate of a dry sump, de Dion car: it has to be that specific.

cars, they have the benefit of affording better protection in the event of an impact. As floorboards, they are loosely fitted into the car, as there is nothing to bond them to; the thickness is still only about 1in (25mm), made up of the chassis' ½in (13mm) tubing and ½in (13mm) honeycomb panelling fitted between. A normal road-going Super Seven has just sheet aluminium floor covered by carpet, with seat and seat runner covering part of it. In a way, this panelling has been one of the main evolutions in the Seven's history, and has rather revolutionized its construction, without altering its appearance or character. A measure of the care taken over the panelling is the fact that all panels are coated with a film of plastic before they reach the fitter who applies them to the chassis.

The honeycomb panelling is the most modern piece of technology in the car's make-up. Revealingly, Bruce describes the Seven as 'Late 1950s, early 1960s technology, which has been improved over the years. A monocoque would be more expensive to produce and not as repairable,' he added. 'As far as Caterham is concerned, the chassis is traditional, and has close affiliation to the Lotus product, which is probably also important to the people who buy it; if it was more akin to the most recent Lotus Elan, they probably wouldn't be interested in it.'

It comes as something of a surprise to discover just how much of the car is made by Arch Motors. All tube fabrications and sheet-metal applications, such as the dash, are made here; front wishbones, cycle-wing stays are also made by Arch. Design chief Don Gadd said that he has on occasion joked with Graham Nearn that Caterham could supply the wheels and Arch would bleed the brakes and drive the complete car to Caterham. I asked Bruce if Arch had ever been tempted to start making its own cars, since clearly they have the manufacturing expertise.

'Not really,' he replied. 'Caterham has the proven product, and it would be very difficult to come up with something fresh. The track record of new manufacturers trying to get into the car-producing game is a bit grim. We prefer to keep a low profile, and we're glad of the work security, I guess. We're the backroom boys really.' Modest words, for Arch can claim to have built chassis for most of the top racing teams over the years: Brabham, McLaren, Lola, Chevron, the Rocket single-seater, a Mark 1 Lola for Stirling Moss, virtually all the Formula Ford people including Van Dieman, and rally cars like the Ford RS2000. 'In the end it became so crazy that now we're actually glad to be doing just the work for Caterham,' said Bob Robinson.

When building a chassis for a customer, Arch would work from drawings supplied, perhaps contributing some of their own advice to the project, and would create the jigs and proceed accordingly. Said Don Gadd:

> We get involved at the design level to a certain extent, although we have our limitations. A customer may suggest something which is beyond the equipment we have, and we would either recommend someone else for the project, or else we could come up with compromises to show how the job could be done with our own facilities; and this could save the customer x-number of pounds. They usually agree to that! We don't get involved in original design, because there's too much work in that. Although there are exceptions with Caterham.

Such a good rapport exists between the two firms that Caterham knows pretty well what Arch is capable of, and by the same token they know the limitations of the fitters assembling the cars at Dartford. 'If something has to be fitted and filed or played around with because of some variation in a component sourced from an outside supplier, between us we design something which will accommodate the discrepancy.' Don had just received some prototype material from Jez

Don Gadd was development engineer at Lotus from 1959 to 1964, and has been technical director at Arch Motors since 1972, making him a crucial link in the Lotus and Caterham Seven saga. He is pictured on one of his expeditions to the South of France.

Coates, and a phone conversation ensued in which Jez asked Don if he had '⁵/₈in round 18-gauge', and Don replied that they had plenty, and the question came back 'Have you got ⁷/₁₆in square 16-gauge?' to which the answer was negative, as Arch don't use it. The upshot was that it would be left up to Arch to sort out what would be the most suitable tubing for the application.

Had they, I wondered, taken apart a Westfield to assess the relative build quality? Bruce is dismissive. 'Frankly, it's a pain they exist, but no, it isn't as good as the Caterham in terms of detail quality, and this is reflected in the price and resale value. Caterham Sevens, on the other hand, don't really depreciate much at all.'

Don Gadd Discusses the Old Days

Don Gadd has been technical director at Arch Motors since 1972. He joined Lotus at Hornsey in May 1958 as development engineer after doing his National Service. He lived at Cheshunt, which was very convenient for him when the company relocated in 1959. At Hornsey, Don was involved with the

Series 1 Seven, the Eleven and the Mk 15, followed by the Mk 17 which was raced successfully by Keith Greene. Two personalities he recalls from Hornsey days are Steve Sanville who was in the engine shop, and Graham Hill. Most attractive of the Sevens, thinks Don, was the Clubman's racer, with de Dion rear suspension and knock-on wire wheels, with Climax power plant. 'A beautifully engineered car and good to look at, too,' said Don.

I suggested that there cannot have been any idea then that the car would still be going thirty years on. 'No,' he said. 'There was always a degree of scepticism in that we always thought so-and-so was cleverer than us, and we were surprised to have won races with it. We tended to underplay things. But as time goes on, you realize just how good the designs were.' As development engineer he would receive the basic idea from Colin Chapman, or the drawing office, and make up the chassis, develop it and modify it as he went along.

I can remember doing the first set of engine mounts on the Series 2 Seven. It was the first one to take the Ford 105E block, and we didn't have time to draw the engine mounts; so we just set the engine up at drive-line height, mounted on some wooden blocks lying around in the development shop, and just bolted the engine mounts and rubbers in place, and joint-tubed up to that. After we'd made a pair, we gave them to Ian Jones in the drawing office, and he sat down to do the drawing. And that was how a lot of it went.

It isn't often you get a chance to talk to someone who was there 'way back when . . .', and I asked Don what it was like working with Chapman. 'I got on very well with him,' he said. 'He had colossal energy, and he was a man you could only keep up with for about three months. Otherwise you would burn out.' All-nighters were commonplace then, and Don remembers flying spares out to Monaco on the evening of the Grand Prix for Jimmy Clark's wrecked F1 Lotus 24, and working all night to repair it in time for the race. Don is full of contemporary tit-bits: like, did you know that back in 1961, Stirling Moss smoked Senior Service?

I asked Don if he remained friends with Chapman after he left Lotus. 'Yes, as far as one could; I'm not saying that in a nasty way. It's just that he never had any really close friends, as he would burn them up in about three months. It was all "come on, let's go here, let's do that", and people couldn't take it for long. The person for whom he had the most affection was Jim Clark, and Jim managed to get under the veneer that Chapman had. He was good fun though, no doubt of that.'

Don Gadd worked with Cosworth in the early days. When Mike Costin left Lotus, Don was poached away to join the embryonic engine specialists.

I'd say the finest engineer I've ever worked with would be Keith Duckworth. He was truly brilliant. But as far as innovation was concerned, there was nothing to touch Chapman. His engineering was nowhere near as sound as the disciplined work of, say, Duckworth; but Chapman's genius was in seeing something and how it could be adapted for a different design. A case in point was the first of the Formula Junior cars; Chapman was over in Germany at the ZF gearbox plant, and they were making gearboxes for forklift trucks. He realized that inverting the gearbox would have the effect of lowering the 'box and raising the driveshafts, and that this would be an excellent system for a powerful car. A forklift truck would have very close ratios anyway. So a ZF forklift gearbox was brought over, holes were drilled and its oiling was altered, and it became the first of the rear-engined gearboxes.

Some vision. Whereas Keith Duckworth would sit down and design something equally as good, if not better. Don Gadd ascribes this genius as coming from the will to win, rather than the result of some make-do-and-mend philosophy borne out of post-war austerity.

His racing was always like that; he knew only two positions for the throttle, and he carried on his business the same way. For instance, you'd be track testing somewhere freezing cold and wet like Snetterton, and the cars would be spinning off all over the place – he'd still be there, and if anyone complained about the weather, he'd wonder what they were on about; it was a sort of tunnel vision on what he was trying to achieve.

By the time Don arrived at Lotus, the Series 1 Seven was a going concern. 'We started on the Series 2,' he said. 'There was a fairly distinct demarcation between the Series 1 and the Series 2, but the Series 3 flowed from the Series 2. The flared wings came in with the Super America, and that design caught on over here.' As development engineer, Don's role was in producing the original chassis

Arch welders make it look easy, but the Caterham chassis demands close attention.

John Dodson and Richard Rogers finishing off a chassis, welding on brackets for roll-bar, exhaust and suspension mounts.

With the chassis upside down, Jerry Course drills holes for rivetting on the undertray.

John Bennett folds the side panel over the chassis rail.

and organizing the panelling for it, as well as liaising with the glass-fibre people to get the wings and nosecones in hand.

Cosworth was supplying the 105E engine at the time, and that grew into the Classic engine with the single Weber carb. The main bearings weren't that good, but good enough for the Seven. One of the sweetest S2s was the A-series Downton-prepared car. We played around with various gearboxes at the time, and the Downton car had an MG Magnette 'box, which, like the A35, had fairly close ratios. In fact the Magnette gearbox was used in the racing Mk Eleven and Mk 15, married to a Climax engine.

Another aspect of Don's work was to look for ways of reducing weight, and reducing costs; this might mean substituting a cheaper radiator, or if a particular component went out of production, he would source another one, and perhaps modify it to suit. Altering and developing parts was the norm. This didn't mean that every car was in some way different to its predecessor; S2s and S3s were made in batches, with variations only in terms of left- or right-hand drive, or engine spec. When something like a radiator changed, the next batch would all have the same component for quite a few months. Cars were made to order, not for stock.

Quizzed about contemporary Seven racers, Don recalls moonlighting and preparing a 7½ copy for American driver Bob Anderson. He was the Amsterdam-based agent for a firm called Nuclear Chicago, and did quite well on the Continent with the car, which Gadd fitted with a Lotus Mk 20 independent rear suspension set-up. Anderson's engine was prepared by a Dutchman called Hank van Zarlinger, and Gadd remembers he marked every mechanical component with red nail varnish. 'On the whole, though, if you were serious, you would race a small sports car, something like the Eleven, 15 or 17: the Seven was a Clubman's car, and it

was a lot less prominent in racing than it is today. There's also more demarcation between each class today. In those days there were fewer people racing, and everything was more relaxed.'

Don left Lotus in 1964, and his wife Sheila, who had been Colin Chapman's secretary, left soon afterwards. Don recounted one of her enduring memories of Chapman:

At the end of the day, Sheila would leave a Mars Bar in her drawer, having perhaps taken a bite out of it; when she went in next day, she would often find a set of teeth marks at the other end. Now at this time Hazel Chapman was anxious about her husband gaining weight; however, there was nothing he liked better than when the lads were working late, and he would go down to the chippy and buy everyone bags of chips and have one himself – and then he'd go into my wife's office and see if there was any chocolate around!

Just before the move to Hethel, Don quit Lotus and went with Mike Costin to Cosworth. 'They were heady days,' he recalled. 'We were developing the SCA engine, the 1-litre screamer which produced such epic duels and spectacular slipstreaming in mid-1960s Formula 3, and we'd just started drawing the DFV when I left. This was mainly because Cosworth were moving to Northampton.' Instead, Don moved to Maldon, Essex, so he could pursue his interest in sailing. Nevertheless, in 1972 he was plucked from his workshop, where he was making Merlyn chassis, by Bob Robinson to help shoulder the increased workload at Arch Motors.

When Caterham took over the Seven, there was no loss of continuity in production.

They handled more Sevens than anybody else by far. The other important dealer was the Chequered Flag, and there were one or two others, but we already had a good rapport with Caterham when Lotus hived it off. When Arch was dealing with Lotus with the Series 3, Caterham was still in the background, and when they took over the rights to the Seven, things seemed no different. In fact it made life a little easier, because by that time Lotus had become a relatively large company, and any suggestion we came up with to make it a little cheaper or easier for us to produce got lost in all the paperwork at Lotus. At Caterham we were dealing with just one man, and a new idea could be suggested, tried out and agreed over a series of two or three phone calls.

Don Gadd and the Robinsons look on the Series 4 Seven as being Mike Warner's project, into which Chapman had little input. Much as I am in favour of rehabilitating it, there is the distinct feeling at Arch Motors that it is regarded as an aberration. Don told me:

> We still look upon the Seven as being derived from the Mark 6, which was purely Chapman – in fact I've got an early Seven drawing here which was checked by Chapman. But the Series 4 was very much a retrograde step; it was all right to drive, and its performance was quite adequate, bearing in mind that Chapman said only one person in ten would use the full potential of a Lotus. But if it had been more traditional, more of a purist's car, we'd be making them instead of the tubular frame.

He went on to list draughtsmen: Ian Jones of course was one of the principal designers, followed later by Alan Styman; Styman went to Jersey to join ex-Lotus project engineer Ron Hickman on the Workmate portable bench project, along with Brian Luff; and Len Terry came in 1962 to design the Indycar. Gadd worked closely with Brian Luff under Mike Costin. 'The Seven was rather low down in our priorities,' said Don. 'It took care of itself really, as there wasn't a great deal of work to be done on it. Most of our work was in

developing the racing cars and the touring cars, and it was not until early 1964 that the touring cars [Lotus Cortinas] were split from the racing cars.' He pointed out that the original Lotus Cortina had a similar A-frame arrangement to the Series 2 Seven rear suspension: 'That was a colossal car to drive at the time,' said Don. 'In those days a hot car on the road was something like an A35 with twin carbs, and the difference between a Series 2 Seven, or indeed, a race-prepared Lotus Cortina, and a hot road car like a Riley 1.5, was most profound.'

When developing the Seven chassis into the Series 2, Don Gadd would have in front of him the drawing of a modified Series 1 chassis, and the fitters would make up two or three before they finally got the right configuration. He explained:

> Most of the work on the Series 2s and 3s was on the various engine options – you could still have a Climax engine in a Series 2. Coming more up to date, there are ways of adapting the Vauxhall chassis to take the K-series engine if that's what you want to do, and the Ford engine will go into the Vauxhall chassis. Before that, we had either a long-cockpit live axle or de Dion chassis, and the engine bay would suit the Ford engine. Then we were doing one which was modified to take the K-series engine, followed by another one designed to take the Vauxhall engine. But even in 1994 you still ordered a Ford, Vauxhall, or Rover chassis.

The other chassis variable is that the pedal box is located according to whether the car is to be left- or right-hand drive; and of course from 1993 the pedal box itself is 2.5in (63mm) longer and 1.5in (38mm) wider than previously.

Racing spec cars are different from standard in their lack of instruments, and in the cars destined for the Vauxhall racing series there are also extra tubular diagonals in the floor under the seats. These are inserted

Completed Caterham chassis piled high; compare the complexity of the tubing with the mountain-bike frame.

because of the formidable power of the 2-litre twin-cam motor and the colossal amount of grip provided by the slick tyres. The chassis never actually betrayed any weakness, but it was felt that the extra diagonals would stiffen things up beneficially.

In Don Gadd's office is an impressive drawing-board, and I asked him how far he thought the Seven chassis could evolve. 'Caterham are loath to change the overall appearance,' he said, 'and quite rightly so. As soon as you start adding extraneous things or raising the bonnet or widening the wings, it ceases to be the same animal. We've had a Seven with a V8 in it here,' said Don, when I cited the Westfield SEight. 'Years ago it was, in the 1970s, built by a chap named Harry Barke, and we modified his chassis so he could shoehorn in a Rover V8, and as far as I know he's still got it.'

The evidence of Don's most recent handiwork was not exactly under wraps when I toured the Arch factory, but I was asked politely by Bruce Robinson to look the other way, and certainly not to take any pictures of it. Don was unable to say anything about it, except that it would be different from the Seven spaceframe, and was being developed alongside it. It would be usable either on the road or in competition, he said, and although it was classified information, it could well be seen at the 1994 Motor Show. I did not realize it at the time, but here was the new 21 chassis in the making.

Don and Sheila Gadd recently returned from a run to St Moritz in Don's 1991 de Dion Caterham 1700 Super Sprint, which took them through spectacular mountain passes and overnight stops in romantic chalet-style hotels. Don prefers the Ford-engined car: 'I'm not all that keen on fuel injection,' he admitted. 'At least with two carburettors you can play around with them, and if anything goes wrong, you know what it is. Having had a complete failure with a fuel injection car which left us stranded by the side of the road, well, you might just as well take the back off a TV set!' The Gadds' next run in the Super Sprint was scheduled for Frejus in the south of France. Count me in!

6   Building the Seven

The Caterham factory is a modern single-storey block built in 1987 on an industrial estate near Dartford – some would call it Crayford – in north Kent, a couple of miles along a new dual carriageway from the southern end of the Dartford Tunnel and the giddy heights of the suspension bridge over the River Thames. It is located just off a busy main road, but you know instantly where you are during the working day by the line-up of brand new Caterhams outside. A glance inside each one shows the steering wheel wrapped in polythene. Some cars have a wax coating. The main block houses the assembly area, engine-building bay, development shop, stores, offices, canteen and also the visitor reception area. Alongside is the building which houses the kits for dispatch, storage racks, crashed Sevens and, up on a mezzanine floor, a dazzling array of classic Lotus products.

Guided Tour

I was given a guided tour by Paul Kite, whose role then was customer liaison although he now works in sales. 'The Caterham is a well engineered product,' he said 'but they are far from cheap now, and customers feel they need to be looked after when they visit the factory.' Generally speaking, the customer age band today is between twenty-five and

A newly finished Caterham Vauxhall racer stands in the spacious Dartford assembly area.

Paul Kite, who looks after customer relations and provided a guided tour of the factory, poses in the Caterham showroom.

sixty-five, and the customer base has changed somewhat from the original Seven enthusiast who would have been prepared to put up with a lot less in the way of creature comforts than today's buyer. So a certain amount of deferential treatment is in order.

Quite logically, the assembly progresses from one end of the hall-like factory to the other. At the top is the engine shop, where you can see new units fresh from the suppliers, awaiting their turn for preparation, plus a couple ready for installation. One or two chassis, panelled and just back from the paint shop, stand by for fettling. Next bay on from the engine shop is the brake department, where hubs and brake assemblies are built up.

Down both sides of the main hall are cars in varying stages of assembly; some with power-train installed, some with suspension being fitted, one or two having seats and trim installed, and finally mudguards and wings

attached. There are a dozen or so cars in build at any given time; also one or two fully built and finished cars are to be seen, ready for dispatch – these are likely to be for export. The majority are being built up to kit stage, to be completed by the customer. The kit stage implies that it has instruments, switches, wiring loom, pedals, braking system and wings all fitted; and rather ambiguously, if it is CKD (completely knocked-down), the hood would be fitted as well. Thus the major elements of production are done for the customer, and otherwise it is a question of bolting everything else together.

Of the 500–600 cars built each year, half are kits, a quarter are fully built, and the remainder are sold in component form with twenty-five hours of work left for the customer to do. This still constitutes a kit from the legal point of view. At the bottom end of the main hall, three or four cars are being serviced, or having crash repairs attended to. Original Lotus Sevens can be dealt with here as well, although they are far from common. There is virtually no competition preparation at the factory; this is done privately, with a large number of cars prepared for Caterham Challenge races by Suffolk-based Hyperion Motor Sport, Arrowstar of Oxford, and Beecroft of Bolton.

Caterham also costs in a three-hour post-build safety check-over for every kit: to ensure that the customer has assembled his kit correctly, he has to bring it back to the factory or to one of the approved service agencies and it seems that people are prepared to travel from the other end of the country to get this done. Principally the check covers steering and brakes, and if there is anything amiss, Caterham will rectify it, for a small consideration, or the customer can just be advised on what needs doing. A fully built car gets a short test run from the factory to make sure everything is in order.

111

The majority of competitors in the Caterham Challenge series have their cars looked after by specialists, but the factory does prepare a few. Here a K-series car has some exhaust work done.

Stores

Alongside the main assembly hall and with direct access to it, are the stores, burgeoning with Caterham components, stacked on shelving on two floors. Everything for the Super Seven is here; the parts which were obvious on the upper floor included spare honeycomb panelling, with boot floor, boot board and rear panel, also bonnets, wings, nosecones, trim sections and exhausts. On the ground floor were hoses, manifolds, carpeting, fuel tanks, driveshafts, dampers, roll cages, wheels and tyres, and bins and boxes full of bolts and screws.

Here is a cache of live axles, looking strangely antiquated and out of place these days, the product of another era. At the bottom end of the stores is a line of bin-racks, a job sheet attached to each one, gradually being filled up with the makings of the next batch of Caterhams.

Next to the stores and the assembly area is the development shop. Any car which is not to standard production spec, or any

Parts bins lined up in the stores, one for each car in build. As the bin fills up, items are crossed off the list on the job-sheet.

Ital live axles complete with drum brake and hub assemblies stockpiled in the stores.

modification under development, would be tried and built in this department; and as you would expect, the public are not allowed in. Nor could we take any pictures of the modifications being conjured up within.

Main Assembly Hall

'Nothing is actually manufactured here,' said Paul Kite. 'We have something like 200 different suppliers, and we assemble

Caterham's Dartford assembly shop during a lull in the proceedings, with the newly completed Vauxhall racer in the foreground.

everything here.' Some parts are made specifically for the Seven, while others are derived from other vehicles. Of Caterham's total personnel, ten actually 'build' the car, three work in servicing, three are building kits. Each person has his own work station, with his name on a cupboard against the wall. I say 'his', because unlike the trim shop which is about equal male to female, it's a bit of a male preserve at Dartford; apart from secretarial and administration staff, only a single woman was to be seen on the shop floor and she was in the stores area.

ENGINE PREPARATION

We started at the engine bay, where examples of the three different engines used were in the throes of preparation. Each engine has its own little stand, enabling it to be carried by two people, and some work is carried out with the engine swinging free on a hoist. Four men who specialize in engines are employed here. The Ford Kent ohv engine, now twenty-five years old and the mainstay of specialist sports cars, gets the most thorough work-over. Surprisingly, Caterham does not use the Zetec engine, for reasons of power and weight, and because it needs excessive damping to cure vibrations. (Some owners do fit the Zetec, however, notably units prepared by Dunnell Engineering.) There are no less than four versions of the crossflow engine: three are 1600s, and the fourth is the 1700. It takes two days to prepare one Ford cross-flow unit. Royston Paskins described the process for the 1700 Super Sprint:

> The engine builder starts by stripping the Ford unit right down to the bare block. The block is sent away to a local machine shop for the ports and the bores to be ground out to match and honed out to 1,700cc, and different pistons go in. Then the head gets

Robert Singleton works on a pair of Webers destined for a 1600 Ford Kent engine. Jets will vary according to which version of the engine is being fitted: the two tuned 1600 engine options are rated at 100bhp and 110bhp, while the 1700 gives 130bhp.

Caterham's own valves and camshafts fitted.

Classic Motoring

The 84bhp engine is the regular 1,600cc unit with downdraught carburettor; the 110bhp version has sidedraught Webers, an A2 cam and modified cylinder head. The austere Classic model, which costs around £8,450, has the earlier chassis configuration, plus live Ital rear axle and basic suspension layout. The 84bhp version of the Ford cross-flow 1,600cc engine uses a four-speed reconditioned gearbox and steel wheels. Spartan is

*Block of a Ford Super Sprint engine
mounted to the bench, having had the
ports and bores ground out and
honed out to 1,700cc. Different
pistons, together with Caterham's
own valves and camshafts, are fitted.*

*This 1700 Super Sprint engine and
gearbox, plus almost mandatory twin
Webers, is fitted with its carrying
cradle and ready for dispatch.*

the word which comes to mind, as there is no
hood and no windscreen, only sports aero-
screens, and consequently no sidescreens as
there is nothing to hang them on; a tonneau
wouldn't go amiss. No wipers, either, and you
don't get a heater or a spare wheel unless you
pay extra.

Those who buy a Classic and are hooked on
Sevens but want to trade up for a new de
Dion car, can take advantage of Caterham's
buy-back guarantee, structured at a rate of
£100 per thousand miles to cover deprecia-
tion, provided the car has been regularly
serviced.

Vauxhall Unit

The fuel-injected Vauxhall 2-litre twin-cam

unit – as fitted in the Astra, Cavalier or
Calibra – is virtually straight out of the box,
but with a different sump and bellhousing to
make it suitable for the Seven chassis. In
standard form it develops 165bhp. Caterham
will fit it with carburettors for export or for
racing, which can lift peak power up to
188bhp. Carbs are still permitted in Japan,
for example, and a number of cars so destined
were to be seen on my visits. There is not
much difference in actual power output
between a fuel-injected car and one with
carbs, but carburettors – twin 45 or 48s on the
Vauxhall engine – make it a different vehicle;
they look good and make a nice sucking noise
redolent of the race track. Injection has a

The 1994 VX Vauxhall Super Seven was normally supplied with fuel injection and full catalytic system, but this 165bhp 2-litre 16-valve Caterham-Vauxhall twin-cam is fitted with twin carbs and no cat.

Engine builder Royston Paskins spends about eight hours on a K-series 16-valve twin-cam. By swapping camshafts, rechipping the engine management system and switching the plenum chamber, output is increased to 130bhp.

number of sensors which contrive to make the engine more environmentally acceptable.

The sump is swapped for Caterham's own product. More significantly, a dry sump lubrication system is a notable option on the Vauxhall unit. Designed and developed in-house by Caterham, it mates the Sierra gearbox to a Vauxhall engine, and the oil tank is an integral part of the bellhousing. It is effectively a double skin arrangement, with the oil sluicing in the outer chamber. A scavenge pump is mounted on the side of the engine, driven by a toothed belt from the crankshaft, and pumps oil back to the tank. This allows an extremely shallow sump, and oil surge and lubrication at high cornering speeds is not a problem – indeed all race spec engines employ this system. It gains around 8bhp, partly by virtue of the crank not running in thick oil. Factory 24-hour race cars ran wet-sump engines because of an 11kg weight advantage, with at worst a 6bhp deficit.

K-series Engine

The K-series, 1.4-litre Rover engine is fitted

Martin Stewart inspects a brand new K-series engine on a hoist prior to changing the sump for Caterham's own shallower version.

in the Super Sport model. It produces 110bhp in standard form, but can be massaged up to 130bhp by switching camshafts, rechipping the ECU engine management system, and changing the plenum chamber to a Caterham bespoke unit. Engine builders Royston Paskins and Martin Stewart spend about eight hours preparing each Rover unit. The sump is changed for Caterham's own make, and pick-ups are different in order for this unit to sit a lot lower in the chassis. The height of the engine is critical on a Seven, in order to retain the original bonnet line, and a flatter sump profile permits a lower-lying engine.

It is connected to a five-speed Ford Sierra type 9 gearbox, with Caterham's own bell-housing for the adaptation, which is made by Titan Motorsport. It has the advantage of being a light, modern engine. Because of its relatively small cubic capacity, the Rover engine had to overcome initial prejudice, but die-hard Seven fans soon became enamoured

of its reliability and trouble-free nature. 'Before fuel injection, when we were doing the Ford-engined cars with a couple of carburettors stuck out the side, life was a lot less straightforward,' said Paul Kite.

Gone are cold-start carburettor hassles, with all the accompanying coughing and spluttering they involved; here is a high-tech engine in a traditional bodyshell. Until 1993 Arch Motors made different chassis for different engines: 'Which', said Paul Kite, 'was a bit of a nightmare for us.' With an eight-week lead time on each chassis, there was obviously a delay if someone wanted a special chassis. The 1994 spec chassis will accept any of the three engine options by shifting movable cross-members; these were previously fixed. It also has a longer pedal box to cater for taller drivers, and there are three potential pedal positions.

The K-series-engined car costs from £14,000. The greater price than the Classic simply reflects the cost of Sierra differentials, half-shafts and de Dion tube and ears, and the five-speed gearbox. The K-series Super Sport is, as the name suggests, an altogether superior car, and is available with the Caterham six-speed gearbox; this enables you to exploit its higher revving potential, and it can be hustled along more keenly than the regular K-series car.

ASSEMBLING A CATERHAM

The task of building a car begins with creating the front corners. There are four types of hub and brake assembly: the most basic use ordinary road discs, while the racing variant has an iron hub. The Caterham's standard brakes are basic Ford Sierra items, and an optional arrangement features AP four-pot racing callipers with ventilated discs at the front, and single-pot callipers at the rear.

Some components are not exactly true when supplied to Caterham. For instance, stub axles are often found to be oversize, and have to be rubbed down on the lathe to make them right; or sometimes the threaded ends on steering columns are too long and have to be shortened. The sub-assembly shop was operated by dapper Maurice Thorne, since retired, and includes the lathe, the drill and the hydraulic press for pushing the bearings into the hubs. The press incorporates a purpose-made tool to press the outer race home.

I watched Maurice put together the front upright assemblies. They consist of the upright, left- or right-handed, plus the inner and outer bearing races and felt seal; also the brake callipers and fasteners, pads, the disc and hub which is bolted to it, stub axle and attendant fasteners like washers, split pins and castellated nuts. Then there is the steering tie-rod lever. All metal components ex-stores are coated with protective wax, which is removed with white spirit solvent. Maurice Thorne has to burnish the uprights

Maurice Thorne torques up a front hub assembly. Some he did earlier sit on the bench.

to take off excess plating so they slide on cleanly. On the workbench, the upright is clamped in a soft-jawed vice. The steering arm and pink spacing washer are bolted to the upright, torqued up to 22 to 27lb/ft. The stub axle passes through the upright, and is fixed with ½in (13mm) nylock nut, tightened to 60 to 65lb/ft. If your car has cycle-wing mudguards, the wing stay has to be fitted to the stub axle under the nylock nut, which is tightened to the same tolerance.

The bearings' outer races are tapered, with narrower sides pressed into the hub, and clearly, care needs to be taken not to damage the bearings during fitting. Caterham's press does the job easily enough for component kits, but if you are building the front corners yourself, it may be as well to get the local garage to do just this one job

Using a purpose-made tool on the hydraulic press, Maurice Thorne presses the bearings into the hubs.

for you. The roller bearings which go at the rear of the hub have to be well greased, as does the track in the hub. The felt dust seal will also be fitted in a press. The brake disc slots onto the hub and is fastened in place with the accompaniment of a squirt of Loctite, by four bolts torqued up to 22 to 27lb/ft pressure.

The upright is then tilted through 90 degrees, and the hub assembly drops onto the stub axle. The small roller bearing set is greased, as is its location, and it fits over the stub axle. The D-washer and castellated nut are tightened to 6lb/ft – and before fitting the split pin through the castellated nut to secure them, the disc is given a trial spin. If it feels notchy when rotated, the assembly is

not quite right and it is dismantled and done again. When Maurice is happy with it, the end of the split pin is bent over and the dust cap tapped in. The brake calliper is bolted in place, and a spacing washer located between calliper and upright on both bolts, in order to get the spacing right between calliper and brake disc. The bolts are then tightened to 40 to 45lb/ft. Every suspension bolt is smeared with Copperslip to make future dismantling easier. The upright assemblies are attached by a spigot on the upright which passes through a spherical joint and is secured with a nylock nut.

Front Suspension

The chassis stands on axle stands now, ready to receive its front suspension components: these include coil springs and dampers, plus an aluminium spacer which is located in the lower eye. Upper wishbones have a ball joint attached, and although they are adjustable, they are factory-set and need no attention. The lower wishbones have spherical (not the classic) joints fitted, with circlip to the underside, and the rose that fits in the lower wishbone needs to be a slide fit. The lower wishbone is wider than the chassis, so that the castor angle setting can be adjusted. Four spacing washers can be inserted to give an initial idea of clearances. An Allen bolt locates the spring-damper unit on the top wishbone with a half nylock nut, and the lower end is fixed by a bolt passing through the aluminium spacer in the lower damper eye. Home builders have to bear in mind that the front suspension assembly is only fully tightened when the car is completed.

The front anti-roll bar has a bracket on which the top front wishbone pivots, and a pair of brackets containing the 'cotton-reel' rubber bush which the anti-roll bar pivots in, are slid onto the roll bar before fitting the balls at either end. The studding is secured into the end of the bar with Studlock, and

Derek Howlett connects the front spring-damper unit to the lower wishbone.

this is used to secure the balls, too. The bar is incorporated into the front suspension system by pushing the ball into the greased joint in the top wishbone. Using a little Studlock on the bolts, attachment is from the rear into threaded bushes top and bottom.

Steering Assembly

This consists of the rack and its clamps, upper and lower lengths of steering column, clamp, rubber bush, track-rod ends and a universal joint. The rack is normally fitted after the engine has gone in, and if the job is being done at home, you have to bear in mind that the location of the oil pump on the specified engine may coincide with the passage of the steering column. Thus, the steering rack might need to be articulated to move the lower section of column away from the oil pump; a finger's width is sufficient gap. And naturally, the steering rack has to be centralized so there is equal lock on either side. This can be done at home simply by turning the steering to full lock on either side, and measuring the distance between the tyre or wing stay and the side of the car; if it

corresponds on both sides, the rack's positioning is correct and it is tightened up.

Rear Suspension

The transmission and rear suspension set-up of a contemporary Caterham turn-key model, rather than a live axle car, includes the de Dion tube, two aluminium ears, long and short brake pipes, brake-pipe union, discs, hubs, hubs, callipers, bearing housings and cover plates to keep dirt out of the ends of the de Dion tube. The constituent parts· are assembled on the bench before being fitted to the chassis.

The differential is fitted before the rear axle is mounted into the car, but in advance of this, a lug is machined off the back of the differential so that the de Dion tube does not foul it when the car is in motion. The propshaft is attached to the front of the differential before it goes in the car, using four blue bolts, torqued up to 40lb/ft. The differential and propshaft assembly are fitted from under the chassis, via the rectangular space between the frame tubes. Two fitters carry out this procedure, with one horizontal on the ground pushing the differential upwards and feeding the prop down its tunnel, while his colleague inserts locating bolts through the differential and relevant chassis ears. Incidentally, the lower differential mounting bolts are ½in (13mm) shank with M12 thread, and are not found anywhere else on the car.

The precise centralization of the differential is achieved by shimming washers, using three to each side of the car. When tightened up, the distance is measured from differential lug to outside of the chassis, and if the distances are within 2mm of one another, the differential is in the vehicle's centre line.

With the left-hand driveshaft inserted into the differential, the de Dion tube is passed through the wheel-arch and centralized – achieved by shimming up either side of the A-frame – and the end of the driveshaft is inserted through the bearing housings in the differential. Then the right-hand driveshaft is inserted through the aluminium ear on the end of the de Dion tube, and thence into the differential. The nuts on the end of the driveshaft are left- and right-handed, coded white and green accordingly, and tightened to a mighty 200lb/ft, using a 1⅝in (41mm) socket.

Other components which have been pre-assembled on the bench go on now, and these include the brake discs, hubs and callipers. For convenience, the rear anti-roll bar is laid in place at this point. Brake pipes are now connected up; the pipe runs on top of the de Dion tube rather than in front of it, where it would be vulnerable to movement of the differential when the car was in motion. Spacers fit between the brake calliper and aluminium ear to achieve the right spacing between calliper and brake disc; in general, washers are fitted between any aluminium component and its fastener, although with cast iron this is not necessary.

Attachment of the major items – the A-frame, spring damper units, radius arms,

rear anti-roll bar and its mounting blocks and pivot mechanism – is relatively straight-forward. The rear axle is attached using the radius arms and A-frame, and home builders should be certain to get the A-frame the right way up and the radius arms the right way round. It is also important to ensure there is clearance between the driveshaft gaiter and spring-damper unit mounting. None of the bolts is fully tightened until the car is complete and sitting on the ground.

Gearbox

Gearbox ancillaries include filler plug, reverse light switch, speedometer angle drive, plus circlip, cable and seal, speedo gear and gear cover. The gear is inserted from the left of the gearbox, and the gear cover locks it in place. The speedo gear seal goes over the

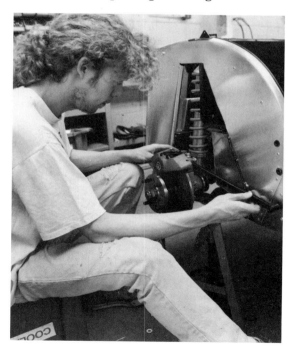

Each Caterham fitter has his own work station: here Gary May fits a radius arm to a car with a de Dion disc-brake rear suspension.

121

Suspension assembly is complete on this Caterham, and Andy Price is bleeding the brakes.

top of it. The angle drive slots into the end of the gear, and is secured by a circlip. The speedo cable is fitted to the angle drive, and the reversing light switch is also fitted at this point. The angle drive is the most vulnerable component when the engine and gearbox is lowered into the chassis, and care must be taken not to knock it accidentally.

Four bolts fasten the bellhousing to the gearbox, passing through the aluminium sandwich plate and gasket. The clutch-cable bush is a simple press fit, and the pivot pin is tapped in place within the bellhousing with a hammer. The clutch fork passes over the input shaft of the gearbox, through the gap in the side of the bellhousing, and the fork engages on the pin. The clutch-release bearing passes over the front of the gearbox, and is pressed into position on the clutch fork, and secured by the sap clips. The clutch gaiter and clip are fitted along with the clutch cable. Left-hand drive cars have a hydraulic clutch, which has a separate slave cylinder.

Engine Installation

More ancillaries are attached in advance, including the oil pressure sender, and the engine mounting brackets and their attendant rubber are fitted – loosely at first – to the chassis rails; also in place is the gearbox mounting rubber. The chassis is now on axle stands and the engine is suspended from a hoist at some 45 degrees.

The gearbox is eased back into the engine bay, and the propshaft is inserted into the back of the gearbox. The engine obviously follows into position, and the engine mountings are swivelled round until they are flush with the side of the block. It is fastened on each side by four set screws, with two bolts securing the gearbox mounting at the rear of the engine. If the car is to have a dry sump-lubrication system, an alternative engine mounting bracket is used on the right-hand side to by-pass the oil pump. Clearly, before the car turns a wheel under its own power, all lubricants and coolants will be added.

If you are building a car at home running

on carburettors, it is as well to check that the air filters correspond with the aperture in the side of the engine bay. Because they will settle slightly as the engine beds in, they ought to be set a little high, and adjustment can be made by shimming the engine mounting rubbers, lifting the engine – and filters – accordingly. If you happen to need to lower the engine, small sections of the mounting brackets can be pared off.

The steering column is fitted, and the bolts holding the rack onto the chassis are tightened up. The blanking plate and box are mounted on the column before it is finally secured with the clamp assembly. A grub screw is tightened onto a flat on the lower column and secured with a lock nut. When the column is inserted through the steering column lock tube – which is riveted to the chassis – care must be taken not to displace the bush at the bottom of it. To secure finally the steering column top and bottom, another bush is pressed into position in the bottom rail of the dashboard. At the rear of the pedal box, which the column passes over, is the sealing box, riveted in place.

Cooling System

The next job is to fit the radiator and cooling hoses along with other ancillaries such as the washer bottle, tubing and jet, and the water temperature sender. It is also time for the cables for the various controls to be connected up, and first is the throttle cable, clipped to the pedal and leading to the injection; or the carbs. The clutch cable is attached to the pedal, and the other end to the fork in the bellhousing. There are two handbrake cables to the de Dion handbrake: the forward one is attached to the handbrake; the rear cable loops around the front cable by a pulley, and the other end is attached to the rear callipers. The speedo cable has two similar-looking ends, one fastened to the speedo, the other to the gearbox.

Radiator hoses like the one being fitted by John Killick are regular trade items.

Handbrake Set-up

The handbrake is one of the most difficult items to fit, because it is located under the scuttle and heater panels. Access is through a slot in the top of the heater panel, and the handbrake barrel is inserted through it, care being taken to make sure it is the right way up, and that the recess in it faces the outer cable. With the lever bolted onto the chassis, using the pivot bolt, the inner cable is moored to the chassis. The handbrake's operation is unusual in that the inner cable is fixed, and it is the normally static outer one which does the work, moved by the lever. The outer cable slots into the lever, capturing the inner in the process, pushes down, and the outer cable goes into the recess in the barrel. Finally the cover is slid onto the lever and locked into position on the handbrake barrel by a grommet and a circlip.

In the course of fitting the pedals in the pedal box, Andy Elcomb incorporates the linkage and master cylinder.

Caterham's wiring looms are made by MES in Birmingham, with one for injection cars and one for carburettor cars. Ian Cowdery connects up the dashboard wiring.

Clearly a handbrake is compulsory in order to be road-legal and to pass the MOT test, but since nobody I have come across actually uses theirs, preferring just to leave the car in gear, in practice it is rather redundant.

Wiring Loom

The front indicators have their lenses removed. The wiring passes through three holes in the lamp, black for earth and a green feed wire. A white trace in the green wire indicates it is for the right-hand side of the car, and a red trace is for the left-hand side. The repeater flashers for the outside of the flared clamshell wings need to have fixing studs removed and replaced with longer ones before fitting. Three green wires and three black wires link virtually all the Caterham's

electrical apparatus, and it is simply a matter of joining green to green and black to black, using bullet connectors. Positioning in the connector is not important, so long as all wires are connected, and may be determined by the neatest method of accomplishing this.

Ancillaries and Trim

Windscreen and instruments and other ancillaries are taken care of now, and the trim goes in, according to what has been ordered. The specification will have been given to Oxted Trimming in advance, and will be ready and waiting for the car in build. The carpet covering the transmission tunnel goes over the gear lever gaiter – or 'witch's hat' – and has darts cut in it for better fitment. It is located on poppers, and glued to the top chassis rail with the edge overlapped by the boot cover. The seat-belt escutcheons are mounted through the carpet to give a neat finish.

The hood sticks are bolted onto the car, with care taken to set the height of the individual bows accurately; aligned with one of the rearmost chassis tubes, the edges of the three sticks or bows just kiss each other and form an equilateral triangle. This establishes the length of the outer stick, which is then attached to the bracket on the car, and the inner hood stick is fixed to the outer one at 4in (102mm) from its base. The hood straps are looped onto the sticks, with the tensioning buckle smooth side to the hood, and the longest length of strap screwed to the back of the car.

The popper bases are fitted at specified distances around the rear of the vehicle and along the windscreen header rail, and the matching poppers to the hood itself: ¾in (19mm) up from the back of the hood, and the same distance in from the seam. Ideally, the edge of the hood will sit neatly on top of the wing beading. After ensuring the sidescreens are correctly positioned in relation to the hood and body aperture, the hinges are fitted on the windscreen stanchions and sidescreens.

For those building their Seven at home, Caterham supplies an instruction manual, and an assembly video fronted by technical director Jez Coates, based around a de Dion spaceframe; this demonstrates clearly what fits where. There's also a technical help-line. Also the finished car should be taken back to Caterham to ensure that it has been assembled correctly. It's included in the price, so why not?

Exhaust Systems

One of the most characteristic and indeed dramatic features of certain Super Seven models is the prominent near-side exhaust, visible for all the world to see, with its four

Using a mastic gun, Chris Weston seals around the Caterham's front bulkhead and scuttle where panels join. The boot floor gets similar treatment.

branches issuing from the tub and ending underneath the passenger's left elbow. The area of pipe under the passenger's access (in right-hand drive form) is protected by a satisfyingly large aluminium cylinder-guard – which, because of its pierced surface, looks like a cheese-grater.

There is a facility for routing the exhaust system underneath the car, however, and a Caterham so equipped is rather quieter. Vauxhalls in particular have under-car exhausts, and the routing was devised as a way of complying with certain European noise regulations. From time to time in Seven history, systems were routed differently; for instance, from 1963 with some

There are basically two types of fire extinguisher and this is the hand-held version, mounted between seat locations.

Series 2s and especially in the Lotus Series 3 and Series 4 days, the pipe ran outside the car, but instead of terminating by the passenger's elbow, it ended out at the back.

DISPATCH

Alongside the main building is the dispatch and storage department. Here is a stock of chassis, ready panelled by Arch Motors, which will be taken the two or three miles to Erith for painting before being taken into assembly. A number of Vauxhall and Rover engines sit waiting their turn, and stocks of wheels and tyres are piled up.

Half a dozen kits are boxed up and ready to go, and this is more than Paul Kite would like, from the point of view of space and access. 'Ideally, four or five is about the limit,' he said. For those who have never bought a kit car, it is instructive to see the form in which it gets delivered. In the cardboard

Static fire extinguisher mounted in the passenger space in a racer, plumbed in and wearing the 'Ready for Use' tag. The contents would be disgorged into the engine bay in the event of a fire.

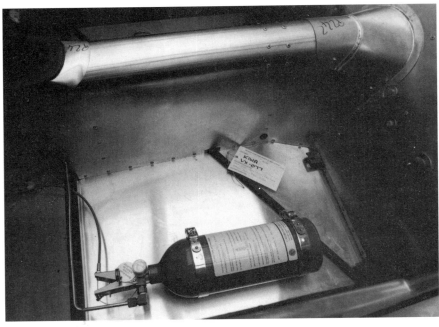

How your kit is made ready for dispatch. The boxes for each car occupy two pallets, with items like the roll-over bar packaged separately. Clearly cartons are a substantial consideration when selling cars in kit form.

boxes are complete kits. Each kit has the body-chassis unit, a set of packages containing all the componentry and a set of wheels; the engine is next door.

A component car is ready for delivery, and a further six or seven kits await collection. They are simply finished chassis, accompanied by a series of packages containing

View of the dispatch bay from the mezzanine floor, with tyres piled high, a Vauxhall-engined racer and stocks of body/chassis tubs fresh from Arch Motors.

engine, cooling, lighting, and everything else to get the car up and running.

One or two race cars are to be seen, stripped down to just the bare necessities with minimal instruments, including a left-hand-drive Vauxhall destined for France. A couple of crashed cars await repair, while up on the mezzanine floor is Caterham's collection of 'classic' Lotus cars. Paul Kite took off the dust sheets – understandably they are always under wraps. This is a delightful Aladdin's cave of Lotus history, immaculately preserved: here is a Series 1 Seven with its BMC engine, a Series 2 and a Series 2 racer; and the Series 3 Lotus Seven with its lower-set headlights provides instant comparison with the Caterhams below. The Mk 6 appears rather stumpy and a trifle ungainly by comparison. The Elite still looks wonderful today, as does the Eleven, such an advanced aerodynamic concept then and now.

WHEELS

Sevens have been supplied with a variety of wheel styles over the years, from wire spokes and Lotus 'Wobbly Web' to the latest VX on Vauxhall-engined Caterhams. There are still several different options: you can specify the KN wheel, which Caterhams have used since the 1970s, with two styles of Super Seven alloy currently available, or a typically late-1980s Revolution or Compomotive example. The 14in Supalite is a Minilite copy, and as far as I am concerned, they don't come any better: the 'period' look of the Minilite suits the Caterham very well indeed.

Compomotives are only ordered in very small numbers, and more often on cars sold to Japanese buyers. The Classic Caterham can be ordered with a new steel wheel, made by Weller; this is quite a heavy item, despite its telephone-dial aspect.

Whatever your preference, there is a good selection of 13in and 14in diameter wheels to choose from, including magnesium alloy Minilites, which are headquartered at Croughton in Northants, and the Supalite.

Modern Caterham wheels are interchangeable, with the 7J x 16 VX wheel a popular choice.

The 14in Revolution alloy wheel is sometimes chosen as an after-market option, shod here with Goodyear NCT 195/60 R14 tyres.

The traditional Supalite wheel suits the Seven's styling.

129

Also regular factory fitment is the optional 6.5J x 15 Prisoner wheel, wearing 195/50 VR15 Michelin XGTV tyres.

The KN alloy is falling out of favour now, although it was a popular choice during the 1980s. Newer, larger diameter wheels are the more popular way to go, and lower-profile tyres on these big wheels match the smaller diameter wheels to a degree; the rolling radius is not that different between a 14in wheel with a 60-aspect tyre and a 16in wheel with a 45-aspect tyre. But to get more authentic handling, a Seven will work better with taller, narrower tyres.

There is a certain amount of machismo about the cycle-wing front mudguards as opposed to the clamshell wings, because they appear more sporting. They are slightly lighter, but the disadvantage is that they tend to throw up the stones more, and the rear-wing stone-guard gets more of a hammering. The other factor is that you lose half a turn of lock, because the wing chafes on the body of the car on full lock, and of course this does not happen with the flared wing.

This HPC model is having cycle-wing front mudguards fitted. Fixing holes have been marked out on a jig, and Chris Bradford is lining them up.

7 Fibreglass, Paint and Upholstery

USE OF FIBREGLASS

First, a history lesson. In the years following the Second World War a new industry grew up making all manner of things from boat hulls to car bodies, and the medium it used was synthetic resin reinforced by glass-fibre matting. It was ideal for constructing car bodies which had separate chassis rather than unit-construction, which was starting to become recognized practice in the early 1950s. While aluminium continued to be used by the traditional specialist coachbuilders, notably in Milan and Turin, fibreglass was a much cheaper alternative, with the additional benefits of strength and freedom from corrosion. One of the advantages of glass-fibre is its lightness, although there are deficiencies such as surface-crazing with age, and the material wears away around fixings such as bonnet hinges and door catches.

By the mid-1950s manufacturers were producing bodies for specials, mostly to fit 1,172cc-powered Ford or Austin 7 chassis. Among these were Rochdale, Buckler of Reading (who distributed the Microplas body), Super Accessories, Convair, Falcon, Auto-Kraft, Cheetah, Heron, Speedex, HG Developments, Tornado Typhoon and Talisman, and Ashley. Many of these were very similar and resembled scaled-down versions of contemporary sports racing cars. In 1954 the first TVRs used Atalanta coupé bodies by RGS Automobile Components of Windsor. It made sense to have your kit-car body emulate a recognized make in some way, as it was the obvious means of attracting the impecunious enthusiast. Some fibreglass special builders attained the status of recognized manufacturers, including Berkeley, Reliant (who turned to fibreglass in 1956 for their three-wheelers), Fairthorpe, Alexander-Turner, Peerless (who produced the Warwick from 1958 to 1960), and Jensen with the 541. Marcos, Ginetta and Gilbern were getting started, too.

In 1957 Colin Chapman's pretty monocoque Lotus Elite was well ahead of the game, technically and aesthetically as well as on the track, and by the early 1960s a wide assortment of fibreglass-bodied machines, including G.S.M. Delta, Diva Valkyrie and Elva Courier, diced with one another in the 1-litre class of sports GT racing. It was also the era of the special minis, led by the Mini-Marcos, Mini-Jem, Ogle-Mini, and so on. New fibreglass-bodied creations were springing up everywhere, and it was quite logical for Lotus, at the cutting edge of vehicular technology, to utilize grp for its cheapness and lightness. In the case of the Seven, it was a practical expedient too, since the aluminium nose and wings were the most vulnerable and expensive sections of bodywork to produce.

Caterham Applications

Super Seven nosecones, and the front and rear wings, both clamshell and cycle-wing types, are made of glass-fibre, and Caterham uses three suppliers for these components: red and black coloured items are made by Fibresports of Basildon, Essex, and all other

The workshops of Dartford Composites, with clamshell wings hanging up to cure and wings and nosecones bubble-wrapped for dispatch to the factory.

colours by Dartford Composites, with carbon-fibre noses and cycle wings for competition and JPE cars produced by Crosby GRP at Silverstone.

I went to see Dartford Composites to watch these being made, and Bill Player talked me through the process. 'We started the company five years ago with the aid of Caterham Cars,' said Bill, 'and to us they're all-important.' Bill has been in the grp business 'twenty-odd years' and he told me proudly that his firm will manufacture any panel for any application, including use of the vacuum process. His extensive portfolio includes right-hand-drive Ford Mustang

dashboards, and a kinetic gearbox produced for BP made entirely of grp, and good for 60,000rpm. Potential applications of this medium are vast, and, seemingly, anything can be made with it. 'Although the design of Caterham components isn't down to us, we altered the Vauxhall air intake so it would fit the bonnet.' They also have the only moulds to produce wings for Lotus models and earlier Caterhams.

They work in Kevlar, too, and produce the racing seat for the Super Seven, and cycle wings and rear wings for the JPE. 'It's done with the vacuum process, where the mould and the Kevlar constituents are put in a polythene bag and then the air is sucked out of it – quite an awkward process, and fairly expensive, because of the basic materials,' said Bill; 'something like an extra £20 per panel, but you do know it's going to be perfect.' The racing seat they were given as a pattern came from a Formula First car, and it was the wrong shape for the Seven, so Bill chopped it into three, and reset it so it would fit properly. Ingeniously, he incorporated the Seven logo into the set-back from a casting taken from a rubber mat. 'Ideally,' he said, 'I'd prefer them to go to a model maker's and provide me with a pattern, as I spend a lot of time on the creative side.'

All the raw materials for the Seven's fibreglass bits start off on benches at one end of the workshop, with the matting on a roll. 'It's always kept in the dry, well out of the damp,' said Bill. The resin is stored in barrels, and the gel-coat pigment comes ready-mixed from the supplier. The Caterham is unusual in that, whereas most fibreglass cars like TVR are painted after the body is made and united with its chassis, the paint is applied into the mould and becomes part of the fibreglass structure, rather than as a layer painted on top of it. Not many grp manufacturers use this method, with panels normally being supplied in the medium's natural colours of white or grey. There is no doubt that the finish is superb, and with each one receiving thirty-five minutes' worth of polishing, that's not surprising: they shine so much you could almost shave in them.

The moulds last for years, and the ones in use are five years old, and are in daily use. 'They are as good today as when we started off,' said Bill, 'and that only comes by looking after them. Look after your moulds, and they'll look after you.' All Caterham panels are produced in split moulds; these come in sections which are bolted together. The problem with split moulds is that the panel is prone to shrinkage, because the gel coat wants to move away from the join; however, Dartford Composites appear to have found the answer to this – a matter of not doing the bolts up too tightly, and curing correctly.

The first step in making a Caterham wing is to line the inner surface of the mould with a clear solution known as 'mould-release', which will facilitate a clean removal of the cured panel; one application is good for thirty panels. The conventional method is to wax the mould each time it is used. Then the inside of the mould is brush-painted,

Painting the gel-coat into the mould.

Dartford Composites' artisans laying up the glass-fibre matting and applying gel-coat into moulds for Caterham cycle-wing mudguards.

133

accurately yet quite liberally, with the required pigment.

Meanwhile another fabricator is impregnating sections of matting with a general-purpose resin, which he lays up in the mould and rolls out completely flat. The matting is 2oz (57g) glass, 600 grams per square metre, and the sheets are 2mm thick. Although some bulky non-Caterham items can be several sections thick, the Seven panels are made with only a single sheet of 2oz (57g) glass. Their strength is derived from the construction method and the shape of the panel: 'the egg-box theory', as Bill Player describes it.

Curing takes several hours, and the Caterham panels are left overnight, which

Using a power sander and rubbing compound, Bill Player buffs the nosecone to a superb mirror finish.

Dartford Composites' chief, Bill Player, uses a jig and power-tool to trim unwanted flashing from a Caterham nosecone, still in its mould. The radiator air intake will also be cut out with a jig.

means each mould gets used only once a day. After curing, the panel is extracted from the mould and Bill Player takes over to do the finishing and trimming. There is no 'flashing' as such – the fine wafers of resin which extrude from more complex moulds – but the nosecone in particular needs some thirty minutes work here. It has to be trimmed with a cutter set at a pre-determined angle and blade length, to obtain a fine edge all the way round. It runs around a jig which is 5mm smaller than the mould size, and spins at 22,000rpm. 'It's like cutting butter,' said Player, having removed a section from a nosecone to create the air-intake aperture. Front wings are done by eye, as the mould leaves trim lines for the operator to follow. Cycle wings and rear wings also have their own jigs, and all panels are placed on two drilling jigs for all the fixing holes to be made. Says Bill:

The actual time to produce one nosecone is about three and a half man-hours. Our job is very labour-intensive, and that is the most expensive part. We're making about 120 panels a week for Caterham, with five panels to a set; sometimes we make flared wings, and sometimes it's cycle wings. Flared wings are preferred by traditionalists, and cycle wings by the competition fraternity.

Trimming is a dusty business, and a respirator is always worn. When Bill is happy with the trimmed panel, it goes to be polished, using an orbital polisher and cutting compound; this removes any blemishes from the gel-coat, and the finished panel is then packed in bubble-wrap for dispatch to Caterham's factory on the other side of Dartford.

PAINTING

The majority of Sevens have just their fibreglass extremities painted, leaving the aluminium panelling of the centre section bare, and of course this is most commonly polished to a dazzling shine. Wings are self-coloured: the colour goes in at gel-coat stage, and there are five designated hues. Some customers choose to have their cars painted, however, and at Seven club events the wildest colour schemes are in evidence. This is the easiest way of personalizing your car, of course.

Because of the logistics of assembly, the tub is painted before any of the componentry, trim and drivetrain are installed, so notionally at least, the route from Arch Motors to Caterham's Dartford assembly plant is via the paint shop, irrespective of whether the Super Seven is being built to kit stage or as a completed car. In theory, cars can be painted whatever colour you like. Photographer Simon Clay and I visited the paint shop at a sub-contractor called TSK, owned and run by Tony Whiting in Erith.

TSK has been Caterham's painter since they moved to Dartford. They 'tried him out' on one or two cars, and, said Whiting, 'It carried on from there. And on the strength of their business I was able to expand and buy

Occasionally painters TSK are asked for something out of the ordinary, and this car awaiting its wings and headlights has a distinctive colour scheme, somewhat reminiscent of the 35th Anniversary model.

135

a new oven.' Throughput varies. One week maybe four cars come for painting, another may see ten; four to six is the average. The bare chassis is sent from Dartford, having undergone pre-prep; this includes having all fixing holes drilled for wings. Wiring looms and brake-pipe runs will generally have been done, and they come in different stages of build, depending on whether the car is destined to be a basic kit or fully built. Whiting prepares and paints them, including flatting and polishing, and then back they go to Dartford. I asked Whiting about the preparation of bare aluminium for painting. 'First we look at all the known areas where they have been welded,' he said. 'These we DA in 180 and then 320. The rest of the car is DA'd in 320 and then padded off with a red Scotch tape.'

They had just done an 'Anniversary' car, green with a yellow stripe, to commemorate Caterham's twenty years as Super Seven builders; this milestone was the incentive for a free paint job and special wheels. A limited edition 'Prisoner' was in the throes of being painted, a particular shade of green with yellow nosecone and red upholstery, and eventually to be autographed by Patrick McGoohan; it struck me how small the wingless tub looked on its trestles in the centre of the spray booth, compared with, say, the all-enveloping body of a TVR Chimaera. Painter Paul Bryant mainly uses a selection of five standard colours, although the range of available shades is virtually endless. Occasionally he is asked for something out of the ordinary, and in his experience it is rare for bonnets to be left unpainted.

Masking up is a simple if laborious process, because Bryant is painting just the outer skins of the body panels, although there are no mechanical components to worry about. It is not like a Morgan for instance, where the wings must be detached to ensure the paint gets between wing and body; there can't be many cars as simple and

Caterhams are painted in the booth and oven at TSK of Crayford. Here, Paul Bryant sprays a 35th Anniversary model.

as economical to paint as a Seven. After masking up, the surfaces to be painted are de-greased using mild hydrochloric acid solution; they then go into the oven. After the body is de-waxed, a wet-on-wet etch primer is applied; this is allowed to flash off, and any specks are 'de-nicked' with very fine wet-and-dry paper. The colour coat is applied next, which is a wet-on-wet process again. Three coats are applied, the fully masked and respirator-clad painter Bryant moving swiftly and methodically around the tub, aiming his gun from side to side at a range of about 18in (40cm). Fine clouds of paint swirl over the car as he works.

When Bryant has finished, the oven is switched on to 'bake'. The car is unmasked while still warm, because the glue on the tape is soft and it pulls away more easily. It is then flatted and polished with 1,200 grade

Painter Paul Bryant prepares to mix one of the five standard Caterham colours. The range of shades available is virtually endless.

paper in soap and water. The paint supplier provides a warranty for TSK's work, which is reassuring; your paint finish is covered twice in effect.

UPHOLSTERY

All Caterham's upholstery is made by the Oxted Trimming company, based just south of the M25 and five miles or so from Caterham. This firm is part of the family, having looked after the Super Seven's fabric requirements since 1973. It was started in 1972, although Oxted boss Eddie Marriott had done trimming work on Series 4 Lotus Sevens and had upholstered Series 3 seats and carpets since 1969. 'We started doing just seats, then we did carpets, and gradually took on more, little by little, until we had the lot,' he said proudly. 'We developed our bits as the car evolved.' There was a certain amount of trial and error, and they even went to the lengths of copying Rolls Royce

As a partner in Oxted Trimming, Eddie Marriott supervises the materials and make-up of all Caterham upholstery.

techniques to get the best result. 'If it wasn't right, we'd rip it out and start again,' Eddie Marriott told me. 'It's like everything; you get what you pay for, and Caterham upholstery is extremely high quality.' Not surprisingly, Marriott inspects every car they trim to ensure the standard is maintained. 'Mind you, everyone tries to keep the quality up, so mistakes are very rare,' said Eddie. 'In the early days, you should have seen the mess we worked in; but the cars used to turn out immaculate.'

Within reason, a buyer can specify whatever colour he likes for trim. Standard rig is fabric-covered aluminium, but S-type trim is something special; seats have a lot of adjustments built in, while trim spec includes leather-covered transmission tunnel, leather-trimmed Wilton carpet, and leather panelling on the inner surfaces. It is an expensive option, however. I asked him if he recalled any 'shockers':

We did a black car for Japan in about 1977, 1978, and it had white carpet with red rising suns machined into the tunnel top. It was awful to trim, but over there it sold like hot cakes. So did the 'hairdresser's car', which was pink with a jade green interior.

Cars come in several categories: there is the car you sell, there is the demonstrator, the press car, and then there is the motor show car; and they are all very different animals. Out on the street the latter is laughable, its colour scheme and trim is so outlandish – but on the motor show stand it looks magnificent, and with the spotlights playing on it, it is obviously right. People will always buy a motor show car for what it is, no matter how horrendous it looks.

The Trim Shop

All the standard trim is cut out and sent to Dartford to be fitted at the Caterham factory. Cars with special trim requirements, such as leather – which can cost £2,500 – is applied

The edging around a piece of Caterham carpeting is sewn on.

The mobile stand in Caterham's show-room displays examples of the special S-type trim options, including seats in red, white and blue leather, leather dashboard kit and padded leather roll-over bar. The chart beyond shows all the sections of the Super Seven carpeting.

directly to the car at Oxted; two hides, or 110ft (33m) of leather are required to trim a Seven in leather and it takes fifty hours to make up seat covers and all the relevant panels for one car. There are a few extra details, not least of which are the seat frames, also made by the Oxted Trimming Co., which have to be taken into account as regards time; these are powder-coated to make a top-quality, long-lasting job.

There are a number of trim options. Caterham's standard kit is black nylon carpet, with seats by Restall, Oxted's own make

known as S-type, or simple slab seats. The half S-type option comprises S-type leather seats, leather dashboard kit and leather tunnel top, with standard carpets and no side panels done. The full S-type package consists of full leather set as above, with Wilton carpet in the boot, petrol-filler covers, map pockets and sound-deadening, all made bespoke to the car. These days, one in five cars has leather seats specified.

Because the half S-type package does not use up the whole two hides, Eddie Marriott is faced with a certain amount of wastage. So for a car requiring half S-type trim, colours are standardized, and these are red, maroon, blue, green or black. If ordering the full works, you can ask for any colour you like – or indeed, a one-off pair of seats can be made in any colour, because they can be made from precisely one hide. Other combinations are possible: leather boot covers, spare wheel covers and leather roll bars together make up the difference between a third and a full hide, and a customer requiring these can also go for whatever colour he or she fancies.

'Most people are fairly staid,' said Eddie, 'but you do get the odd one that's a bit different. And Caterham always does something special for the Motor Show.'

I asked where the hides came from. Marriott was absolute in his dismissal of the product supplied by Britain's best known leather purveyor: although the two companies are only twenty minutes apart, Marriott considers it would take at least six weeks for an order to be fulfilled, for the simple reason that Caterham is not seen as a prime 'blue chip' client. So Marriott gets the leather from the Bridge of Weir company in Scotland, where an order can be processed in twenty-four hours, 'door to door, free delivery and no hassle'. Marriott goes further, maintaining he can rely on Bridge of Weir quality: 'At worst, I may end up with 15 per cent wastage with a bad hide, as opposed to 25 per cent wastage from elsewhere.'

Design and Technique

A great deal of thought has gone into the Caterham's seat design. Eddie Marriott explained that they started by looking at the need to get the driver as low down and as far back from the wheel as possible, and then studied how best to support the human frame.

> We started from the neck down and underneath the body to behind the knees. To get the legs back, you also have to adjust the rake. If you sit someone in an upright plane, with his back following the rear bulkhead, the head will go out through the roof, so there has to be a compromise between where the back of the seat touches the bulkhead, and where your spine is. The angle of rake is not the same as the bulkhead.

Evidently this level of care and attention is reserved for the best seats in the range, and the first K-series car I was lent was fitted with the basic flat squabs which may have accounted for why I didn't feel entirely comfortable in it.

Oxted make all trim except for the Restall seats, and an in-house replacement for those is in the pipeline. All trim for top-of-the-range models is made at the Beatrice Road workshop (which also carries out antique furniture restoration), while hoods, tonneau covers and trim are cut out and made up at a workshop in the centre of Oxted. In total, twenty-two people work for Oxted on trimming Caterhams, most of whom are long-serving staff; Carol Overall for example has worked at Oxted for twenty-one years.

'We never do "stack cutting",' explained Eddie, 'when twenty or so hood panels are piled up and a band lathe cuts out the lot in one go. The trouble is they move about slightly and you get variations and inaccuracies, which won't do.' Oxted mark up and cut out all trim pieces individually, which takes a bit longer, but it guarantees that every hood is going to come out the same, so there are never any fitting problems. To produce a hood, the rectangle of material is laid out and marked up, and it is then allowed to 'recover' – that is, it is left for a while so it can regain

The busy machining area at Oxted Trimming, where in the foreground, Carol Overall stitches up a hood cover. In the background, Sheila Lowry and Christine Agate work on hoods.

The hood material is unrolled, and using a selection of curved templates, Andrew Heath marks the shape of the component sections prior to cutting them out.

the size it was before it was rolled up, which causes it to shrink slightly; after this process, it is cut out. The machined-up hood is then fitted with its windows. Barbara Reekie, who has been with Oxted for nine years, sets them adeptly in place using a high-frequency welder. The machine is guided by a hand-held template.

Templates are used to mark out the smaller pieces of trim for specific areas. These are then cut out and the edges machined up.

Barbara Reekie using the template and cutter to create the distinctive rear three-quarter window in the Caterham hood.

The Caterham's sidescreens have been cut a bit higher to incorporate greater window area, thereby giving taller drivers better visibility – which I, for one, applaud – and there is a pod to accommodate the driver's elbow. Sidescreens used to be made in glass-fibre, but supply problems caused Caterham to change to a manufacturer of polystyrene sidescreens. These have the advantage of being lighter, they fit more accurately, are covered in matching cloth and trimmed accordingly. Other items made here are boot covers and front mats.

The sewing machines used are heavy duty compared with regular household machines: everything about them is larger than normal, and they are described as 'double walking foot' because they have two treadles as opposed to a single one. Oxted use mainly Japanese equipment, Seiko and Juki. The latter is used for sidescreens because it has greater 'throat-depth', the space between the needle and the back of the stock; otherwise the machinist would not be able to get the section through. The difference is only 10mm, but apparently it makes all the difference.

Cladding the roll-over bar in leather is a rather difficult job. 'It's like a leather-rim steering wheel in some ways,' said Eddie Marriott. 'It has to be absolutely smooth over the curves.'

When the items of trim are delivered to the Dartford factory, it is the job of Caterham fitters to install them. Sections like the tonneau covers and hoods have to have their press-studs fitted, and the Caterham fitter has to locate the studs on the car and match them with the poppers on the fabric. 'With the boot cover, it's a case of centralizing it on the car and gradually going from there: it is practice, skill, experience – and luck,' said Derek Gilbert, a veteran of twenty years at Caterham. He rivets the studs to the body, using a jig to mark the correct positioning, so they are the same on every car. The cover is then placed centrally on the car, and the front poppers fixed on first, then it is pulled down to the back of the car and stretched so that it fits flat and neat.

8 Driving the Seven

There is nothing like living with a car for a few days to get to know its foibles; a couple of hours gives you the flavour, but not the essence. Caterham very kindly lent me a car for a week, and as luck would have it, the weather in Norfolk was kind. I took the opportunity of using it on all types of road, with and without the top on, and by day and by night. My conclusion? You don't know what you've been missing until you've driven a Seven: it's that good!

As I have already explained, my original experience with a Seven was in a Series 2 Lotus model belonging to a friend, and my first impression was that the contrast in the level of creature comforts was considerable compared to those in the K-series car that I clambered aboard. As you snuggle down into a semi-recumbent posture in the cockpit, the immediate feeling is of the intimate relationship between driver and car, and the close proximity of all the controls and instruments. All unmistakably purposeful: the Caterham leaves you in no doubt of its intended function which is to thrill, and to go extremely fast indeed. There is the near-to-the-ground factor too, of course, although you only notice that when in amongst other traffic.

The Seven's bonnet is not as long as the Morgan's, but the louvres and two huge chromium-plated orbs ahead of you give a similar sort of impression. The rounded flares of the front wings are not as integrated into the design as are the Morgan's, obviously, but again, there is a certain comparison between the two vehicles. The driving positions are totally different. You sit

The most spartan Caterham of all is the base-model Classic, powered by the 84bhp Kent engine. Tipler tried one of the first to be built, assembled by Which Kit *magazine in seven days.*

143

The view down the Seven's bonnet is of louvres and two huge chromium-plated orbs, flanked by the rounded flares of the front wings.

considerably lower in the Super Seven than you do in the Morgan, and not half so close to the wheel.

Never leave the keys in the car, as I did when parking at Caterham HQ; 'Once you've lost one, you never do it again,' said Simon Nearn. Having settled yourself in place, you start to hunt for the ignition lock. This is located somewhat awkwardly directly under the steering column, and the key is fiddly to insert. Many Sevens these days have a Vecta anti-theft ignition cut-out switch, which requires more deft probing even before the ignition can be tackled. Fail to get the ignition key inserted within ten seconds, and you have to go back to the immobilizer slot again. I view these devices with a degree of scepticism, and prefer the far larger racing-type cut-off switch – which I had on my racing Alfa GTV6 – which has a bigger 'key' of course, but is more accessible and less troublesome. However, the Vecta is an insurance company-approved device, and you can't insure a Seven without a Vecta in London or the south-east of England.

The clutch is sharp by comparison with my current Alfa Romeo family hack, and I cannot recall ever having driven a car with such

a small gearstick. You move it around in a tiny little well, using just your fingers (which I was once reminded were 'for fish and chips, not for gear levers'); though this was no disadvantage, because the gear lever on the K-series car seemed to know where it wanted to go, dropping into place with unerring accuracy. The minimalist flick switch which serves as the turn indicator control caused my eyebrows to raise: it is utterly simple and foolproof, except there is a tendency to knock it 'on' when moving your left hand from gear knob to steering wheel.

Driving solo, you are soon aware that your left elbow is cradling the transmission tunnel, invading the passenger space; when you have a passenger, the degree of intimacy is greater than you find in most cars. Your right elbow nestles in the niche in the restyled sidescreen. Your right knee is almost always in touch with the scuttle, your left shin with the bellhousing.

The pedals are quite close together, making me glad I'd opted to wear my size nine Sparco racing boots instead of the old Doc Martens; docksiders (just about fashionable at the time of writing) will do, but as I was told at a Seven club meeting, if you participate in any sport, you wear the appropriate footwear, and the Seven is no different. On most ideal Seven roads your clutch foot will be permanently poised for action, but on a long straight it can tuck away under the clutch pedal in the long pedal box of the latest models.

UNCANNY AGILITY

Steering is acutely sensitive, picking up every nuance of the changing road surface; it tells you exactly the nature of the ground the car is travelling over, be it on black-top or concrete, and you are aware of the smallest dip and bump. Also, the slightest movement of your hands on the steering wheel telegraphs a degree of directional input: you can make the car weave from side to side with uncanny agility, and fly through a series of bends with the sort of handling precision to be found only in a kart, which is direct indeed. I admit to nearly overcooking it once, opposite-locking desperately to catch the back end in a hairpin, but that was my over-exuberance rather than discovering the car's limit; they say understeer is characteristic at high speed, leading to gentle oversteer (depending on the rear anti-roll-bar setting) but it all seems eminently controllable. As I recorded my impressions into a tape recorder, my wavering voice on playback testified to the stiffness of the ride. An uneven road surface such as a neglected country lane gives a bouncy ride even in a de Dion car, and when travelling to and from Caterham on the wretched M25 I found an unpleasant wave-like motion took hold on sections of concrete motorway.

AURAL PLEASURES

The K-series engine idles nicely, and sings a booming note rather than a guttural rasp.

Although I was sometimes taking it round to 5,500rpm in each gear, I settled for changing at 4,000 as a rule, and the aural pleasures of this engine arrive with each shift: accelerate hard and sharp and you get a 'boom, boom' each time, reminiscent of the F1 turbo era. You can, of course, choose not to 'bury your toe' and the throttle response is completely smooth. The K-series is the civilized Seven. It is quite low-geared, giving about 20mph (32km/h)/1,000rpm in fifth. In practice, fifth gear at 3,000rpm gives 65mph (105km/h), and I needed to use the gears a bit otherwise it seemed a little sluggish going up a gradient in top; it wasn't struggling, but it wasn't exactly saying it was pulling hard. Just drop a cog however, and the urge returns. Anyway, 4,600rpm in top equals an indicated 100mph (160km/h). Despite the buffeting, or rather because of it, this is the best velocity for dealing with motorways; get them out of the way as quickly as possible.

Brakes on the K-series Super Seven are excellent, always reliable and inspiring confidence when at high speed, and with no trace of fade or pulling to one side. The only real emergency I had with the K-series car was when an elderly Mustang in front of me on a dual carriageway burst a tyre, and chunks of shredded rubber were scattered everywhere. The three-wheeling American veered sharp left for the hard shoulder, and I had to anchor up pretty smartly to avoid its detached hubcap, hurtling backwards in my path.

K-series headlights can only be described as adequate up to 80mph (125km/h) on dip beam, with main beam being fine at that sort of speed. The dazzling blue, main-beam warning light was almost as bright as the' headlights themselves, and it was tempting to stick a piece of masking tape over it. There was a flasher switch on the extreme right where I expected the horn to be; and that was, logically, located in the steering-wheel boss.

As I have said, I wasn't faced with a wet journey during my tenure of the car, but the wipers performed well enough on the flat screen in conjunction with the washer, and there is an intermittent wiper setting too. However, the heater on 'my' Seven was almost non-existent; you could tell the blower was on, but it delivered very little warmth, which I could have done with on the runs between Caterham and Norfolk. (I had not checked, but maybe the heater valve wasn't open.) My apparel consisted of leather biker jacket and army surplus tank-driver's cap, the kind with ear flaps, and this was only just adequate in late summer; I could have done with a scarf or roll-neck pullover too. Doubtless a waterproof coat would be an appropriate accompaniment for longer-term use.

BRILLIANT FUN

The Seven was brilliant fun on the switch-back roads of the South Downs and the quieter A roads and back lanes of north Norfolk. The faster I went, the harder the wind buffeted, and I endeavoured to hunker down deeper into my seat lest I should lose my hat. With sidescreens in place there is less turbulence, but the revised window arrangement still leaves a cross-piece at eye level.

I was surprised how little room the Seven took up in my garage, normally occupied by the family saloon; its very petiteness fosters a desire to cuddle and cosset it like a toy.

After visiting some equestrian friends who live at the end of a long gravel drive, I discovered the lower chassis rails inside the engine bay had filled up with stones, in spite of slow progress with no wheelspin. So, if you don't wish to carry unwanted ballast, check for gravel after similar forays.

OVER-TYRED

Fat tyres and exotic wide wheels have always been fashionable among sporting motorists. However, the current wisdom among seasoned Sevenistas is that the cars are generally over-tyred these days. The K-series car had wide 195/50-section boots on 15in 'Prisoner'-style wheels, and it seemed to stick like glue. But I am told that 185-section rubber is entirely adequate, and provides a nimbler car. With wider tyres there is a risk of aquaplaning, and some say the car is too light to exert enough pressure on the tyre to make it work properly. The factory does not agree with this hypothesis, it has to be said. However, the Norfolk contingent of the Lotus Seven Club once tossed their keys into the centre of the room, and instead of swapping partners, drove each others' Sevens; the verdict of regional co-ordinator Steve Davidson was that the lighter the wheel and the narrower the tyre, the better the car's responses. He thinks optimum choice is probably 185/60 x 13 Yokohamas.

THE VAUXHALL EXPERIENCE

I was let loose in a Vauxhall-engined car by Lotus dealers Haydon Cars, a British Racing Green car with a lemon-yellow tip to its nose. It was running on tall, 16in wheels, and I could not fault it in respect of grip and handling. It could be placed exactly where I wanted it to go, and the minutest steering inputs had the desired effect of directing the car; although I felt the tiny diameter but plump-rimmed Momo wheel was, well, just a bit too fat for ease of use.

With 4,500 miles (7,240km) on the clock it felt like a new car, and was happy to give its all. The Vauxhall unit produces a much more guttural noise than the K-series engine, and the roar under acceleration was

Tipler was let loose in a VX by Haydon Cars of Salisbury, and predictably, he was suitably impressed by its performance. This Super Seven VX has the 2-litre Vauxhall/Opel twin-cam engine, de Dion rear suspension and is fitted with Caterham's 7J x 16 HPC alloy wheels shod with 205/45 VR16 Michelin XGTV tyres.

unquestionably that of a high performer. In traffic it was docile, give or take the odd backfire, purring like a lion along undemanding sections of road; but it is fast as well as tractable: prod the accelerator and you are whisked off up the road very rapidly indeed. It puts the K-series-engined car pretty firmly in the shade, although this is not to denigrate the handling of the 1.4-litre car. When you need to move on quickly it delivers snappy acceleration, and the whole ambiance is more dynamic than the 1,400cc car. And how well does it stop? Perfectly, although you need to be pushing hard as there is no servo-assistance; and there is no hint of fade after a number of high-speed *ralentando* situations.

To the recently initiated, there was considerable entertainment to be derived from watching the cycle-wing mudguard-clad wheels changing direction and bobbing up and down as the suspension rode the bumps; just the fascination of observing what the front wheels are doing would be a strong incentive to go for such a configuration, rather than the clamshell wings. Childish

really, since all wheels do this; it's just you can actually see them with the Caterham. Besides, it is probably the closest most of us will get to an open-wheel single-seater. Moreover with its chrome headlights, the VX provides a surreal experience, offering the driver and passenger distorted views of themselves.

This car just likes to burble along, and the slightest touch on the steering wheel effectively directs it. If the steering is finger-tip sensitive, then so is the gear shift; it is the tiniest arrangement I have come across, with virtually no stick visible, just the gear knob, but it slips into place in the most satisfying way in short movements between ratios. Torque is impressive, as you would expect from 2 litres, and the car pulls cleanly and strongly in fourth when ideally you might have changed down to third. Fifth just gives you that effortless burble: this car positively sings to you!

A few seconds with the foot buried is enough to convince you of its capacity to exhilarate, and I was transported by the kinds of delight available in a TVR Chimaera, armed with twice the engine size. With the Seven though, you are receiving quite a considerable buffeting, even with sidescreens installed.

Filling the Seven up with petrol requires a little patience, as you cannot just jam the filler nozzle into the filler pipe and squeeze the trigger. It will quickly click itself off, with the accompaniment of a splash back, so you have to be much more delicate with it. This came as no surprise to me, as the fuel filler tube on my Alfa is equally short, and takes an age to top up. As with the Seven, you insert the nozzle only part way in and only squeeze the trigger slightly until you have a continuous flow of fuel. You'll find the pump's nozzle doesn't go in that far anyway.

The switchgear is laid out, from left to right, with hazard warning, rear fog, petrol gauge, exclamation mark, fan, water temperature, oil pressure, indicator switch, washer, wipers – a pair of flip-over toggles – then rev-counter, speedo, three warning lights, the light switch, plus main beam

flasher, and the horn, surprisingly located where the little finger on your right hand might find it. The ignition switch is right underneath the dash, below the steering column, and is a bit awkward to get the key into. There was no automatic immobilizer on this HPC car, unlike the K-Series model.

HOODED FIGURES

There is a similar disregard for weather protection on the part of both Seven and Morgan owners, and I relished driving the Seven with the top off. At night this has a particularly romantic appeal, when the stars twinkle overhead in a clear sky and you catch wafts of familiar but indefinable agricultural aromas. The downside has to be diesel fumes on a crowded trunk road – best plan your journey to avoid such routes. I was pressed to erect the hood by my five-year-old daughter Zoë, and undoubtedly the Seven feels distinctly cosy and cocoon-like with the top up, but it's of dubious benefit except when

Cockpit of the Vauxhall-engined Caterham, with all the important instruments and switch-gear present, but virtually nothing in the way of creature comforts. But who cares?

148

The K-series Caterham is the civilized Super Seven. The car lent to the author is shown in three guises: firstly with hood down, but sidescreens fitted, then with hood up, and thirdly, with full tonneau cover on, and hood installed in hood-bag.

weather conditions dictate, as you get lots of resonance and the engine is even more booming and the transmission noise is more prominent.

On the whole, Seven driving is at its most civilized – if that is the right word – with the top down and the sidescreens in place. The sidescreens simply unbutton and swing around the screen frame hinges to rest on the bonnet, and you lever yourself in or out. You cannot run with the tonneau and sidescreens in place, unless you don't mind the sidescreens being loose, as the tonneau prevents access to the sidescreens' fastening poppers. Fitting the tonneau is straightforward – give or take a bit of a tug – and you need to remove the seat headrests. I suppose from the security point of view, if you are confident enough to leave any sports car parked with its tonneau on, you'll probably be equally happy about leaving sidescreens in the car.

PUTTING THE HOOD ON

It never rained during my playtime with Sevens, so I never had to erect a hood in an emergency. Doing it at leisure, though, I wouldn't expect to encounter any difficulties. There's none of the quick action 'pull the top over your head and batten it down at the traffic lights' which is entirely feasible with a car such as the Alfa Spider, or even, bless its heart, the MGB. With the Seven it's all or nothing as far as the hood is concerned, and I have the feeling Seven owners are a breed more closely related to hardy Morganeers than the cosseted types mentioned above. Whatever, sooner or later you have to face it that your ability to put up and take down a hood is proof of whether or not you are cut out to be a real sports car owner.

Your hood is likely to be stored in a hood-bag attached to the boot cover behind the roll-over bar, or it could live under the cover in the boot. To start with, you pull up the lightweight hood frame into a vertical posture, and drape the tilt over it. It will want to collapse, so you have to support it a bit. You then peg the bottom of the hood around the edges of the cockpit. I found it quite easy to start from the rear, pressing the 'lift-a-dot' fasteners on to their studs, taking care not to miss one out. Then the hood is stretched forwards to meet the front of the windscreen, and (taking care not to skin your knuckles in the process), you work your way along the screen front. It's dead simple, and pretty much fail-safe too (unlike the Elan S4 I once had, which did the job of taking the hood down by itself; it had the habit of undressing at around 90mph, when a semi-circle of daylight would appear between the screen-top and the leading edge of the hood, growing ever larger the faster you went, until at around 110mph, the entire hood whip-lashed back over your head. After a few such demonstrations, it finally shredded itself, and from then on, hard-tops and coupes didn't seem quite so sissy.)

Taking the Seven's hood down is simply the reverse procedure of putting it up, beginning with opening the sidescreens, and swinging them forward to rest against the sides of the bonnet. Then you unbutton the fasteners all the way around the windscreen and rear panel, then lift it off the hood frame, folding it neatly and stowing it in the hood-bag or rear compartment.

Gaining access to a Seven is an art form in itself, especially one with the hood up. Thus equipped, it is sufficiently idiosyncratic to warrant a mention, and I evolved the following contortions: with doors swung back, stick one leg in, double up with head against stomach in order to clear the hood, hoisting yourself in and using the side of the car and transmission tunnel for support, while simultaneously bringing the second leg inside the car. Once inside you close the sidescreen in the normal way, using its two press studs to secure it. Your visibility is not

To put the top up, first raise the hood sticks. Then the hood is stretched over the sticks (below), and buttoned onto its fasteners around the back of the car and above the windscreen.

at all bad: ahead is the low windscreen, now seemingly even shallower with the hood clasped in place, providing somewhat tunnel-like visibility, and I found it rather akin to driving with sun visors down in a saloon car. The hood frame is just over your shoulder, and to the side at eye level is the top of the sidescreen plus the hood where it overlaps it. This does mean you are forced to peer underneath it for maximum side vision. But if you move your head back slightly, the taller rear three-quarter window effectively gives you an adequate view sideways. Extracting oneself from a Seven with the hood on provides a huge source of mirth for the casual onlooker. At one point I became firmly convinced that the way to do it was to stick both legs out first in advance of the rest of the body. But this system did not work satisfactorily as a means of getting in: and bottom first left one floundering helplessly.

There's a lot of macho nonsense spoken about riding around with the top down – although I think Morgan owners have the worst reputation for this – and frankly,

The art of getting in with the top on. First, stick one leg in, then double up with your head against your stomach in order to clear the hood.

Hoist yourself in, using the sides of the car and transmission tunnel for support, while simultaneously bringing the second leg inside the car.

Nearly there, but you cannot allow any false modesty here.

Extracting oneself from a Seven with the hood on is good for a laugh. Tipler tries sticking both legs out first, and it appears to work.

although I enjoy a blast with the top down as much as anyone, especially in the summer, I wouldn't think twice about putting the top up if conditions were anything like inclement. I wonder if I'm alone in thinking the Seven looks really rather good with its top up.

BACK TO REALITY

After driving the Super Seven for a week, my reaction when returning to the Alfa was predictable. Its seating position seemed so high up, everything so vast and remote from the road, enormous movements necessary to reach things; the vagueness of its power steering, in this, a sports saloon, was a real contrast. The Alfa 75 may be a fine drive compared with most saloons, and considerably more powerful than the K-Series car – with 3-litres and 192bhp – but vivacious it is not. There is no doubt about it, the Super Seven spoils you for driving anything else.

ARCHETYPAL SEVEN: THE 1700 SUPER SPRINT

At Caterham one day I was admiring an orange car with contrasting black Minilites, mudguards and nose cone, and Paul Kite asked me if I wanted to buy it. Having already formed the opinion that given sufficient funds, a Caterham would certainly top my shopping list, I was far from disinterested. However, when told about the spec, I was keen to sample this Ford Kent engined live-axle car, and was lent it for a blast up the road. 'It's got a different cam,' said Kite, 'so it'll go a bit.' And he wasn't kidding. Good for 160bhp, he said.

It was a far more rorty proposition than either Vauxhall or Rover-engined cars, and frankly, it sounded exactly like a racing car. All breathy and cammy, backfiring on the over-run. Acceleration was truly phenomenal. It was red-lined at 7500rpm, and it went all the way there with no complaints, just solid hard thrusting power. Wonderful stuff. It was such a beast that on several occasions I had the impression that I wasn't quite in

Another car driven by the author was this Ford Kent-powered, live axle, four-speed Caterham, with high-lift cam. Its animal-like behaviour and stunning acceleration convinced him that this had to be the archetypal Super Seven.

153

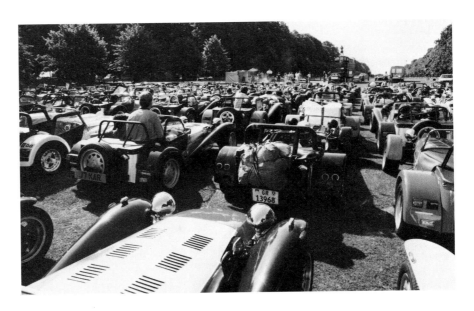

Massed ranks of Sevens gather for prize-giving at the 1991 International. The Swiss driver appears to have forsaken his spare in the interests of luggage-carrying capacity.

control. There was a tight notchy four-speed gearbox, and steering was by a tiny Momo wheel. Its full racing harness lent credibility to the race car impression. The live axle certainly gave a harder ride than the de Dion cars, and I was fairly bouncing over the humps, feeling every one through my backside. Caterham would have let me take it home for £12,000, and I'm not sure that I wouldn't have been more tempted by this rather than a de Dion car. It was so raw, and in many ways it epitomized what I perceive to be the quintessential Seven. It was certainly an amazing piece of kit, and it appealed directly to my worst boy-racer instincts.

GOING CLUBBING

In 1958 it would cost you 25s to join Club Lotus, but then during the course of the year you could attend regular monthly meetings at the Paviours' Arms in Page Street, Westminster, and fire questions at Lotus celebrities like Colin Chapman, Graham Hill, Cliff Allison and Mike Costin about the company's latest developments and race plans. In 1959 the annual dinner-dance was held at the Casino Hotel, Taggs Island, Hampton Court, with dancing to Barry Dean and his orchestra; the club's trophies were presented, the Ian Smith Lotuseer Cup won by Jimmy Clark in 1960; and the John Coombs Lotus Trophy, which went to Elitist Peter Lumsden. In the course of the evening in 1960 Lumsden, accompanied by Bette Hill, drove a Seven onto the dance floor. Lotus' recreational affairs invariably included an element of recklessness; I attended at least a couple of Lotus balls in the JPS days, when Team performed to their pop record with a stripper, and many bread rolls were thrown. Chapman was a legendary crack shot. In 1960 other attractions included a competition sponsored by the *Sunday Dispatch* newspaper in which the prize was a Lotus Seven.

Enthusiasts were catered for by the excellent magazine *Sports Car and Lotus Owner*, the wide-ranging and thoroughly entertaining content of which was put together by author Ian H. Smith and photo-journalist

David Phipps, among others. Advertising manager was Patrick Stephens, a long-time specialist publisher. Club competitions secretary was Jack Richards, who owned a Series 1 Seven (TBY 484) fitted with a stage 1 tuned 1,100cc Climax engine, good for 200bhp/ton, and running a 4.9 differential and de Dion back end for better traction and acceleration.

SEVEN NEWS

In January 1974 the official club magazine was called, simply, *Seven*; it cost 15p, or was free to paid-up members. Graham Nearn was publishing director and Arthur Francis was editor, with Peter Cooper as technical editor. Most of the photography was by Caterham salesman Adrian Thomas, and features included club news, sports forum, technical hints, readers' letters and revealingly, details of the Miss Seven 1974 contest. Only three issues of the magazine were ever

published, so tantalizingly, a result was never declared. Caterham Cars' adverts on the inside front page of *Motor Sport* gave the monthly venue and time of the next Seven club meeting; this was usually a pub in the home counties like the Headley Arms, Warley in Essex, or the White Hart at Godstone, Surrey.

LOW FLYING

British owners are well catered for with the Caterham and Lotus Seven racing series, with events at circuits all over the country. In addition, the Lotus Seven Club of Great Britain provides a good range of activities for owners to participate in. The club has an extremely enthusiastic administration team, and it also produces an excellent monthly magazine called *Low Flying*. Where some magazines are individualistic and lacking in intellectual content, *Low Flying* is, like the machines it represents, a breath of fresh air.

Members of the Lotus Seven Club Deutschland are just as passionate about their cars as British owners.

The 1994 International meeting was billed 'Super Seven Summer Safari', and it was held at the Fire Service Training College in the Cotswold town of Moreton-in-Marsh. It looks quiet here: that's because members are revelling in attractions like grass-karting, archery, swimming and buggies, followed by supper and dance in the Mess Hall.

Its contents comprise a healthy, no-nonsense compilation of race and sprint reports, technical tips, track days and general motoring features, members' adventures abroad, outings to all sorts of places at home and away – such as Monza or the Lake District –

factory updates from Robert Nearn, and regional reviews, with of course, adverts from all the Seven traders and private sales and wants.

This is not very different from most club magazines, but *Low Flying* differs in the

A Dutch visitor at the Lotus Seven Club's International event at Moreton-in-Marsh, 1994.

Steve Davidson's Zetec-engined Caterham blasts away from the start of an autotest at the 1994 international gathering; the giraffe is part of the 'safari' theme. Exclusively Sevens sponsored drag strip runs, and the autotest was down to Arrowstar.

jaunty and amiable way it is written and produced. It doesn't patronize or overwhelm the reader, and the only bias is an undisguised antipathy towards Westfields; but on the whole it makes interesting and entertaining reading supported by good pictures and drawings. In a way, it follows appropriately in the tyre treads of the long-defunct *Sports Car and Lotus Owner*.

I cannot imagine owning a Seven and not being in its car club: the Lotus Seven Club of Great Britain has 1,500 members, and its meetings are extremely popular, particularly the international gathering at Moreton-in-Marsh in the Cotswolds. At these, the array of Sevens decked out in their varied colour schemes is truly inspirational. Guy Munday has been responsible for the commentary for the last eight years, imbuing it with an insider's intimate knowledge of both the cars and the biographical details of many of their owners. The Seven is very much a car which brings out the owner's personality, and for most, the togetherness of the club is an important aspect of Seven ownership; the car is not just a means of transport, it is a hobby

as well, and the club is a major part of it.

Low Flying gives information as to what is going on in the provinces, from which it is possible to gauge how each region is built up. For example, Guy Munday looks after the Surrey section, formed in November 1987; this region boasts no fewer than 140 members, which is 10 per cent of the entire club, and its regular monthly meetings draw forty or fifty owners.

SEVEN X 4X4

Low Flying also reports on 'odd-ball' Sevens, such as the one-off four-wheel-drive car built by Dutch member Arno Huberts. This conversion is based on a 1990 de Dion chassis, using a Sierra Cosworth 4x4 drivetrain and 1700 Super Sprint engine. Although not too many changes were made to the chassis, the Sierra's front differential has been moved forwards instead of running in the sump. Sierra front uprights were incorporated, with ventilated discs. The owner is quoted as saying that his conversion has taken the fun

Possibly the most bizarre engine conversion in a Seven is club member Jim Brooks' Mazda 13B rotary-powered, 1989 live axle Caterham. Mated to an RX-7 gearbox and Caterham remote shift, similarly neat installations have also been done in the US and New Zealand.

out of driving, but installation of a 220bhp Cosworth motor should redress the balance.

ROTARY POWER

Another somewhat bizarre installation is that of Jim Brooks. Jim, who raced a 1,650cc Series 2 Lotus Seven in the States in the mid-1960s, has fitted a Mazda 13B rotary engine into his 1989 live axle Caterham. Mated to an RX-7 gearbox and Caterham remote shift, this extraordinarily neat power-plant is said to be good for 200bhp. When I saw it in action at a club sprint, it emitted an uncannily smooth engine note. Jim acquired the ex-Mazda saloon motor from Jap Engines of Bury St Edmunds, and the specification includes aluminium flywheel and polished porting. 'Exhaust timing is critical,' said Jim, 'although there is no need to balance it under 8,500rpm, and it could be safe to 15,000rpm. It will certainly run for twenty-four hours at 7,500rpm. The standard crank is solid steel billet, so it's unbreakable.'

Apparently this conversion is not unknown in Sevens in the US and New

Zealand. The rotary engine sits lower and further back in the Caterham chassis than conventional power-plants, weighing in at 290lb (131kg) complete, and Jim used ordinary Caterham rubber mounts and the Ford mounting points. He had to alter the chassis diagonals in the engine bay by some 4in (102mm) to clear the manifolding and oil filter, and create a special bracket to locate the gearbox mount. Other modifications include a shortened propshaft, a right-hand exhaust pipe, stronger rear springs to counteract front end lift, and a massive ex-Footwork F1 oil cooler. The battery is underneath the fuel pressure regulator at the rear left engine bay.

On his bench is Jim Brooks' next project, a turbo short-block rotary unit – stronger than the non-turbo, he says – which may be fitted next year.

Cars like these may be individual, but they are yet another facet of the fun nature of the Seven, and it is easy to see why anyone with an engineering bent would be tempted to try something a little different. It's that maverick bubbling up again!

9 Buying and Selling

SELLING THE SEVEN

Colin Bennett was the first Lotus sales manager, and he reappeared on the Lotus scene as a guest of honour at a function a couple of years ago. He was followed by Robin Read, whose personal reflections on the years 1959 to 1962 in his book *Colin Chapman's Lotus* provide a fascinating window into life at Lotus in those days. His tone is sometimes aggressively anti-Chapman and conveys much about Read's feelings concerning the treatment of Lotus personnel, dealers and customers alike. Whatever you make of this aspect, however, it is nevertheless an important read for the Lotus *aficionado*. Today, Read hails Chapman as having had 'More influence on motor racing than any other individual – ever.' He also considers that finance director Fred Bushell has always been underrated: 'He kept the thing going all through the difficult periods, and Chapman trusted him to do that. Fred was able to go near to the ragged edge, and stop Chapman from going too far.' In the final tragic dénouement, however, he wasn't.

Robin was responsible for sales across the board, which included retailing the Seven and the Elite, and his deputy at the time, Peter Warr, sold the racing cars. Robin recalls:

We were fighting for our lives at the time. The company was being dragged down by the Elite, and if Chapman hadn't insisted on going ahead with the Formula Junior 18, the doors would have closed in 1960. As it was, the Lotus 18 was the all-purpose racing car which could do the business in Formulas One, Two, Three or Formula Junior, and it saved the company. That was because each one made 50 per cent profit; they cost £750 to build and we could sell them for £1,500.

Dealer Network

Almost from the first instant, Robin Read recognized that a problem existed with sales of the Series 1 Seven, a relatively specialist car which at that time could only be bought from the factory. A dealer network would alleviate this situation, more especially because it would also allow part-exchanges to be taken, against sales of new cars. So on 1 October 1959 Lotus Components set up the first dealerships in its proposed network. There were seventeen of these 'Lotus Centres', namely: Boshiers of Norwich; Bovey Motors of Bovey Tracey, Devon; David Buxton Ltd of Spondon, Derby; Connaught Engineering of Ripley, Surrey; Downton Engineering in Wiltshire; Dicksons of Perth; Holbay Sports Cars at Woodbridge, Suffolk; Frost's Cars of Shoreham, Sussex; Kirk's Motors of Lincoln; Lotus Sales of Haddenham, Bucks; St Andrews Motors at Newcastle-upon-Tyne; Selsey Motors in Sussex; John Evans Sports Cars in Liverpool; Sports Motors Of Manchester; Woodyatt of Malvern; and the Chequered Flag (Midland) Ltd, at Nottingham. By spring 1960, Ian Smith's Caterham Car Services Ltd at Town End, Caterham-on-the-Hill, was also a Lotus Centre. You could, of course, still order your car direct from the factory at Delamere Road, Cheshunt. Read's statistical records show that of the 149 Sevens dispatched in 1961, twenty-one were sold in November, presumably in the wake of the Motor Show. January and February were bleak, with only six and four units going in those months. But on the home market, Seven sales earned considerably more for Lotus than the Elite, although the latter was a better seller abroad than the Seven.

Tax Avoidance

They were sold in kit form, since that way the swingeing purchase tax on fully-built items – not applicable to racing cars – was avoided; and because of rigorously applied tax laws, they were ostensibly sold through the rather complicated expedient of three Lotus off-shoots supplying various componentry. The aim was to sell a Seven a day, and it seemed that the target had been exceeded by 50 per cent even before the network got going. In order to stave off rush orders at the factory, each outlet was to have a crate of parts in hand for immediate delivery, and a demonstrator available for promotional purposes.

However, because Lotus was still losing money on it, one of Robin Read's first tasks was to do a costing on the Series 1 Seven, and it was immediately clear that economies had to be made. More than any other factor, this is really what brought in the Series 2 with its simplified chassis and cheaper rear axle. According to Read:

> Unfortunately it lost some of its technical excellence, but it was the first popular Seven. Before that, the Mk 6 was the first serious attempt to create a commercial Lotus, and it was popular demand that made them introduce the Seven, which was essentially a contraction of the Eleven; a lot of people put Climax engines in them and went racing, but after that, Chapman wasn't really interested. More relevant to the direction the Seven would take was the development of the stock Ford engines – the 105E screamer and 109E from the Classic, which, developed by Cosworth, turned the

Seven into a real road-burner. They were the real ancestors of the Caterham.

Some 75 per cent of Seven exports was allocated for the States, of which Read commented:

> Jay Chamberlain was our man over there, in Hollywood to be precise, and he was largely ignoring the Seven – the Elite was the car he was trying to shift, and the Eleven was the race winner. I told him he'd got it wrong, because although the Americans were, quite rightly, dismissive of the old flat-head engines, they hadn't played around with the Sprite engine. So we brought out the Seven America with the Sprite engine, and the cars started selling in the States. This model was also influential in the development of the Series 2 car. A reasonable service network for Sprites was already in existence, so American Seven owners could get their maintenance done there. The US market fluctuated, with sales picking up in the spring as the racing season got under way.

Overall, Read believed export prospects for the Seven were patchy because the specialized nature of the car meant it would only appeal to the 'rabid anglophile abroad'.

Lotus sales director from 1963 to 1970, and again from 1976 to 1980 was Graham Arnold, who runs Club Lotus from East Dereham, Norfolk. 'In the early days of Lotus Components, the sales people like Robin Read kept it close to their chest,' said Graham, 'whereas when I joined in 1963 it came under the Lotus banner alongside the Elan and the Cortina.' Apparently it was hard work selling Sevens in the late 1960s; one a month was the norm, but Arnold's target was six or seven. As an oarsman he advertised the cars in a rowing magazine, to some effect; the slogan was 'Out of an Eight, into a Seven and carry One', which was highly suggestive of the Prisoner's enigmatic numerology, in a way.

In the hands of Peter Gammon, this 1,497cc MG-Laystall-powered Lotus Mk 6 – UPE 9 – won most of the races it entered in 1954. Its aluminium body was accurately repanelled by Len Pritchard for Graham Nearn, including those wonderful rear wings. It is driven here by the late photo-journalist Chris Harvey.

This Series 1 Lotus Seven is chassis number 856, and has the BMC A-series engine. It was built at Cheshunt, and is owned today by Graham Nearn. Surviving Series 1s are very rare today: 251 were made between 1957 and 1960.

This Series 1 was built in 1959 by Brian Luff, who as Lotus chassis project engineer, sourced many of its components secondhand from Lotus' suppliers such as Williams and Pritchard and Progress Engineering. The colours were Ford Goodwood green and sunburst yellow, and its registration LOT 7 came from a scrapped moped.

The Series 2 Lotus Seven was frequently fitted with the Cosworth-built version of the Ford 109E 1,340cc engine, and equipped with twin Weber carbs; the battery is missing from this car in Caterham's own collection.

The Series 4 was designed by Lotus stylist Alan Barrett, incorporating more than a hint of contemporary racing car lines into the traditional Seven's basic elements, especially around the rear of the car. The full-length front wings lacked the elegance of the clamshell type, but protected the passenger's ankles from the exhaust pipe.

The Classic, introduced in 1994, is the entry-level Caterham, powered by the 84bhp 1600 Ford Kent engine. It is Seven motoring at its most basic, and lacks any such niceties as hood, tonneau, sidescreens or windscreen, let alone creature comforts like a heater.

Thirty-five years of Lotus and Caterham Seven production was commemorated in 1994 by the limited edition '35th Anniversary' model, painted in traditional yellow and green colours.

In 1983 Caterham brought out a limited edition model called the Silver Jubilee in celebration of twenty-five years' involvement with Sevens. It was finished in silver, with striping on nosecone, front and rear wings designed by James Whiting. The specification included stainless exhaust, nickel-plated wishbones, chrome headlights and roll-over bar. Jeremy Bagnall-Oakley's car has only done 11,000 miles (17,702km).

This 1989 'big tube' Super Sprint is powered by an 1,800cc Ford Zetec engine built by specialist Paul Dunnell and supplied by James Whiting. Owner Steve Davidson is set to swap it for a 2-litre Zetec allied to a six-speed Caterham gearbox. Wheels are magnesium alloy Minilites, shod with 185/60 x13 Yokohama tyres.

Patrick Havill powers his 1700 Super Sprint through the Bombhole at Snetterton, 1994.

Officially only 13 SS Twin-Cams were produced, and apart from Graham Nearn's NRN 7, this may be the only other SS in the UK. The original invoice from Caterham Cars to Mr M.L. Smith, dated 2nd January 1970, was for £1252 10s 0d. Chassis number is SC 2621/TC6, engine number 20972. Wheels are Brand Lotus – the same pattern as Dunlop's, machined by Kent Alloys from a GKN casting, and the rear wing protectors are nothing more sophisticated than black rubber mat.

Details of the SS Twin-Cam logo.

Britax-made rear light cluster of the SS is recessed into a niche in the rear wing to provide a flusher fit.

The 1,558cc Lotus-Holbay twin-cam engine has an alloy head, specially cast cam covers, four-branch exhaust, high-lift cams, and produces 125bhp. The SS bonnet cover has a special air intake to feed the twin 40DCOE Weber carbs.

The Seven was catapulted onto millions of TV screens as Patrick McGoohan's personal transport in the Prisoner *series, set in the fantasy architecture of Sir Clough Williams-Ellis at Portmeirion. A modern, limited edition Caterham 'Prisoner' model, bearing the famous KAR 120 C number plate, visits the shrine.*

Lotus sales manager Robin Read, left, organized a competition at the SCCA's New York region Motor Show in 1961, in which visitors had to guess the time it took mechanics from Lotus' agents Grand Prix Imported Cars to assemble a Seven; the prize was the car itself, which was built in well under twenty-four hours.

The demonstrator at the time was fitted with a 1.5-litre Coventry Climax push-rod engine, ex-Jo Siffert's Lotus 21, from the Swiss star's early days in F1. Said Graham Arnold:

> The basic design of the Seven was sacrosanct, and only evolved through component sources drying up. If anyone attempted to institute any changes, they were out, double quick. That's what happened to Len Terry. He showed Chapman some plans for a revised Seven and there was a swift exit. Len Terry then proceeded to build the Terrier sports car from a shed in Epping Forest, and it trounced the Lotus Sevens around at the time.

OWNER PROFILE

Graham Arnold's recollection of the typical Seven buyer was male, mid-thirties and reasonably well-off, the frustrated racing driver – and here's the psychological sting – with a need to build the car himself as a surrogate baby. He also remembers Graham Nearn as a highly accommodating person to deal with, who would take more cars than his quota if Lotus needed to shift them, and would invariably have the wherewithal to pay for them. When Warner proposed a second dealership for Sevens, before the Series 4 era, Arnold rejected the idea because it would clearly compromise Caterham Cars.

Although the nature of the beast has not altered, the buyer profile has changed over the years. As the specification has improved, so the price has risen, taking the Seven out of the reach of the impecunious enthusiast. Hefty insurance premiums levied on anyone under twenty-five have thinned the number of eligible owners, too. Thus a modern Caterham is the province of the comfortably-off and the middle-aged, who would have one as a second or third car for weekend use or to go racing with. Around £8,500 gets you in

One happy Caterham customer is rock musician Chris Rea, who is also a successful competition driver.

with a new car, a basic kit with reconditioned back axle and engine, up to the top of the range at about £23,000.

Today there are still very few outlets for Caterhams and Lotus Sevens; as far as the factory is concerned, there is just the one. The Nearns have kept a tight rein on brand new cars, preferring to retain complete control over sales and distribution. 'We don't have any selling agents,' said Graham Nearn. 'Although we do have half-a-dozen approved service agents, which is particularly useful for the racing fraternity. People want to go somewhere more local to have their car tuned and looked after. Otherwise, we just sell direct.' The factory also sells spares and competition accessories, on special offer from time to time.

Marketing Overseas

Overseas, Caterham appoints one agent per country, except in Germany where they have three. Although there is only one importer for the States, he looks after three sub-agents: this is a way of 'testing the water', and setting up the makings of a network before selling in earnest. The agent's major task is to get the car homologated and approved in that particular country, and he then has the 'territorial rights' for his country as a reward.

In Japan they drive on the left, as in the UK. TVR sell a great many left-hand-drive cars to Japan, because there is considerable kudos to be derived from being seen in an obviously imported left hooker; Caterham's exports, however, are all right-hand-drive cars. The Japanese are very enthusiastic about Sevens, and the Japanese agent regularly sells 150 Caterhams a year, in the most traditional guise possible; you can perhaps visualize the leather flying helmets, the goggles and white silk scarves behind the aero-screens.

If Caterham does get established in the States, the US price is likely to be $28,000, but Graham Nearn is all too aware that caution is vital. Lotus made the mistake of overpricing the Elan: where an Elan at $30,000 was acceptable, at $40,000 it was not. They never found out what the market in between was.

BUYING YOUR CATERHAM

Over the years, Caterham sales staff has included Guy Parry, Andy Steele, Guy Munday, Mike Lawson and Simon Wheeler, to name but a few, all extremely knowledgeable of course, and there is much to be said for dealing direct with the factory rather than an agent when ordering your new car.

The procedure is straightforward. The customer pays a deposit, and his order is processed. Within two or three months he will be sent a final specification, and a request for a bigger deposit. From this point Caterham is committed to building the car, and the customer to his chosen spec. The specified car goes into the production schedule, and will be built up in three or four months, or six months for a fully-built car. It is necessary to keep to the brief because there are so many variations available, and to change one's mind would upset a chain of suppliers and indeed, throw the whole assembly train out of kilter.

Caterham's Secondhand Stock

There is always a stock of secondhand Sevens at Caterham's Town End headquarters, and Caterham will buy back late or original condition Sevens. Simon Nearn told me that sometimes there are as many as fifteen, though I rarely saw more than half a dozen on my visits. They are Caterhams for the most part, ranging from a 1700 Super Sprint at £12,250 with 22,000 miles (35,405km) on the clock, a J-reg Vauxhall HPC for £17,950 with 25,000 miles (40,233km), but occasionally there will be a Lotus model. During the course of writing this book, a certain yellow Series 4 worked its way into my subconscious as a potential second car, but it was eventually sold to a Belgian enthusiast.

SPECIALISTS

There have been Seven specialists for as long as the model has existed. Lotus specialists in 1958 were the three stalwarts the Chequered Flag and Performance Cars, both in west London, and the Car Exchange in Brighton. By 1960 ex-Team Lotus staff at DRW Engineering in Kensington were specializing in tuning and race preparation. The fastest Lotus Sevens ex-works used Climax power. But you could go equally quickly with a well tuned example, and Daniel Richmond's Downton Engineering was one of the best sources for a 948 BMC A-series unit.

Richmond was to make his name tuning Mini Coopers, but in the days of the Series 1 Seven he was the Elva specialist. Richmond's own A-series-engined Lotus Seven had the motor mounted slightly further forwards than production models and included all the right modifications: balanced bottom end, lightened flywheel, flat-top pistons and high compression 10.8:1 head, high-lift cam, large inlet valves, double valve springs on the exhaust valves, twin SU H4 carbs on tapered inlet pipes, plus Downton's special manifolding; fitted with Lotus close ratio gears, double remote gear shift and Dunlop R5 racing tyres, this was a fast yet tractable device. When testing the car for *Sports Car and Lotus Owner*, David Phipps remarked on the Springrim wood-rim wheel and chronometric tacho, and achieved a top speed of 96mph (102km/h) with 60mph (100km/h) in second gear accompanied by 'impressive rubber marks'. A full Downton tune cost £150 in 1959.

Another Lotus expert, Willie Griffiths, tuned up Sevens. Operating from Finchley, north London, Griffiths went in more for the 'blueprinting' approach, which ensured everything was put together at correct tolerances, and worked out cheaper than the modifications provided by Downton, for instance. Some head work was carried out.

163

He fitted twin 1¼in (32mm) SUs, opened out the ports, skimmed the head by 60-thou, and shortened the exhaust system. This produced not only a crisper exhaust note, but a much tauter feel to the engine as well. An option was a three-speed Buckler close ratio gearbox.

As is fairly well known, Cosworth Engineering was formed in 1958 by Keith Duckworth and Mike Costin, although the latter resigned early on because of his Lotus commitments. Duckworth, having raced a Mk 6, worked with Chapman full time during 1957–8 to develop a five-speed gearbox. In the autumn of 1958 Duckworth installed a Heenan and Froud dynamometer in Cosworth's new workshop in the north London suburb of New Southgate, and with Les Spilsbury began preparing engines for private customers as well as Lotus racers like Innes Ireland and Alan Stacey. Their speciality at the time was tuning and preparing the Climax FWA and FWE units, in 1,290cc and 1,100cc form, but Duckworth soon made good his intention to establish the company as a creator of Ford-based racing engines.

Small Lotus specialists have always been around, doing servicing and maintenance, and selling used cars, and some specialists offer to build cars for private customers. In the Midlands, just by the M42, is Paul Matty Sports Cars, a concern which has specialized in the Lotus marque for nearly twenty years. Like Kent Sports Cars at Littlebourne, Canterbury, Matty is a Lotus specialist rather than just a Seven man. Both generally have half-a-dozen or so good Sevens, both Lotus and Caterham, in stock at any time, and Kent Sports Cars are in the throes of a Series 2 chassis-up rebuild.

Mike Abbas used to be noted for Sevens in the 1980s, and still uses the Seven as his logo; he sold cars mainly for export to Japan. One of the many talents of Mike Brotherwood, specialist in period Sevens, is the ability to rebuild and supply Coventry Climax engines. Barry Ely of Leyton, east London, is another Lotus specialist with a Seven or two for sale; and if you happen to be looking for a classic racer, Chris Alford of Hassocks, in west Sussex, is a leading specialist in period racing cars. Salisbury specialists Guy Munday and Vincent Haydon are now Lotus main dealers, and have Esprits, Excels and Elans alongside their line-up of Sevens.

All these advertise prominently in the classified advertisement section of the specialist press and in the club's magazine *Low Flying*, and I visited a number of firms to gauge the level of involvement, customer profile, and how the Seven stands in the marketplace. Only a few enjoy Caterham-approved status, but all have something to offer the enthusiast and the Seven owner.

Woodcote Sports Cars

The only solus Seven dealer I encountered in the UK was Stuart Wylie, who has run Woodcote Sports Cars pretty much as a one-man show for nearly ten years now. Wylie, formerly a Fleet Street printer, began by offering a Seven for sale which he owned with a friend, and his phone, in his words, was 'red-hot':

He sees the typical buyer profile as a person in his or her mid-forties, who has wanted a Seven since their twenties, but was thwarted by a growing family; with the birds having flown the nest, ownership of a sports car becomes viable. As far as Stuart Wylie is concerned, the customer that got away is comedian and sometime car journalist Rowan Atkinson.

He rang up one day, interested in a Cosworth-engined car, but the closest I had was a virtually brand new 1700 Super Sprint five-speed. I didn't recognize his voice on the phone, and and he turned up and tapped on the window. I was gob-smacked! You can picture it, Mr Bean standing there! He said 'I'm Rowan Atkinson', and I said 'So you are!' In the end, though, he said he'd wait for a Cosworth-powered car, which was a pity as he'd have been the ideal customer.

That was Wylie's loss, for in the event, Caterham sold him one.

The most exotic car Wylie had in stock when I called on him was a 1989 Super Sprint fitted with a Lotus twin-cam motor. 'Bit of an enigma,' said Wylie. 'This is a real animal, and yet the previous owner's wife didn't know there was anything special about it. It's been a race winner in its day, too.' The list of modifications sounded like a performance tuner's catalogue, for it was equipped with a steel crank, phosphor bronze valve guides, five-speed Quaife gearbox, hydraulic puddle clutch, limited slip differential, dry sump lubrication, all adding up to a healthy 160bhp, which translates itself into a 0–60mph (0–100km/h) time in under 5 seconds.

The rarest car which he has traded was a concours Series 2 Lotus Seven, which went to Japan.

But I don't tend to get involved with Lotuses, because they are classics now, although I wouldn't object to a restoration project of that sort to keep on the back burner. The real disincentive is the sort of money people ask for Lotus Sevens these days; like £12,000 for a Series 3, which is all very well for a fanatical collector, but a sum like that buys you a very good Caterham, which is going to go better and be more reliable than the Lotus. Why spend all that money and buy yourself all the inherent problems you get with an old car?

Redline Components

Redline Components Ltd was formed in October 1989 by two ex-Caterham employees, and is at the foot of Caterham Hill, close to junction 6 on the M25. Peter Cooper had been Caterham's production manager since the early 1970s, having joined the company in 1968; one of his claims to fame is that he and Reg Price developed the 1700 Super Sprint engine. Mick Lincoln had been with Caterham since 1974, and was stores manager for much of that time; their colleague John Payne, who had also worked for Caterham since 1974, mostly in the stores, joined them soon afterwards. Like all the

Mick Lincoln, Peter Cooper and John Payne set up Redline Components in Caterham in 1989, after the factory relocated to Dartford. As officially approved servicing agents, they do a lot of servicing and maintenance work for Caterham, as well as supplying spares all over the world.

Caterham locals, they had a close understanding, having been together for the last fifteen years, unlike the new personnel intake from the Dartford area. This appears to have been the major factor in their decision to leave Caterham Cars to 'go it alone'.

While the Caterham headquarters is up on top of the hill, Redline is down in the valley at 19 Timber Lane, Caterham. Redline remain Caterham-approved, however, and cars may go down the hill to be serviced there, rather than along the M25 to Dartford.

Peter had his own workshop in the mid-1960s and began doing servicing and sales preparation of Sevens before actually working for Caterham. He started running the service workshop, and subsequently the service end of the production workshop.

Because Cooper and his colleagues had been so closely connected with Sevens for such a long time, and because they were just down the road, Caterham Cars perceived that there were distinct advantages in having some pre-delivery and routine servicing done by Redline. There can't be many firms as clued up as they are! Thus, some fully built cars come down from the factory for pre-delivery servicing. 'We also do servicing for people who've just built their own car,' said John Payne. 'We check it out to make sure they've put it together properly. The post-build check is costed into the price of the car, for safety's sake.' The proportion of Lotus to Caterham models dealt with by Redline is by far in the latter's favour. Peter explains:

Most Lotus Sevens have been exported now or renovated, and we rarely see a genuine Lotus Seven here, partly because the owners are very much hands-on people who prefer to do their own maintenance. However, we did once rebuild a Lotus Seven for a Swiss chap, a car which had a Dolomite Sprint engine. It wasn't a good fit, so we improved that aspect of it! It had a four-speed box with overdrive switch on the gear knob!

In the 1960s you could get just a chassis on its own from Caterham, so there were a lot of Series 2 replicas about even then, cars which didn't have a genuine chassis plate, but which to all intents and purposes looked like Series 2s because all the parts were available to build them. There are certainly more Series 2s about than were ever built by Lotus! Genuine Series 3 Lotuses are quite rare because it was only a short production run. As for the Series 4, in its day I quite liked it, but you have to remember that as with any car from a particular period, some of them look quite gross. Without sidescreens, it was loosely competing with things like the beach buggy, and they were troublesome, unnecessarily fussy cars. It was Hobson's choice, as that was the only Seven available at the time. The Germans and the Swiss are the biggest market for the Series 4s nowadays; the president of the Swiss club runs a Series 4. It's a slightly different culture, so maybe the Series 4 suits them.

'When there's a club event, we tend to get a number of enthusiasts in for a service who've driven over from Switzerland and Germany,' said John Payne. Apart from servicing and accident repairs, which is mostly on a local basis, Redline's main business is supplying parts, and customers come from as far afield as Japan and Australia, with a fair volume of orders from the EEC and Scandinavia, as well as the US and Canada. Said Cooper:

We source parts for owners of Lotus cars, which we're more *au fait* with; but we have a working knowledge of Sevens of all ages, so we cover all models. I was instrumental in developing the early Caterhams, adding strength to the chassis, more or less following the original Lotus concept, but taking out all the weak points.

His view is that the first cars were in some ways the best ones because they retain the real 'wind-in-the-hair' rough edge.

Haydon Cars

Haydon Cars operates from a smart, compact garage and filling station site in parkland just inside Salisbury's busy ringroad. A former BMW franchise, Haydon took on a Lotus franchise in April 1995. The showroom now contains immaculate Elans, Sevens and an Esprit or two, with a dozen Sevens parked outside. In the workshop are two Esprits, an Elan and a Seven up on the ramp, all being fettled and serviced. There is an adjoining workshop dedicated just to Sevens where, at the time of our visit, two new cars were being fettled for customers; one was a 1994 Super Sprint-engined de Dion spec car, and the other a live axle 1600 GTS four-speeder. There is a lathe where small components are honed to suit; as I watched, Hugo was modifying some wheelnuts.

Vincent Haydon's partner is Guy Munday, who spent six years at Caterham as used car sales manager. The pair also have a passion for classic Lotus matters, with a Lotus 69 F2 car formerly driven by Emerson Fittipaldi on the books, and rear wing sections of a works Lotus 72 F1 car in JPS colours on the showroom wall. They also have an F1 Lotus 78, one of the ground-effect models which Andretti, Peterson and Nilsson drove in 1977 and 1978.

The business has been in existence for seventeen years, formed by Vincent Haydon and his wife, and run as a full-time operation for the last seven years. 'As long as it's got a Lotus badge on it, we'll deal with it,' he said. They have just restored a Formula Junior Lotus 18. Behind the garage is another building known as the engine shed, where a range of machinery is undergoing rebuilds; there are Lotus twin-cams, Vauxhall HPC units, Super Sprints and even a 3-litre Ford Cosworth DFV F1 engine.

Vincent Haydon's career in Sevens started off when he acted as a purveyor of second-hand specimens to the factory, liaising with

Former Caterham used-car sales manager Guy Munday (right) teamed up with Vincent Haydon to form Haydon Cars, based in Salisbury. Guy does most of the commentaries at Lotus Seven Club of Great Britain events.

Munday when he was sales manager. Haydon scoured the country for Sevens, and if the car was good enough for the factory to sell it, he was paid a commission. Eventually he became sufficiently confident to sell the cars himself. By mid-1992 the liaison between Haydon and Munday had gelled, and the new partnership moved into its current premises in April 1993. One of the nice things about the Seven is that, although its origins go back to the 1950s, there is always a sense of progress as new blood joins the club; this appears to be happening at a faster rate than ever before, with fresh concerns like Vincent Haydon's taking off.

Haydon and Munday reckon to sell

between five and twenty Sevens a month, depending on the season, and the annual turnover is 'well into three figures' according to Guy Munday. Customers range from the less well-off – and that means a great many of us, I would imagine – who have saved all their pennies to realize a dream, to company directors, millionaires even. Guy told me:

> We've got a chap aged sixty-six who's just like a child, flashing around the place. And there are young people who have just scraped together enough money for a 1600 GTS. Whatever the buyer's income, these cars are about having fun, right across the range. The JPE is the factory's own top-of-the-range model, whose sole purpose in life is to be the fastest thing on four wheels to 60mph [100km/h]. And we've just built a Vauxhall-powered car for a customer with 250bhp as a road car. That included uprated everything, crank, cams, pistons: fully loaded, as they say.

Guy prefers to nurture potential customers with a full explanation of what the range consists of, and the history of the model: 'We have a prominent site here, and a lot of people come by who know what a Caterham is, but have no idea of its origins and the options available. After a ten-minute chat they might well end up being interested in buying a car from us.'

Apart from the British market, I wondered whether they sold many cars abroad, and whether there are any legislation problems:

'There are no problems selling complete Caterhams abroad,' said Guy. 'Our principal overseas market is Japan, with a certain amount going to Europe, and older cars especially going to the States; their regulations make anything post-1967 difficult to get in,' explained Munday.

Ratrace/Vegantune

Based in Hendon, north London, Mark Oliver's Ratrace company specializes in all manner of spares and accessories for Sevens; it also put together a team of Caterham Super Sevens to win the 1994 Birkett Six-Hour relay at Snetterton. Ratrace is linked with Richard Marshall's well known engine preparation company Vegantune. Until recently Vegantune was also responsible for building the Evante, a striking update on the original Lotus Elan; it made its name in the 1960s building hot Lotus twin-cams, and latterly, the Ford-based VTA twin-cam engines, which it still carries out. Between 1979 and 1980, Caterham sold thirty cars fitted with the VTA unit.

Classic Carriage Company

Derek Moore has specialized in Sevens for twenty-three years, having started the Classic Carriage Company on a part-time basis in Brighton, while working as marketing director of a major plc. He relocated to Leicester some eight years ago, bought the old hotel behind Mallory Park's hairpin in early 1994, and his company goes from strength to strength.

'I specialise in all Lotuses made before 1973, and have had full factory approval to service Lotus Seven models for five years now; and I am confident we shall get factory approval for servicing Caterhams, too,' said Moore. There is a weekly delivery of spares from Caterham, and the Classic Carriage Company sells genuine Lotus and Caterham parts and accessories as well as discounted items such as K & N filters, plus sundry secondhand components, to Midlands enthusiasts.

As well as the busy workshop, Moore also has a trim shop specializing in trimming classic cars, and particularly earlier Sevens. He builds cars for customers: there is currently a Vauxhall race car and a K-series car for his wife in build, and he generally has a couple of Sevens for sale during the summer months, with maybe five in the spring. Moore prides himself in being able to pinpoint just the right car for customers. For example, he had just acquired a Holbay-engined 1968 Series 3 car from Jersey for a customer.

> My heart is in pre-1973 cars, and I would happily do Sevens and nothing else. I have restored the odd Healey and Porsche 356; I make early alloy parts, and we specialize in rolling aluminium, which Arch Motors don't care to do. So we manufacture front and rear wings and nosecones for Series 1 Sevens. All Series 1s were subtly different, so I wouldn't care to quote a price without seeing the car first.

Many of Derek's customers come from overseas: he has recently sold Lotus Sevens to clients in Denmark, Holland, and Luxembourg. The British are spoiled for choice when it comes to Sevens, he thinks. The home market is mostly comprised of people in their late thirties to early fifties, who maybe had a Lotus model when they were young, and despite the heartaches involved in Lotus ownership in the 1960s, view the cars today through rose-tinted spectacles. Now they can afford one again, these people almost inevitably end up with de Dion Caterhams rather than classic Lotuses, because they are so much more civilized.

When giving a talk to Lotus Seven enthusiasts in Bath, Derek was criticized by one member for selling 'our heritage', a Series 4 Seven, to a Frenchman in Lyon. Derek's response was that since the Frenchman had made the journey to Britain with little knowledge of English, and had sought exactly the model he wanted, he was a truer Seven enthusiast than many British. 'It is too easy for us to buy Sevens,' he said. 'We take it a bit too much for granted. My cus-

tomer in Luxembourg cannot licence his Series 4 at home because of legal restrictions, so he brings it here once a year for an MOT and tax and insurance, and runs it on British plates.'

Many of Moore's customers run interesting models: the owner of a Series 2 car whose father Vic Campion made wiring looms for Series 1s in the early days, discovered a pair of bare, unused chassis and Climax engines in the parental garage, and has one of them up and running.

James Whiting

Not many tuning specialists have their own coat of arms, but James Whiting does, and genuine, too. It started in 1977 when he was involved with drag racing, pitching a 1,750cc-engined Austin A40 against the mighty American V8s; his team was known as Knights in Armour, and the A40 was the Silent Knight and featured the Whiting crest on the bonnet. As drag-racing regulations changed – as they always do when an outsider does things better – he persuaded Caterham to let him have a Seven to challenge the Americans again. At the time only David Bettinson was showing the flag in his bespoiled ModSports machine, so it was an ideal opportunity for some publicity for the marque with a standard-looking car. Fitted with the 1,750cc engine, Whiting's Super Seven won its class at Santa Pod in 1978, taking 11.83 secs to cover the quarter-mile (0.27km) dash, reaching 110mph (177km/h). When the rules changed again, he went in for sprints, and collected more customers for his Lotus Seven tuning business.

A Rolls Royce mechanic by training, Whiting first worked on a Seven in 1972, and in 1979 set up to tune and prepare both Lotus and Caterham Sevens. He gave up on Lotus models in 1985 because supply of parts from Hethel became too erratic; they would only re-manufacture parts if there was sufficient

Shaken not stirred? James Whiting gave his Caterham the Martini treatment with one of his special colour schemes. Here he puts things into perspective on the MoD test track at Chobham.

demand. Among his commissions from Caterham was to produce some special liveries for limited editions. One such was the Silver Jubilee model of 1982, with its distinctive striping on the nose and front wings, a design which James has applied to his own car in Porsche Martini colours.

Whiting's Exclusively Sevens business is about bespoke servicing: 'I aim at guys with more money than most Seven owners,' he admits. 'People who appreciate something a bit more special, for whom aesthetics are more important than engineering, especially under the bonnet. Hence I do polished tanks and Aeroquip brake lines, with tidy pipe runs. It's about engineering craftmanship to get around problems with components.' There are usually five Sevens at Whiting's workshop in Ashford, Surrey; some are in for routine servicing, others for suspension tuning; one was being fitted with a state-of-the-art Dutch White Power suspension system, with its click-stop settings and hydraulic adjustment for corner weights;

another gets an aluminium nosecone and wings – the nosecone alone costs £700, as against a fibreglass one at £70.

Jim's other speciality is the fitment of the Ford Zetec engine. These are supplied to order by Paul Dunnell of Stowmarket, Suffolk, and cost £2,400 in 1,800cc form. The pedigree could hardly be better, as Paul is the son of Roger Dunnell, founder of Holbay Engineering, and in October 1992 Dunnell and Whiting effectively joined forces to promote the Zetec package. Whiting waxes lyrical:

> For someone wanting more power, there are the Vauxhall and the Zetec, both yielding 150bhp, and a BDG fitted with Cosworth pistons and head could also achieve this figure. But it would cost more, possibly £5,500, and at the end of the day would be much more of a racing engine.

The potential of the Zetec was demonstrated at the North Weald Lotus Seven Club sprint I went to, where the fastest three cars

The Ashford, Surrey, workshops of James Whiting's Exclusively Sevens are always full of cars in the throes of preparation. Whiting, principally an engine specialist, has a partnership with Paul Dunnell to fit and supply Ford Zetec engines for Sevens.

were running Zetec engines – though I have to say, in the absence of competitive Vauxhall-engined cars.

So for the Seven owner wanting to upgrade his car, the 16-valve Zetec is a cost-efficient way to go. Not only is this engine used in Mondeos, Orions and the top Fiesta – so future sourcing of secondhand units will be good – but it does fit all Caterham chassis.

In Dunnell form, it retains the black box, but comes with side exhaust and carbs – 40DCOEs on the 1,800cc and 45s on the 2-litre – although injection will be available by mid-1995. For this, Dunnell's intention is to retain the air cleaners so you still get the characteristic sucking sound, fit a Lambda sensor in the tail pipe, and incorporate Caterham's catalysed system.

Jim Whiting makes a convincing case for the Zetec:

It's shorter than the Ford BD engines as it has no timing case and pulley. Also its life-span is good for the next decade, yet it fits straight onto a 1960 vintage gearbox. Internally it has fine tolerances and neoprene seals, and like Japanese engines, it should be good for 100,000 miles [160,930km] with no major attention.

All problems with Sevens are to do with people trying to get too much power out of their cars; it used to be with the Ital axles which would break, now it's crossflows, as owners try to keep up with faster cars. The Caterham Classic is a beautifully reliable car, but it's not quick, and the simple alternative engine is the Zetec.

The reason Caterham did not fit the Zetec in the first place had to do with deals being in place at the right time, and in their case it was with Rover and Vauxhall engines. Vauxhall was heavily committed to motor sport with the Vauxhall Lotus single-seaters and the BTCC, so Caterham's racing series suited them very well. Besides, the Zetec was late coming on stream because Ford had gone down the lean-burn route and had to come back to catalysed engines. Then when it first

171

appeared, the Zetec was allegedly down on power: certainly Morgan was loath to commit it to their 4/4 model until various problems had been sorted. Meanwhile, in spite of the Vauxhall twin-cam's demise, Caterham has access to sufficient numbers for the foreseeable future; and who knows, the 1,800cc K-series twin-cam may be another possibility for Caterham.

INSURANCE COMPANIES

It may come as a surprise that insurance is relatively affordable for a car of this performance; in fact the Caterham may even be the cheapest high performance sports car to insure by virtue of its record for not being involved in accidents that often. This is mainly because owners are enthusiasts, and therefore perceptive drivers. Moreover the nature of the car is such that, being nimble and swift, it can be extricated from potentially dangerous situations more easily than most. And if it is damaged, it doesn't cost that much to repair; parts can be bolted on and off, and chassis can be rejigged. Premiums are reflected in the age and record of the driver, as is the norm, and a Vecta immobilizer is considered a bonus. A few specialists advertise in the club's *Low Flying*; these include RCM Associates of Crowthorne, Berkshire, and Adrian Flux of King's Lynn, Norfolk.

BUYING SECONDHAND

For those of us who would like a Seven but cannot afford a new Caterham, there is a flourishing secondhand market (the leading specialists are identified earlier in this chapter). Clearly, if you want a Lotus Seven, it will be over twenty years old now, and as a 'classic' these suffer from inflated values. And no Seven is cheap any more. You can buy slightly more cheaply by going privately, for example through the classified advertisements in *Low Flying* to purchase a club member's car, otherwise you accept the dealer's margin and either go direct to Caterham or a specialist.

Early Lotus models are charming cars, marginally simpler than a modern Caterham, and spares are obtainable. You will have gathered by now that all Sevens are relatively easy to work on, and accessibility to all componentry is second to none; no matter which Seven you buy, it is difficult to get it wrong. Even if you get one with a faulty motor, and most are Escort-derived, you can scrap the engine and start again; being a spaceframe chassis, it is a straightforward matter to slice out the offending part and braze a new section in. They are hardly ever subject to corrosion, apart from the Series 4 cars. Whereas a fifteen-year-old Elan's backbone chassis would almost certainly need replacing, the Caterham's spaceframe is treated and powder-coated at Arch Motors and is therefore well protected, especially where aluminium meets steel. For example Guy Munday has an original 1961 Series 2 Seven, which has a touch of surface rust on the chassis, but is otherwise surprisingly unscathed in this respect. A regular competitor at Lotus Seven Club events, Guy points out that 'any problems with a Seven are going to be pretty obvious. Clearly there are no electric windows or air conditioning or gizmos to go wrong.' His advice is to check that engine number and chassis numbers tally with what the documentation says; maybe the original specification has been updated and uprated, which may be no bad thing, unless you particularly want originality.

If you satisfy yourself there is no corrosion on the chassis tubes, having paid particularly close attention to areas around the suspension mounting points, you just have to look out for signs of general wear in the suspension bushes and wheel bearings, and

The search for a secondhand Seven can take you to a specialist, like Haydon Cars, where they know the models inside out.

adverse tyre wear. You need to make a detailed examination of wishbones, track rods and anti-roll bars and their mountings to make sure they are straight and undamaged.

The Test Drive

Guy Munday's advice at this point became more specific, particularly regarding a test drive:

Even if you buy a car with a faulty motor, you can easily source a replacement, from a humble 1600 Kent engine to a Raceline or Dunnell-built Zetec like this.

173

All mechanical parts are easily accessible, as are most of the chassis rails, so a closer inspection can be made of the inner structure than on most vehicles. Like this Cosworth-powered example, many club members' cars are so clean you could eat your dinner off them.

On Series 2 and 3 cars, look at the A-frame mounting on the underside of the differential to see how worn the bushes are; and the casing on the Series 2's standard axle can be cracked. Also check whether the engine is smoky or rattles. Take it for a decent test run, but don't be seduced by the excitement of the drive; be objective about the car. This is vital, since a visual check of chassis alignment is not adequate, whereas a drive in the car will reveal any serious defects. For instance, does it creak or groan during acceleration or braking? This is acceptable with the fibreglass Series 4, but not with other Sevens. Does the car pull to one side under braking? Can you drive it hands off in a straight line, and does it feel spongy rather than taut over a bumpy road, assuming that the tyre pressures are accurate to start with? You need to get the tonneau and hood out to assess their general condition, too. Remember that an unpainted aluminium body will need polishing once a month to maintain its sparkling mirror finish.

On all Sevens, chassis tubes are relatively

easy to view and assess for straightness and signs of corrosion or breakages at frame joints. On earlier Lotus models, the lower tubes either side of the cockpit are the ones most likely to have been affected by rust, and pop-riveted patches covering this area would suggest that sections of bodywork have been cut away to replace lengths of damaged chassis tube. Pre-Caterham Sevens relied on their panels to supplement chassis rigidity, whereas Caterham's revised gearbox mounting transferred some of the stresses directly to the spaceframe. Therefore you need to check the panels for signs of tears, cracks, and loose or missing rivets, especially in the floor and transmission tunnel: seats should be removed for this operation. Cracked bodywork, both aluminium and fibreglass, may be the result of accident damage or chassis weakness caused by vibrations. If you are bent on restoration, have a read of Tony Weale's book *Lotus Seven Restoration, Preparation and Maintenance*.

Provenance is important, and a fully documented history in support should confirm whether a Seven is genuine. This car is, on the face of it, an enigma, having a personalized number plate (with no letters) and both Lotus and Caterham identification.

Good Provenance

Confirming originality is mainly a matter of checking provenance; if the car has been built as a kit, you need to ensure that it has been assembled properly, using correct parts. Guy Munday told me that he is occasionally offered cars which have been bought less engine and gearbox from Caterham, and subsequently fitted with a poorly prepared Escort engine. It is therefore a good idea to look for an engine built by a specialist if considering a Q-plate car. A fiche of receipts points to a good car, and clearly if it came from Caterham originally, that is a good start. You need to be sure where the engine, gearbox and front uprights came from if they were not supplied by Caterham.

Vehicle Registration offices are not always sufficiently alert or informed, and the occasional car slips through which should have a Q-plate, and is registered with a regular letter by mistake.

Discussing Costs

When buying secondhand, the first thing to establish is the budget available. For £3,000–£5,000 the Series 4 Seven has all the handling attributes of the Seven family: whereas the majority of Sevens and Caterhams are, on the face of it, timeless, the Series 4 is a period piece, encapsulating exactly the era from whence it came. 'It may be a heavier car because of the steel inner skin, but the suspension is quite up to the job. Just be sure to ask for your free flared trousers when you buy one,' quipped Munday.

The Series 4 presents its own set of problems for the restorer, however, being more vulnerable than the true spaceframe cars. All sports cars ship water from time to time, and in the case of the Series 4, water can collect in the space between the inner body tub and the steel panels which clad its more rudimentary spaceframe, particularly along the lower edges. Corrosion attacks the chassis tubes at the rear of the cockpit, spreads along the lower tubes and thence into the steel side panels. It can take years for this to happen, but then Series 4s are more than twenty years old now. Restoration involves removing the fibreglass outer body and most likely the steel panels in order to repair any damage to the chassis rails and to fit new panels. If you are examining a Series 4 and these areas are coated with underseal or similar compound, be prepared to expect the worst. It is relatively easy to check the sheet steel panels inside the engine bay, but the box-section cross-member under the radiator and supporting the front suspension turrets needs careful examination. If considering a restoration, the car should be in as original and complete condition as possible; in the case of the Series 4, its windscreen surround, sidescreens, seats and instruments need to be present as they are almost impossible to source now.

The car buyer's usual cut-off seems to be £10,000, which is apparently a difficult figure for a dealer like Guy Munday to work around. For a little bit more, you could go for a de Dion car with five-speed gearbox and the Super Sprint engine, and for a little bit less you would buy a four-speed, live axle 1600 Sprint; but at £10,000 you would be looking at a very nice live axle car, or an untidy de Dion car. A compromise would be to aim for a de Dion car plus five-speed box, but running with a slower engine, because it is always feasible to uprate an engine at a later date, say 1,600 to 1,700cc whereas altering suspension and gearbox is not really viable.

Sevens start at £3,000 for a Series 4, with other Lotus models in a class of their own; disregarding the Series 4, Lotus produced the Seven from 1957 to 1970, and eight years of that period were taken up by the Series 2 car, so you can judge accordingly which is going to be more plentiful, and which more sought-after. Perhaps the most desirable today would be a 1,500cc Cosworth-powered Series 2. Rarest are the Series 1 cars, since only 242 were made, and they tend to find their way into private collections.

In restoration terms, Series 1 cars are the most problematic and most costly because they are all aluminium, and wings and

Short of getting a Series 2 Lotus to restore, the cheapest way into the Seven market is to buy a Series 4 car; and you could even race it, like John Pringle and John Rees, seen here at Mallory.

nosecones have difficult compound curves to reproduce; they can be made, but are expensive, for example £600 for a nosecone. It also entails using obsolete parts during a rebuild, and as a usable classic with a good turn of speed, a Series 2 car is a better bet. The Series 2 also looks appreciably different from a Caterham, as everything from wing sizes to wheels and drivetrains is different. Values of these cover a broad spectrum, and depend on condition and provenance; a fully restored car will be worth £15,000 or £16,000. Although a basket case may be picked up for £3,000, hardly any Lotus Seven other than a Series 4 in fact comes on the market under £10,000. Prices for Series 3 Lotus Sevens are similar to Caterhams made between 1973 and 1980, and are highly desirable classics. Most valuable of all the Lotus models is the twin-cam engined Series 3 SS, as only thirteen were built. Price new was £1,125, compared with a regular Series 3 at £775.

Caterhams start at £6,000 for a reasonable fifteen-year-old runner with MOT; £10,000 gives you a nice live axle car, £12,000 buys you into de Dion territory, and from £16,000 and above you are into state-of-the-art Vauxhall-powered cars, probably with hardly any miles on the clock. Then the prices soar up to £33,000 for a top-of-the-range JPE.

Cars produced between 1973 and 1980 are in a sort of twilight zone, having taken on a collector status in their own right. These early Caterhams had the older-type dashboard layout, and were fitted with the Lotus twin-cam engine with the old 2,821E gearbox. They are relatively rare, since output was often no more than eighty to a hundred cars a year. By the late 1980s output was up to 500 units, and obviously they are more plentiful.

On the basis of more for less, it is hard at first to understand how the JPE costs so much more than the Vauxhall HPC car, particularly as the chassis is no different to the HPC; but when you consider that the engine alone, with its Weber-Alpha injection, costs £10,000, that is a sizeable chunk of the price. There are a few Kevlar bits, too, for instance nosecone and wings, and the R & D which has gone into it has also been costly.

The bottom line is that no Lotus or Caterham Seven comes cheap, although the Series 4 is within more people's reach. There are no hard or fast rules about price, of course, especially with such a potentially varied specification; clearly the higher the spec of engine and ancillaries, the more will be asked for the car, so that a Vauxhall HPC should fetch more than a 1700 Super Sprint. Also, later de Dion cars tend to command higher prices than live axle cars, and as a rule, cars with five-speed gearboxes sell for more than four-speeders. Leather trim or more exotic wheel options also alter the equation, as does a good sound provenance.

Broadly, here is a table to give some idea of the top and bottom of the Seven market, based on advertisements in classic car magazines and the club's magazine, *Low Flying*. There is no guarantee that the prices asked were actually achieved, and the more recent cars from 1990 onwards remain close in value to their factory prices.

Model	Year	Price band
Lotus Seven Series 1	1957–60	£17,500–£10,000
Lotus Seven Series 2	1960–8	£15,000–£5,000
Lotus Seven Series 3	1968–9	£18,000–£10,000
Lotus Seven Series 4	1970–4	£7,500–£4,500
Caterham Super Seven	1974–82	£8,500–£6,000
Caterham Super Seven	1982–90	£18,000–£8,000

THE *PRISONER* SERIES

Among sundry activities that constitute a mis-spent youth, those of us of a certain age will have watched the *Prisoner* television series in the mid-1960s. Amid surreal scenes of Patrick McGoohan being chased along the weirdly romantic sea front at Portmeirion by giant bouncing balls, with characters speaking equally perplexing dialogue, we have the most enduring piece of Seven publicity and legend. This series has done more for the image and status of the Seven than any amount of promotion could hope to achieve, and it is now enshrined in folklore. An example of its trendiness is that pop musician Jools Holland was prompted recently to make a mildly entertaining spoof of the story, using a replica of the *Prisoner*'s Seven, of course. The whereabouts of the original car or cars used in the series is also a mystery.

The car features only occasionally, although much has been made of its appearances, and indeed, the nature of the Seven is crucial to the plot. An Elan, which Chapman was keen for McGoohan to use, would not have done, and indeed, the actor wisely insisted on the Seven. The true maverick demonstrates his independence: 'I am not a number, I am a free man' was the cry. As the *Prisoner*, McGoohan was keen to grasp the essence of the motoring experience in the raw, rather than have it diluted by the fripperies of walnut dash and superfluous creature comforts. KAR 120 C was a 1965 Series 2 car, powered by a Ford 116E Cosworth 1,500cc engine. For the record, the chassis number was SB2,036 and the engine number was S42,4194E, and it had been the Lotus 'press' car. Lotus employee Peter Brand used to deliver the car to Elstree for filming, and it appeared in the opening sequence of most episodes. Its starring role was in just three: 'Many Happy Returns', 'Do Not Forsake Me, Oh My Darling', and 'Fall Out', which, incidentally, features a certain Graham Nearn in a cameo role polishing the car.

Patrick McGoohan, left, starred in the Prisoner *television series during the mid-1960s, and he chose the Lotus Seven as his car because it fitted exactly the rebel ethos of the main character. Graham Nearn, right, stood in as driver for a short sequence, and McGoohan's reward was a photo session in Trafalgar Square.*

Graham Nearn presented a delighted Patrick McGoohan with the keys to a Prisoner *replica on the Caterham stand at the 1991 Motor Show; and McGoohan hinted at a new TV series in which the Super Seven would feature.*

Now here comes part of the mystery: the car used in the introductory sequence has its registration numbers fixed to the radiator grille, whereas the car that appears in the above episodes has a front number plate. Weird or what? Bolton *Prisoner aficionado* Darren Green has made a study of the episodes concerned, and suggested to me that there may have been three cars involved. There are other differences: if car number one was the original KAR 120 C, number two used in 'Many Happy Returns' has rubber stone guards on its rear wings, and number three, the 'Fall Out' car, has no stone guards, and was in fact a 105E-engined car supplied by Caterham – hence Graham Nearn's appearance.

The opening sequence was filmed on location in London in August 1966, with the *Prisoner*'s home identified as number 1, Buckingham Place – pretty close to 'Palace', and making an interesting analogy, don't you think? The opening sequence shows *Prisoner* McGoohan driving north along Westminster Bridge, along Abingdon Street, past the Houses of Parliament and right into Great College Street, then down the ramp of the NCP car park. In the first episode, 'Arrival', shown in June 1967, we are treated to a glimpse of the Park Lane car park, and the pedestrian subway leading away up to Marble Arch.

'Many Happy Returns' was filmed during the summer of 1967, twelve months after the shooting of the opening sequence, and features KAR 120 C outside 1 Buckingham Place. By this time it seems we are looking at another car, and there is a possibility that this is the immaculate 116E Cosworth-engined car on show at Peter Nelson's 'Cars of the Stars' museum at Keswick in the Lake District.

The third car, seen in the 'Fall Out' episode, was prepared by Caterham's David Wakefield in just one weekend, using a 105E Classic-engined car from the 'used car' lot. The original Lotus demonstrator is said to have been exported to Australia, and subsequently written off. Maybe we shall never know. But whatever the truth, the number plate KAR 120 C is owned by Graham Nearn and is used on a modern Caterham.

Meanwhile, the magic of Portmeirion and its extravagant rococo architecture continues to lure Sevens to the narrow streets and broad sandy beaches. Members of the Lotus Seven Club of Great Britain go on a pilgrimage there every year, and it has become a sort of shrine for Sevens.

There is another postscript to the *Prisoner* story. At the Birmingham NEC in 1991 Graham Nearn presented Patrick McGoohan with the keys to a replica of the car he had driven in the series. Appropriately enough, it was chassis number six in Caterham's limited edition run of *Prisoner* cars. McGoohan, who was visiting the UK from the States for the first time since making the series, commented that, nearly twenty-five years on, he felt it was still the right car for the *Prisoner* series. He also hinted that he was about to embark on a fresh series, similar in concept to the *Prisoner*, and that he would seriously consider using a Caterham in that, too. The maverick is alive and kicking.

10   Sevens in Competition

The Seven was conceptually a racing machine, and naturally it was campaigned on the circuits right from the start. It has been in production for so long that its competition history would require a book on its own, so what follows is of necessity something of a sketchy précis of the main events.

The first Seven protagonist was the debonair Edward Lewis, who had a racing background in a variety of machines before he raced a Mk 6 in 1954. Lewis used his Northampton shoe manufacturing business, the Ebony Polish Company, to fund his sport, and his sport also promoted the driving shoes and racing boots he made. After racing a Mk 9 and an Eleven, he took on the first Seven in 1957. Prepared by Peter Wright, its advanced specification included disc brakes, a de Dion rear end and Coventry Climax engine. Lewis had made hill climbs, and Prescott in particular, his speciality, and that was mostly where he took the Seven. An amusing aside is that Lewis's son George was the first person to spin off in a Formula Ford race – the inaugural event in July 1967, when the entire field was composed of Lotus 51s.

In standard trim, and powered by the Ford 10 engine, the Seven ran in the 1,172 formula, a series sponsored by the 750 Motor Club. Originally, this discounted high-lift cams and anything like a de Dion rear suspension, and it was an excellent category for anyone wishing to drive his road car to the track and have a go.

The Seven was eminently capable of excelling itself among much more powerful machinery, and a fine example of this was provided by Graham Hill at the Brands Boxing Day meeting in 1958. Hill's car was the works' Super Seven demonstrator, registration 7 TMT, sporting a 75bhp stage one tuned 1,100cc Climax engine and drum brakes, and B-type BMC gearbox with close ratios, and with it he easily vanquished the cream of British sports-racing Elevens (of David Piper and Peter Ashdown), and Elvas and Lolas; his advantage lay in 'unrehearsed manoeuvres in the corners' since he was outgunned on the straights. Maybe his new Firestone tyres had something to do with it. But what was perhaps more remarkable was that Hill's time in practice was quicker than he achieved in the Lotus 16 F2 car.

In 1960 the 1,172cc formula was changed to permit high-lift cams and four-speed gearboxes, and the leading contenders realized that it was pointless spending funds modifying a side-valve engine, and accordingly traded up for an A-series or 105E-engined Seven Series 2. One such was John Derisley, who gave his new S2 its debut at the Boxing Day Brands meeting in 1960. The car had a Cosworth modified Anglia unit, with two twin-choke Webers. A storm had rendered the circuit more akin to an aqua-park, and exiting Druids during practice, Derisley spun ten revolutions without hitting anything or leaving the track.

Running on three cylinders during the race, Derisley could not catch the Climax-engined cars, and finished eighth, but he still equalled the fastest time he had achieved in his old Seven. Standard-issue seats lacked sufficient support for racing, so Derisley fitted a Mk20 F Junior squab for his next outing, at Goodwood. It is interesting to note that despite starting from the back because of severe clutch slip, Derisley trounced all the opposition, which included not only 100E- and 105E-engined Sevens, but GSM Delta, Sprite and Turner. Not bad, winning second time out in a new car!

Another interesting account I came across was written by Rollo Fielding for *Low Flying* magazine, and described how his BMC-powered Seven would lose out to Cosworth-engined Sevens, not to mention Astons and Jaguars along the straights, but out-perform them in the corners. His main opposition came in the form of Sebring Sprites, MGAs and the occasional Turner. Race preparations consisted of little more than taping up the headlights and revolving them for less wind resistance, fitting an aero-screen, and donning the latest aerodynamic

crash helmet from Herbert Johnson's of Bond Street. Later on, with a Bob Gerard-tuned Cosworth motor, Fielding hit a magic 130mph (210km/h) on Silverstone's Hangar straight, and although he bounced a valve doing it, Lotus offered him a brand new Seven if he could repeat the feat. The offer was rejected.

Other famous names who started their racing careers in Sevens include Derek Bell, Piers Courage and Peter Gethin, and in France, the sons of Jacques Lafitte and Jean-Pierre Beltoise compete today in the French Caterham series. Milestones in the Seven's history include the 7.20 (or 7½), and the Three-7, with its Elite-type suspension and dry-sump 1,340cc engine, raced with great success by John Berry and Tim Goss. Its

Colin Chapman in 1D prepares to receive the sash from Clive Lacey at the 750 Motor Club's Birkett Six-Hour Relay at Silverstone, 1962. They were third in the Sports GT class. Chapman's car is the Cosworth-Ford 997cc Lotus 'Seven-and-a-half' (or 7.20), developed by Don Gadd and Hugh Haskell around a Series 1 chassis with adjustable front wishbone suspension and fully independent rear set-up with Eleven differential and Mk 20 hubs.

The Three-7, which superseded the 7½ (7.20) in 1965 as Lotus' Clubman's prototype, used a five-link, Elite-type rear suspension set-up and differential, incorporating inboard disc brakes. It was raced with great success by John Berry and Tim Goss.

successor was rather more specialized. Encouragement from Goss prompted Mike Warner to commission the 7X, essentially a front-engined F3 car based loosely on the Series 4 Seven chassis, and Goss duly won the 1970 Clubman's championship. Part of Warner's motivation was to counter the inception of a new mid-engined F100

Tim Goss and Co look apprehensive in the Mallory Park paddock prior to giving the 7X an outing. Goss won the Clubman's series in 1970.

183

category, which would inevitably raise the financial stakes of Clubman's racing. The 7X was designed by Martin Wade and Mike Pilbeam, both of whom have been in the 'first eleven' of racing car designers, and it was intended that a customer-version known as the Series 4 Clubman would be sold by Lotus Components. Times were changing rapidly at Lotus, however, and this model was the first casualty.

RACE BAN

It is rarely the case that competitors make the rules, and when sports car regulations were written for production cars according to a pricing structure in 1973, the Seven found itself out in the cold. The car was potentially quicker than its ProdSports rivals in the same price band, which included MG Midgets, Spitfires and the Ginetta G15, so there was no contest. But amazingly, it was also excluded from the modified, ModSports series for equally spurious reasons, mostly centred on the notion that it was simply too fast. This was largely academic in any case, because the RAC chose to prevaricate over the Seven's legitimacy as a production car now it was built by Caterham rather than Lotus, despite the inclusion of other 'kit cars' such as TVR and Ginetta. In 1975 the RAC somewhat grudgingly made the Seven eligible for ModSports racing, where almost anything goes, and Reg Price built a one-off, lightened, Holbay-powered car for Clubman's racer Dave Bettinson. Running with revised suspension and state-of-the-art racing tyres, Bettinson was class winner in 1975; but not without a host of trivial protests from aggrieved fellow drivers competing in more exotic machinery, who felt it belonged in the Clubman's formula.

BLACK BRICK

After a further four gritty seasons, Bettinson passed this car on to Rob Cox-Allison at the end of 1979 as a wreck. Cox then rebuilt the remains on a new Reg Price-designed chassis, using an 1,800cc Racing Fabrications twin-cam and Chevron F2 front suspension. Handling was evidently superb, but such was the Seven's disadvantage along the straights that Cox's mechanic Ted Williams dubbed the car the 'Black Brick'. After writing it off at Thruxton, Cox commissioned Geoff Rumple of Dastle Engineering to build a new Black Brick on an Arch Motors' spaceframe, using a 300bhp Brian Hart F2 motor, for use in GT racing, and riding on Chevron suspension. The 1,800cc engine was retained for use in ModSports events.

Over the next five seasons, Cox moved through a sequence of ever more exotic Black Bricks. The first car's bodywork featured an air dam and revised rear end; the second Black Brick sprouted aerofoils either side of the nosecone, side pods and a rear wing, details which were refined for Black Brick 3; for Black Brick 4, they grew to huge proportions, almost dwarfing the little Seven tub. The final incarnation was Slippery Brick, a 1,500cc, 210bhp BDA-engined car, built by Ian Jones and George Wadsworth of Racing Fabrications in Bury-St-Edmunds. The sweeping bodywork, made by Lotus F1 bodywork suppliers Glassfibre Engineers of Wymondham, gave it the appearance of something verging on a CanAm Lola. This was surely the Seven at its most extreme.

Meanwhile, back in the dark ages of the 1970s, the eligibility of the Seven for Prodsports continued to be argued over. For a couple of years Graham Nearn pressured the authorities into accepting that the Seven was very much a production car, without success. One of the gimmicks was the production of a T-shirt bearing the legend 'Too fast to race'. He was on the point of approaching the

James Whiting puts his Caterham through its paces at a BARC sprint at Goodwood in 1979.

European Court of Human Rights, when he gained the support of Caterham's MP Sir Geoffrey Howe. The MP wrote to the head of the RAC pointing out the absurdity of excluding a British-made car from the UK production championship when it was quite all right for Japanese cars to compete. The RAC got the message, and in 1980 Caterham was allowed to run a Kent-engined car in the top class, where of course it stood little chance against the Morgan Plus 8s and the TVR 3000Ms. The following year the Caterham was slotted into the correct category, and class wins resulted for John Mayne in 1981 and John Stenning in 1982. Maynard Soares won the ProdSports title outright in 1984, having been the moral victor in 1983. In 1983 and 1984 teams of Caterhams finished second in class at Snetterton's Willhire 24-hours' race.

When ProdSports racing collapsed in 1984, the BRSCC promoted the one-make racing series, taken up by virtually every manufacturer from Alfa Romeo to Volkswagen, and indeed Caterham's own Challenge Series was soon to follow. The pity of it is that the one-make series makes it less clear how competitive the Caterham is, compared with other cars. You have to look at the lap times of somewhere like Cadwell Park to see that the Caterham Vauxhalls are doing similar times to the lusty TVR Tuscans.

RACING LOTUS SEVENS TODAY

Lotus Sevens are not eligible for the Caterham series, being 'classic cars' now, but they have their own race series, called the

John Rees in his 1600GT-powered Series 4 leads John Hutchison's 1500-engined Series 2 at Mallory Park during a round of the QED Lotus Seven Club pre-1973 Challenge.

Winner of the 1994 QED Lotus Seven Club Pre-1973 Challenge was John Henderson, whose 1,560cc dry sump Lotus twin-cam Series 2 is leading the field at Mallory during the HSCC meeting on 2 May 1994.

John Pringle's 1600 Series 4, sporting cycle-wing mudguards, leads Peter Burgess' similar car at Russell bend, Snetterton.

Lotus Seven Club Challenge. Originally instigated in 1991 by Guy Munday, prime mover today is John Rees. It qualifies for the 'historic' category, as clearly all Lotus Sevens pre-date Caterham's 1973 take-over, and it is run under the auspices of the HSCC, which organizes the calendar. The series is sponsored by QED, Quorn Engine Developments, the company belonging to Ken Snailham, an ex-Seven racer. QED is based at Leicester, and specializes in Lotus twin-cams, as well as preparing Vauxhall and Ford Zetec engines.

There have been eight or nine rounds each season, held at most UK circuits: Mallory, Thruxton, Cadwell, Donington, Silverstone and Brands; though there are one or two notable exceptions. John Rees has a low opinion of Snetterton, regarding it as 'boring, and unsuitable for Sevens because of its long straights', and is in no hurry to race there.

Together with Rees, Munday looks after the scrutineering and eligibility side. Ken Snailham of QED provides a hospitality unit at all such club events, and the club's suitably liveried double-decker bus is also present, courtesy of chairman Lol Pilfold. There are fifteen Lotus Sevens registered for the series, and ten race regularly. This is not sufficient for a full grid, so for the time being they combine with another series, the 1970s Roadsports which includes Elans and TVRs. 'This means we go where we're sent,' said John Rees. When racing his Series 4, Rees uses the number 47 which appropriately enough stands for 'Series 4' and 'Lotus Seven'.

This 1,500cc Series 2, shared by John and Sarah Hutchison, has independent rear suspension made from Formula Junior components.

The runners comprise a mixed bunch of Lotus Sevens. There are pre-crossflow Series 2s, Series 3s with twin-cams and crossflow engines, and similarly powered Series 4s. The original concept was that owners could take a normal Lotus Seven and race it; but it wasn't long before tuned cars appeared. Although there is a relaxed attitude to development, some regulations had to be applied. The engine cubic capacity limit is 1,630cc, with 30mm chokes and 150mm main jet, a 6in (150mm) minimum ride height and a 1,080lb (490kg) minimum weight. Maximum power output is between 145 and 150bhp, which enables a lap of 55 seconds around

Mallory Park, putting the faster cars ahead of some K-series Caterhams. The cars run on Avon Turbospeed CR28 control tyres, scrubbed but road-legal.

If a car is wrecked, it is never written off, but resurrected using as much of the old chassis as possible; they won't create a new one. Rees' S2 used all its old chassis tubes in a rebuild, despite rust-pitting in evidence; the only time new tubes are used is if the old ones are crushed. If a Series 4 has an accident, it is still salvageable, as Caterham has the fibreglass moulds to make new body sections.

Series 4s are still reasonably available,

and at least four have been campaigned in the series by John Pringle, Peter Burgess, Ian Chalmers, and Andy Shepherd. John Rees' car was written off at Lydden, and was rebuilt using a brand new, Arch Motors-built chassis. I was strongly tempted to buy it from him, as for one thing, the Series 4 is the cheapest way of racing a Seven, and with a new chassis and 711M Mexico engine, it would be virtually a new car.

CLUB SPRINTS

The Lotus Seven Club holds sprints at three or four of the UK's best known venues, including Curborough, Scammonden Dam, North Weald and Wellesbourne. I went to watch one of these events at North Weald aerodrome, to see the Sevens being put through their paces round two circuits of a coned slalom course. There were morning and afternoon sessions, and some cars were driven by more than one driver, as in the case of racer John Rees, for instance, where his Series 2 Lotus was also driven by his daughter Natalie – winner of the novice lady award in 1993 – and Sarah Hutchison. The sparkling and instructive commentary was by Guy Munday, and it was a chance to see a splendid variety of Sevens ancient and modern. Interestingly, the three fastest cars of the day were Ford Zetec-powered, mainly, I suspect, because chief protagonists such as Jim Whiting were there to promote their particular interests in this area – whereas there were no comparably competitive, Vauxhall-engined Caterhams.

THE CATERHAM CHALLENGE

The Caterham Challenge started in 1986 with a bunch of privateers using their road cars on the circuit in the Colin Chapman memorial race, and grew through to 1990 by which time 140 drivers were registered for the series. At this point the Vauxhall-twin-cam-engined championship was launched, with the attendant chassis modifications; the K-series was in the pipeline and the Kent-engined cars were, arguably, getting too old to be reliable as race engines. In any case, they were not going to meet future road-going regulations, nor would they be able to match Caterham's planned sales volumes world-wide.

Keeping very much to its roots as a sports racing car, by the mid-1990s Caterham had three race series taking place at British circuits, virtually every weekend of the season. There are races in France and Japan, and the company is hopeful of getting a series up and running in the States. In the UK the Caterham series are administered by an independent firm called Entreprix, based at Diss in Norfolk, and run virtually single-handed by Belinda McDougall.

Roll Cages

All Caterhams run with roll-over bars, *de rigueur* in any racing machine, and most are made in T45 aerospec material by ex-rally driver Tony Fall's Safety Devices company at Soham, Cambridgeshire. Some are in mild steel by Arch Motors. They are roughly four times the price of a regular steel cage. While the K-series cars can have a relatively straightforward hoop and diagonal arrangement covering both driver and passenger seats, the Vauxhall-engined cars have a low-slung driver-only hoop and diagonal support, with side impact bar outside the driver's side of the cockpit. A couple of accidents have called into question the effectiveness of the roll-over protection: the possibility of fractures at the point where the diagonal support meets the hoop in crashes has meant a rethink, which may entail a much more complex arrangement, more like an open dragster cockpit, with overhead rails incorporated. This would prove unpopular with competitors, since it would impair aero-dynamics – never that brilliant in a straight line, losing 2 or 3mph down a long straight – and make access to the cockpit more difficult, which presents problems of another kind in the event of an accident.

K-Series Challenge

Class C is for the K-series Rover-engined cars which are road-registered, running with engines sealed by the RAC, which is intended to keep down costs and ensure competitive racing with cars on an equal footing. The cars can be driven to and from the circuit, as I did when racing an Alfa Romeo GTV6 a few years ago; apart from having to behave your-self on the road, the disadvantage is that you have to be sure there is a bus or train service home if you wreck the car at the circuit. Fortunately, my progress was sufficiently pedestrian for the car to survive its few excursions into the scenery intact. Class C is seen by the factory as an entry-level race series, while the Rover car company is keen to promote the use of its engines, and

supported the championship in 1994.

Being a modern engine, the K-series unit is reliable, and is virtually service-free. In race trim, it has an LSD, free-flow exhaust with no catalyst, and as well as the roll-over bar, honeycomb panelling and fuel tank protection, there is a full harness, fire extin-guisher and ignition cut-off switch. Spring rates may be adjusted, but cars used on the road often have standard spring rates. Interiors are generally stripped out, includ-ing passenger seat and heater, and race seats fitted. In such circumstances all transmis-sion noises are audible – they are barely disguised in normal use – and the intake and exhaust notes are amplified accordingly.

Class B

Class B is for cars with modified Ford engines up to 1,700cc, and within limits, modifications are permitted. The cars are generally bought less engine and gearbox, and special racing engines acquired from specialists such as Steve Parker Racing, Scholar Engines of Stowmarket or Vulcan Engineering at Hanwell, to name but three.

Typical Snetterton paddock scene in 1994 as the 1700 car of John Grant and K-series model of Danny Audritt are prepared for battle – in separate races.

Keith Starr, 7, Graham Griffiths, 9, and Patrick Havill, 5, lead the Ford 1700-engined racers in the Snetterton paddock for a practice session before a round of the Arrowstar Caterham Challenge. The 1994 Series was won by Clive Richards.

A hectic time at the Russell complex as the 1700 Ford-powered cars of Mark Garner and Peter Fiddes lead the pack during a road-legal Caterham Super Seven round, August 1991. Garner was badly injured and the car written off at Cadwell in 1992 – the only serious Caterham casualty since 1986 – while Fiddes went on to be Class B champion in 1993.

A gas-flowed race spec engine will run up to 7,500rpm and deliver 150bhp through a competition clutch. Even with a limited slip differential a Class B car is capable of spinning its wheels in the dry, let alone the wet, in any gear. This class is well contested as, predictably, there are many Ford-engined Sevens around.

Vauxhall Challenge

This used to be known as Class A, but is now simply known as the Caterham Vauxhall Challenge; it is a dedicated racing category, organized by the BRSCC, for cars with racing spec 190bhp Vauxhall engines. Again, these are sealed units – a couple of cam-cover studs are drilled and a tagged wire passed between them – and the cars are stripped right down to exclude spare-wheel carriers and windscreens; they have a single roll-over

bar protecting just the driver. It is a prime example of what is possible with a standard road car without too much outlay to turn it into a competitive racing car. Unlike the Classic C cars, Vauxhall Challenge cars are not road-registered.

It is a very closely contested championship, with cars racing on slick tyres, with throaty twin-48 Webers; they are as quick as Formula Fords on most circuits. Like the TVR Tuscan series, it attracted Sky TV coverage in 1994, and is one of the fastest one-make championships on the go today. After nine rounds, only six points separated the top three drivers – Paul Milligan, David Walton and Keith Farrance – which demonstrates the closeness of the contest. I have seen a couple of rounds at Cadwell Park, Lincolnshire's mini-Nurburging, and the swarming Sevens were quite as fast as the thundering V8 Tuscans.

Low Flying *Caterham: Graham Morris gets airborne at Cadwell's Mountain, 1994.*

High tech hits the Caterham Challenge. The HPC Vauxhall of Graham Morris on Arrowstar's portable weighbridge in the Snetterton paddock, 1994, having its corner weights checked and balanced.

I happened to be racing my GTV6 in an Alfa Romeo Club Challenge race at Cadwell in 1990, and in the Caterham event which preceded it there was a dramatic shunt just after the start. A fireball erupted when a fuel filler cap was knocked off one car, pointing up how vulnerable the Sevens can be in a massed situation; they are so competitive in any case. Happily no one was injured, but this flash fire led to the fuel cap being redesigned as a flush fit.

I spoke to several of the teams at a Vauxhall round at Snetterton. Russell Morgan's three-car team is sponsored by Mobil, and the cars look pretty good with just the single word written large and simple. Russell's other cars are driven by Oliver Walker and Graham Jones, and 1994 was their second full season. At the time of writing, Blackburn-based Russell was fourth in the series, which is quite some achievement for a privateer who does most of the preparation during the evening. 'My ideal is just to go racing for fun,' said Russell.

Although basic chassis are the same as the standard car, suspension pick-ups are slightly different, and anti-roll bars are thicker back and front on Vauxhall-engined cars, and shock absorbers much beefier. Other variables are camber, castor and throttle, and ride heights are critical, more so than all the other settings, according to Russell's experience: 'The main criteria are the minimum ride height and minimum weight, and of course because the engine is sealed, power output is more or less even; so if the car isn't set up right, you're wasting your time.' Only one engine builder is franchised to build the engines, and that is Auriga.

THE BIG THREE

Other drivers go to the three big outfits, Hyperion – official status, Arrowstar – approved status or Beecroft – freelance, and buy their expertise and knowledge. Among the half-dozen cars in the Hyperion Motor Sport tent was the BP-liveried car. This is actually a quasi-works car owned by Caterham and sponsored by BP, and driven by Robert Nearn at this meeting. Its regular driver in 1994 was Steve Parrish, truck and motorcycle racer. Based at Little Maplestead on the Essex–Suffolk border, Hyperion was started in 1990 by Magnus Laird, and is Caterham's official motor sport dealer and service agent. Laird started off preparing and running 1700 push-rod and BDR-engined cars in the road series, and in 1991, Hyperion began pioneering the new stock block Vauxhall and Rover engines; the Arrowstar and Beecroft teams followed suit. When I spoke to him, Magnus was keen to point out that Hyperion had won thirty-five of the forty-four races run so far, making it the most consistently successful of the Vauxhall-powered teams. Laird himself won the championship in 1991, and a Hyperion car was second in 1992, and first again in 1993 in the hands of Robert Nearn.

At the Arrowstar enclave, Graham Morris sat in his car on a miniature weigh-bridge. It says something about the sophistication of Caterham racing at this level when they have the facility to adjust and set corner weights for each circuit. Said Morris:

> This can be critical, and it becomes almost a science. If you make other adjustments to the car, you have to reset the corner weights. This is only my first full year in this, and there's so much to learn; I just try to get a feel of the car to get a bit of an edge. They're as sophisticated as single-seaters now, and it's very close racing indeed, which is why we're getting a fair bit of panel damage. It happens just as much in the K-series races, too.

Apart from the three Vauxhall-engined cars run by Arrowstar, which are owned by individuals who may be the driver, they also have a hire car. This is owned by Arrowstar, which is run by Pippa and Jack Newland; Jack also drives one of the cars, and in theory it is hired out to drivers with influence and potential. Ex-motorcycle racer Barry

Bullen from Blackpool has had a monopoly on it all through 1994. The other drivers – Paul Kite and Graham Morris – pay Arrowstar for a support package, which includes race preparation, technical back-up and transportation of their car; all four cars travel in the same transporter. Serious it may be, but Caterham racing is not without moments of levity: Newland's car sat under the awning with a banana taped to the roll-over bar, bearing the legend: 'It's not that you're an ape, it's just that you could do with the energy.'

1994 was a year with plenty of ups and downs for Graham Morris. After a dreadful start to the year which cost him the bulk of his sponsorship money, he went to Arrowstar and the car was properly sorted. Graham's confidence was not misplaced: he won both Caterham's continental races at Zandvoort and Spa Francorchamps, which was good for team morale as well. Despite a heavy roll into the tyre wall at Oulton Park, which wrecked the car and bent the roll-over bar, Graham was looking good for the remainder of the season, and talking confidently of the championship for 1995. Sponsorship inevitably plays a big part in fielding a potential race winner, and for that you need between £20,000 and £30,000. One or two small teams run on a shoestring. The only driver running things entirely on his own in 1994 was Peter Bell, who was lent the car by Jack Brabham for whom he is a mechanic.

All competitors run with aero-screens, since obviously they offer less wind resistance, and fuel tanks are replaced by foam-filled flexible cells, which is state-of-the-art F1 technology: in the event of an accident there is no explosive vapour in the cell, and it retains its integrity in the direst of rear-end shunts. The BP-sponsored car had recently undergone just such an accident, and when the car was dismantled, the fuel cell still retained 18 litres (3.6gals) of fuel. After a while it resumed its proper shape.

Graham Morris took the honours at Spa Francorchamps when the Caterham Challenge went to Europe in 1994. He also won at Zandvoort on the same tour, but 1994 Vauxhall champion was Paul Milligan.

Value for Money

From the point of view of lap times per pound, the Vauxhall-powered Super Seven is the best value in British club racing. In 1992 lap times were identical to the front runners in the British Touring Car Championship and Formula Ford series, and at somewhere like Cadwell, virtually on a par with the massive TVR Tuscans. Engine developments have meant that the BTCC cars and FFs are a bit quicker now, but their performance is nonetheless very impressive. I asked Magnus Laird how long he saw the Vauxhall unit being viable. 'The Vauxhall engine is incredibly reliable, and is rapidly becoming one of the great modern classic designs; it should go on in some form or another for perhaps fifteen years, with derivatives and evolutions, no doubt. After all, the Kent engine has lasted thirty years.'

Hyperion runs cars in other series apart from Caterhams, including the VW Ventos, and employs six full-time people, with a number of part-time helpers bringing the crew up to fourteen. Laird's altruism is entirely genuine:

When I was working full time and trying to prepare the car myself at home in the evenings, I had seven mechanical failures out of ten starts. People in the paddock are quite friendly, but nobody gives any serious help to a novice. I wouldn't wish it on anyone to waste so much money on their first season, and I decided something had to be done to help people with no family connection with the sport; that's how Hyperion was born. We offer a high level of service to people who take their racing more seriously, to the extent that we're in danger of losing sight of the original concept – as in the series as a whole, but it's an inevitable consequence of its own success. We're increasingly expected to provide a Formula Three service for privateer money, which is a tricky balance to strike.

Magnus told me that to provide a 'turn-key' service for a season costs in the region of between £8,000 and £15,000. The driver brings his own sponsorship to support the car, and Hyperion prepares and delivers the car to the track.

Caterhams participate in the two-day BBM (Best of British Motorsport) meetings, which attract lots of the better race series such as Tuscans and Clios, and are meant to bring in TV and lots of punters. In practice, they fail to do this adequately, because most spectators only come on one day, and many competitors cannot afford the overnight stop it imposes. Thus the majority are pulling out of the circuit the moment their race is over.

Nevertheless, Caterham racing is a great

training ground, and it is probably fair to say that you can't go any faster for the same sort of money in any other category of racing.

SEVENS ABROAD

In the early 1960s the Super Seven was highly successful in the Australian Clubman series, and in 1964 Ford France bought twenty Series 2 cars for a promotion staged by the eminent journalist and author Jabby Crombac. Several top racers emerged from Crombac's initiative, including Henri Pescarolo, Johnny Servoz-Gavin, and Patrick Depaillier.

To get the flavour of racing in the States in the good old days, Dennis Ortenburger's book *Legend of the Seven* provides a good insight into how things were on the far side of the ocean in the sixties. As soon as imports got going, the Super Seven became successful in SCCA (Sports Car Club of America) racing,

The HPC Super Seven which won the 1992 SCCA 24-hour race at Nelson Ledges, Ohio, driven by Jez Coates, Reg Price and Robert Nearn, with George Alderman carrying the star-spangled banner. They completed 990 laps at an average speed of 85mph (135km/h).

Caterham and Arrowstar personnel work on the brand new HPC Vauxhall, driven by Coates, Price and Nearn at Zolder, Belgium, in the 1993 24-hour race. Wearing hardtop and a nosecone fitted with two spotlights, the car finished seventh overall, and won the 2-litre class outright.

and if the driver was reasonably competent it was a match for any of the heavy metal on a twisty circuit – and that still holds good today. The Caterham factory took a specially prepared Vauxhall HPC Super Seven to the States in June 1992 for the SCCA 24-hour race at Nelson Ledges, Ohio, and although there was much amusement in the paddock at the sight of the diminutive British racer, drivers Coates, Price, Robert Nearn and Delaware agent George Alderman made the home crowd think again, as they won the race outright. In the course of this astonishing achievement they completed 990 laps

(1,980 miles/3,186km) at an average speed on the track of 85mph (135km/h), with ten re-fuelling stops.

The same crew, minus Alderman, took a freshly built Vauxhall injection car to the Belgian circuit of Zolder for the 24-hour race in 1993. Caterhams have performed well in similar events at the Nurburgring and the Willhire at Snetterton in the 1980s, but Zolder was different because of the regulations and the very newness of the car; it had run for barely an hour prior to the race, and preparation, carried out by factory and Arrowstar personnel, was only finished in

Graham Morris on his way to victory at Zandvoort, 1994.

the small hours leading up to race day. Fitted with hard top and a night-time nosecone fitted with two spotlights, it was qualified eighteenth out of seventy-two starters. Despite gear selection problems, the Caterham ran most of the race in fourteenth place, finishing seventh overall as more exotic machinery dropped out, and winning the 2-litre class outright.

The Lotus Seven Challenge took a trip to Croix-en-Ternois in northern France in 1994, and for the last three years the Caterham series has included races at Spa Francorchamps, and Zandvoort in 1994.

Down under in 1994, Australian importers Monarch Motors of Melbourne entered a Vauxhall HPC in the Targa Tasmania, and against top-class opposition including Sandro Munari and Aussie champions Jim Richards and Neil Bates, the Seven – driven by Robert Nearn with Andrew Smith as navigator – ran in eighth place over some pretty arduous terrain, until contact with a tree knocked it back to 13th out of 115 finishers.

11 Finale

Ardent Seven fans are unlikely to be swayed from their passion, and loyalty to the marque scarcely comes stronger. However, two recent models (in addition to the new Caterham Superlight and Anniversary) will provide the Seven buyer with serious pause for thought. Both are from Lotus and Caterham: the latter's fabulous 21 was launched at the Birmingham Motor Show in 1994, while the Lotus Elise, designed by chief stylist Julian Thompson, made its debut in 1996.

The Elise seems to represent a new generation of sports cars while the 21 harked back to more traditional themes. Embracing a more minimalist concept, the Lotus's chassis is constructed in extruded aluminium on the toothpaste tube principle and is bonded together with epoxy resin. Its Rover K-series (non-VVC) powerplant is carried amidships on a steel subframe. Brake discs are made in ground-breaking aluminium steel composite, and alloy side impact bars and pedals further reduce unsprung weight. At just short of £19,000, it is definitely at the top end of Caterham money, and there is no question its looks will seduce. But Proton notwithstanding, times are currently uncertain at Lotus, while you do know where you are with a Caterham.

THE 21

The number '21' is meant to signify the number of years they have been building cars at Caterham. For the 21, technical director Jez Coates started with a clean sheet of paper, and he described its development to me. 'It was something Graham had wanted to do for a long time, and to an extent he was interested in building a new car utilizing the Seven's proven chassis. However, that was rejected on the basis that it wasn't a legally viable car because of its headlamp height.'

Development work began in earnest in January 1994, and was carried out by Jez and his assistant Reg, working with Caterham's homologation engineer – and out of a staff of fifty-six, the presence of a full-time homologation specialist shows how important that aspect is – and it was the production engineer's job to iron out problems on that particular front. Development costs for the prototype were around £130,000, which is modest by corporate standards. Jez continues:

> When Graham said he wanted to produce another car, it was like a *Boy's Own* dream come true for me. But before I could begin, there were other issues to sort out, and over a period of time I had my sights set firmly on aspects such as obtaining low volume type approval, long distance racing, and so on. The Seven itself could never be neglected, and even now there are programmes of work being carried out on that.
>
> We're a relatively conservative company, so deciding on the format for the new car was important; we therefore didn't build something completely over the top, or something people wouldn't buy or that we couldn't bring to the market place for some technical reason. That formalized in my mind that the new car should be based on the standard Seven chassis, building on the race-proven mechanicals that we've got here. So the suspension front and rear, and the drivetrain, is virtually carried over, although the chassis is in fact heavily

revised to give more stiffness. It includes Toblerone-style triangular strengthening along the sides.

The tracking is different to the Super Seven; whereas the Seven's front track is narrower than the back, the 21 is parallel, which allows greater width in the body at shoulder level. We agonized over whether we should drop the sills, but in the end we didn't do that because we wanted to offer really good side impact protection, and we wanted to keep the beam stiffness of the car.

The 21's front suspension is the same double wishbone set-up, although the anti-roll bar is wider. A Vauxhall Calibra steering column is used because it provides more 'sophisticated' stalks and an adjustable wheel. Rear light clusters are sourced from the Mondeo, door handles are ex-Astra, and door mirrors are from the Metro parts bin. Most surprising of all is that the front sidelights are from the tiddly Suzuki Cappuccino. The wrap-around windscreen and side windows are specially made by Triplex. According to Jez:

It's a driver's car in the true Seven tradition, and if you have to negotiate a high sill to get in, so what? People can live with that. We wanted to involve the minimum of compromise, and focus it on being a driver's car, yet at the same time, it's obviously a more practical touring car because it's got doors, boot and eventually it will have full weather equipment. Having made that decision, we toyed with making the rear track wider, but rejected that because the whole car would end up being wider. Why not carry over the Seven's rear suspension? If we separated the driver and passenger with a broader transmission tunnel, we'd lose out on side impact protection.

Having reached that stage with the concept of the car and its underpinnings, the project was a lot more focused; Coates and his team knew what they were going to do with the suspension and running gear, and the big thing then was to put an attractive body on it. It was vital to make it look pretty: if a car is not attractive, it doesn't matter how sophisticated it is under the skin, people won't buy it. Witness the unfortunate Reliant Scimitar SS1, which is excellent mechanically, cheap too, yet despite its body having been designed by Michelotti and updated by William Towns, both hailed as two of the world's top stylists, it won't sell because its shape doesn't excite the majority of sports car enthusiasts.

Decision-making on buying sports cars has much more to do with aesthetics than issues of practicality and common sense, and other markets have different priorities; thus someone shopping for a hatchback might reject the pretty Peugeot 306 and go instead for the more staid but better built VW Golf.

On the Drawing Board

The new Caterham 21's lines were drawn by Iain Robertson, who knew the company culture, having been at one time on the marketing team. These days Iain works on *Autocar* as deputy news editor, but he originally trained as a car designer, doing a three-year industrial design course and two years at the Royal College of Art. His credentials were excellent, and he was commissioned to provide Caterham with four proposals for the new car; however, having done the first one, he had great difficulty in bettering it with the other three, mostly because he was so pleased with his original scheme. Caterham agreed and chose the first design, and the first step in transforming the rendering into a reality was to make a foam version of it.

This operation was carried out in Jez Coates' barn at his home because of the need for secrecy, and because to have done it at Dartford would have been too disruptive.

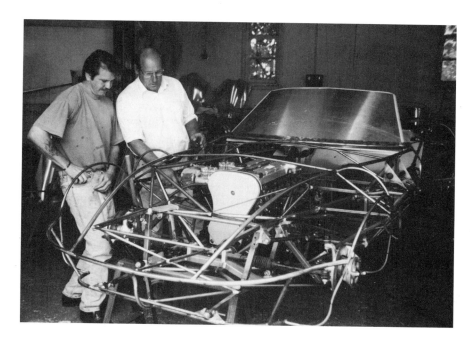

Coates and Robertson took a Seven chassis and made a full-size polystyrene foam buck on it; the body was literally created out of the same polystyrene foam that televisions and so on are packaged in. Car designers use vastly more, of course, and pare it down using chain-saw, surform plane, hacksaw and hammer and chisel until the desired shape is achieved. Details can be experimented with simply by adding more foam and chipping away again. Iain did most of the styling work, with Jez acting as foil to give some practical judgements on aspects such as headlamp and indicator heights. Everything is as low as it could possibly go; the car is only 40in (102cm) high. Says Jez:

I'm a great fan of Iain's work, and I think he's done a great job for us. The rear three-quarter view is almost completely faithful to the original artist's impression. I wanted the bodywork to be spare, as if it is pulled out to stretch over the wheels; there's no more to the car than there needs to be, which is what the Seven was all about – clad in basic aluminium panels, with just the minimum amount of car there.

Shut lines will remain as you see them in the prototype. The nostrils provide cooling for the radiator, with outlets above and out of the side; you need more cross-sectional area on the output than you do on the input. And the side vents are not only a styling feature, they're functional as well. The production car will have simple exterior push-button door handles.

After the 21's debut, it was scheduled to go to the wind tunnel, to see if the shape needed to be altered at all to obtain a better drag coefficient, thought to be cd 0.32 for the prototype. Those aerodynamics should enable a Vauxhall-engined car to top 150mph (240km/h).

The brief for the styling was originally conceived through a series of interviews between Iain, Jez, Andy Noble and Graham, where words such as lithe, taut, lightweight, nimble, Englishness, tradition and quality bubbled up, plus a list of attractive designs from the past or in existence now; armed with these criteria, Iain developed an accurate feel for what Caterham was after, and set to work. The 21 is indeed a masterpiece, although I confess, with an art historical background, one is always looking for parallels and precedents, and I thought I could perceive influences of Ginetta G4, Evante, TVR Griffith and Marcos, to name just four. Iain Robertson identified the Eleven as his chief inspiration.

The show car was in bare, polished aluminium, since that is always going to be rather more spectacular than painted grp. Caterham interviewed potential aluminium panelling specialists, and with single-minded intent went to see their premises; out of a shortlist of three firms, they chose Keith Roach's Roach Manufacturing, based in the New Forest, Hampshire.

The body is mounted on a superstructure carried on the chassis, and it was produced quickly in order to get the prototype ready for the 1994 Motor Show. The prototype's aluminium bodyshell is in 16-gauge, making it more durable for the rigours of a show situation where a car is easily dented, whereas a production body might well be in lighter 18-gauge. 'It will be available in aluminium if you want it,' said Jez, 'or composite.'

The composite grp body would be manufactured in eleven sections, comprising the bonnet, boot and door-skins, inner boot lid, inner door panels, a section including the rear wings and sills, dashboard and front wings, and it would be mounted in the same way as the aluminium body.

Roach produced a hand-wheeled aluminium body for the prototype, just as production versions will be. This material does not come cheap, however, though cost will be dictated by public reaction and, more specifically, the level of orders for the car. According to Jez:

If we're talking about hundreds of cars, the extra cost of an aluminium body will be under £10,000, maybe only £8,000. But if we're only going to build two or three a year in aluminium, it may be as much as £20,000, which would make a Vauxhall-powered car around £40,000. And although it looks stunning in aluminium, personally I think there's a limited market for four-cylinder

A Caterham with doors? Yes, and the interior of the 21 is no bigger than the Super Seven, but its finish is far more opulent.

The 21's curvaceous polished aluminium body has a far better drag coefficient than the Super Seven.

sports cars at £40,000; but only the market will tell us that, and the more cars that are ordered in aluminium, the more prepared we will be to commit ourselves to expensive tooling in order to bring the unit cost down.

That's a Catch-22 situation for Caterham, as the buyer's decision to order a 21 in aluminium would probably be based largely on how close it was in price to the grp-bodied version. The starting-point for a 21 in painted composite bodywork, with 1700 push-rod engine, five-speed gearbox and alloy wheels, will be about £19,000.

One engine option mooted in club circles is the 2.5-litre V6 version of the Rover K-series, and of course a 250bhp JPE motor would take the 21 to 60mph (100km/h) in just 4

seconds. Having driven the prototype for an *Autocar* exclusive, Andrew Frankel reported that the 21 was less blatantly impetuous than a Seven, yet 'unmistakably Caterham, attacking the corners with the same eagerness, changing direction with the same alacrity'. Frankel's hypothesis was that this 'compact Dodge Viper' could reach 180mph (290km/h) at 8,000rpm.

It will be sold as a component car, with Caterham having fitted tricky closures such as doors, bonnets and boot-lid where panel gaps are crucial. The customer will have the opportunity of assembling the mechanical components, including engine and gearbox, axle, front and rear suspension, steering, cooling and lighting; and subject to demand, Caterham will build a 'low volume' turn-key

Designer Iain Robertson was inspired by the classic lines of the 1950s and '60s, and the Lotus Eleven is possibly just discernible in this rear three-quarter view of the 21.

car. 'There's about a 95 per cent chance that we will do an LVTA car,' said Jez. Happily for the gorgeous aluminium bodywork, LVTA doesn't involve a crash test.

'There's more structure at the front of the car, so it's impact performance should be superior to the Seven,' he added. He continued:

> I'd be quite happy for it to go to production with no carpets or suchlike in it. All that additional frippery such as power steering, air-conditioning, electric seats, electric windows and mirrors, all add weight, and they don't make the car any better to drive; in fact they corrupt it because you have to

compromise it by fitting bigger brakes and giving it more power than it really needs. The secret is to make it really lightweight – the 21 is only 680 kilos [1,499lb] and the target was for it to be just 100 kilos [220lb] heavier than the equivalent Seven, though it looks as if we might be able to do better than that. A composite body should be lighter than aluminium in any case.

It will be interesting to see how the two models fare side-by-side in the market-place. The purist may well take the Super Seven, but if the prices are close, the curvaceous 21 will make a very tempting prospect. But can it ever be the raw racer that the Seven epitomizes? I rather doubt it.

Appendix: Comparative Performance Chart

OWNER	ENGINE	CC	DIFF.	TYRE SIZE	GEAR BOX RATIOS:1					WHEEL REVS PER MILE	MPH/1000 RPM 4TH GEAR	MPH AT 6,000 RPM IN:					REAR WHEEL BHP	ESTIMATE FLYWHEEL BHP	VEHICLE WEIGHT LBS	FLYWHEEL BHP PER TON
					1ST	2ND	3RD	4TH	5TH			1ST	2ND	3RD	4TH	5TH				
B. Soper	BMC 'A' Series	1300	3.63	165–55 × 13	2.57	1.72	1.26	1.00	–	8.84	18.70	43	65	89	112	–	69	104	1082	215
D. Dixon	Ford Pre-C/flow	1500	4.11	175–60 × 13	2.50	1.66	1.23	1.00	–	978	14.96	35	54	73	89	–	81	109	1207	202
J. Hugget	Rover 'K' Series	1400	3.92	185–60 × 14	3.36	1.81	1.26	1.00	0.82	911	16.80	30	56	80	100	123	86	123	1236	223
A. Shaughnessy	Ford Super Sprint	1700	3.92	185–70 × 13	2.97	2.01	1.40	1.00	–	881	17.46	35	52	75	104	–	102	131	1212	242
P. Coneley	Ford/SPR	1800	3.92	185–60 × 13	2.39	1.54	1.21	1.00	–	955	16.11	40	62	80	96	–	126	169	1302	291
S. Davison	Zeta 16v	1800	3.63	185–60 × 13	2.39	1.54	1.21	1.00	–	955	17.30	43	67	86	103	–	129	170	1276	298
D. Cheshire	Vauxhall 16v	2000	3.92	205–45 × 16	3.36	1.81	1.26	1.00	0.82	894	17.12	30	57	81	102	125	150	218	1397	350
A. Elliot	Vauxhall 16v	2000	3.92	205–45 × 16	3.36	1.81	1.26	1.00	0.82	894	17.12	30	57	81	102	125	185	236	1168	453

Performance table courtesy of the Lotus Seven Club of Great Britain's 'Low Flying' magazine carried out by Oselli Engineering of Oxford. There is a 30 year age difference between club members' cars.

Index